D0858298

WITTGENSTEIN AND MORAL PHILOSOPHY

WITTGENSTEIN AND MORAL PHILOSOPHY

Paul Johnston

Routledge
London and New York

First published 1989
by Routledge
11 New Fetter Lane, London EC4P 4EE
29 West 35th Street, New York, NY 10001

Printed in Great Britain
by T.J. Press (Padstow) Ltd, Padstow, Cornwall

British Library Cataloguing in Publication Data
Johnston, Paul
Wittgenstein and moral philosophy.
1. Ethics. Implications of theories of philosophy of language of
Wittgenstein, Ludwig, 1889–1951
I. Title
170

ISBN 0 415 00155 2

Library of Congress Cataloging in Publication Data
Johnston, Paul
Wittgenstein and moral philosophy / Paul Johnston.
p.   cm.
Bibliography: p.
ISBN 0 415 00155 2
1. Ethics.   2. Wittgenstein, Ludwig, 1889–1951 - Influence.
I. Title.
BJ1012.J64   1989
192—dc19

For my parents

It is from this side, in the first instance, that objection may be made to modern philosophy; not that it has a mistaken presupposition, but that it has a comical presupposition, occasioned by its having forgotten, in a sort of world-historical absent-mindedness, what it means to be a human being. Not indeed, what it means to be a human being in general; for this is the sort of thing that one might even induce a speculative philosopher to agree to; but what it means that you and I and he are human beings, each one for himself.

(Kierkegaard, *Concluding Unscientific Postscript*: 109)

Let us be human.

(Wittgenstein, *Culture and Value*: 30)

CONTENTS

PREFACE

Wittgenstein's position in the history of twentieth-century philosophy is a somewhat paradoxical one; for, although he is widely respected as one of the greatest philosophers of the century, it is clear that he would have little sympathy with what are considered the most important of contemporary developments. Thus, while isolated parts of his work – in particular, the so-called private language argument – are assigned a seminal status, the wider thrust of his work is ignored or implicitly treated as eccentrically misguided. This is particularly true of Wittgenstein's comments on the nature of philosophy – for example, his claim that 'if one tried to advance *theses* in philosophy, it would never be possible to debate them, because everyone would agree to them' (*PI*: para. 128).[1] Such claims are rejected by most contemporary philosophers. My starting point, however, is the belief that these comments form the crucial underpinning of all Wittgenstein's later writings. As Gordon Baker and Peter Hacker have argued, Wittgenstein's real achievement was his development of a new conception of philosophy and a new philosophical method. Wittgenstein applied this method in various areas of philosophy, but one important area which he left largely untouched was ethics, and my aim is to explore what conclusions his method might yield when applied to this topic. The aim of this book therefore is to show what implications Wittgenstein's approach has in moral philosophy and in so doing to cast light on that subject-matter itself. A further aim is to provide support for Wittgenstein's conception of philosophy by seeking to illustrate its fruitfulness, trying as it were to justify his method by applying it.

Since Wittgenstein's conception of philosophy constitutes a radical break with the past (and since it also diverges from the conception which governs most contemporary philosophizing), I begin in Chapter 1 by considering the nature and basis of this conception. As this chapter makes clear, Wittgenstein saw philosophical problems as the reflection of conceptual confusion and hence thought they could be resolved simply through clarification of the conceptual structures in which they arise. Applying Wittgenstein's method to ethics, I argue that one of the central sources of conceptual confusion here is the difficulty of gaining a philosophical understanding of the concepts involved in human action. To explore this point I consider Wittgenstein's criticisms of Sir James Frazer's writings on ritual (Chapter 2) and suggest that very similar criticisms apply to much contemporary moral philosophy (Chapter 3). Here one point that emerges is the existence of a major gulf between moral concepts as discussed by philosophers and the moral concepts used in our everyday moral practices. Thus the most distinctive aspects of moral claims seem either to be ignored or rejected. To clarify this puzzle, I consider the early Wittgenstein's comments on ethics, for these embody a determined but ultimately unsuccessful attempt to clarify the nature of the moral claims we actually make. I then seek to use the method developed by the later Wittgenstein to illuminate why both the early Wittgenstein and contemporary moral philosophers run into the difficulties they do.

Although the points I make about ethics are very simple, I would argue that they are fundamental and that a failure to recognize them vitiates much contemporary moral philosophy. Here, as in philosophy in general, conceptual confusion may lead one to deny basic truisms – indeed, the failure to appreciate the significance of these truisms may itself be at the root of one's difficulties. The attempt to eliminate confusion will therefore involve underlining fairly straightforward points, but points which gain their importance from the confusions to which neglect of them can lead.[2] This has two consequences for the form of my discussion. On the one hand, it makes it necessary to approach certain central issues a number of times from different sides and this involves a certain amount of repetition. On the other hand, it also makes it important to underline the significance of my remarks by contrasting them with claims advanced in non-Wittgensteinian accounts.

In writing this book, I have received much generous assistance. In particular, I would like to thank Alan Montefiore, who supervised the thesis which provided the basis for this book, Mike Egan and Adam

Swift who read the manuscript and made many constructive suggestions, and Ann Sawyer and Karen Hess who gave me secretarial assistance. My greatest debt is to Stephen Mulhall whose philosophical criticisms always gave me much to think about and whose encouragement helped me finish what occasionally seemed like an endless task.

WITTGENSTEIN, PHILOSOPHY, AND ETHICS

> Our task is only to be impartial, i.e we have only to show up the ways philosophy is biased and to correct them, but not to set up new parties and creeds.
>
> (Wittgenstein *BT*: 420)

Philosophy's perennial lack of progress has been a source of irritation to many philosophers, and anger at this 'open scandal' has been the origin of many different schools and systems. For Wittgenstein, it was a problem in need of radical solution, and the desire to put an end to philosophy's endless self-questioning underlies both his early system contained in the *Tractatus Logico-Philosophicus* and the very different ideas put forward in his later writings. On both occasions, Wittgenstein sought to uncover the roots of philosophy's problems in the hope of finding a definitive means of resolving them. As he said to M.O'C. Drury in 1930, 'my father was a businessman, and I want my philosophy to be businesslike, to get something done, to get something settled' (Drury 1981: 110). In the *Tractatus* Wittgenstein thought he had achieved this goal by offering definitive answers to all the philosophical questions for which an answer was logically possible. Other philosophical questions he condemned as nonsensical attempts to capture the ineffable in words, transgressions of the fundamental principle that 'whereof one cannot speak, thereof one must be silent' (*TLP*: 7).

Like its many predecessors, however, Wittgenstein's early system proved unsatisfactory: difficulties arising from an apparently minor technicality concerning the logic of colour predicates led to the gradual unravelling of the whole system. Returning to philosophy in the 1930s, Wittgenstein radically criticized his earlier approach. Now he argued that the attempt to answer philosophical questions was itself misguided since it involved failing to recognize that philosophical questions were not genuine questions but rather the manifestation of conceptual confusion. Developing this idea, Wittgenstein contended that the proper aim of philosophy was not truth but clarity – what was needed was not a system of definitive answers but a method which would allow the philosopher to achieve a clarity in the face of which the questions which troubled him would themselves disappear.

To many this idea seems to trivialize philosophy; in the words of Bertrand Russell, philosophy seems to be reduced to the level of 'an idle tea-table amusement' (*My Philosophical Development*: 217). In the sphere of ethics, this objection seems to have an even greater force, for how could one seriously claim that in moral philosophy all that is at issue is linguistic confusion? If anything, consideration of this area would seem to indicate just how limited the Wittgensteinian approach is. The aim of this book, however, is to refute this claim by showing that Wittgenstein's approach is both necessary and fruitful in precisely this area. As we shall see, the complexities of ethics are much in need of clarification; indeed, we shall claim that many of the debates of modern moral philosophy reveal a startling failure to grasp the nature of the issues here at stake. Before examining ethics itself, however, we need to consider briefly the nature and basis of the new approach to philosophy which Wittgenstein advocated.

The fundamental premise underlining Wittgenstein's method is the claim that philosophy should be descriptive, that it should advance no theses. According to Wittgenstein, the philosopher is not called upon to discover profound truths nor to offer explanations; rather, his task is to eliminate conceptual confusion by carefully depicting the relations between concepts. On this account, philosophy is a non-deductive activity involving neither proof nor justification and having as its positive aim the achievement of clarity. To understand Wittgenstein's conception of philosophy therefore we need to grasp how and why Wittgenstein thought philosophy could be non-substantive and why he thought such a non-substantive investigation was necessary and important. The best way of doing this is to analyse the nature of philosophical problems.

One distinctive feature of such problems is that they seem to raise difficulties which are at once fundamental and yet somewhat peculiar. In contrast to empirical or scientific problems, new information seems unlikely to contribute to their solution, for what they seem to call for is, as it were, metaphysical insight. When the philosopher asks 'How is it

2

possible to speak of that which is not?' the presentation of everyday examples of that possibility seems both a trivial and an inappropriate response. Similarly, when G.E. Moore raised his hands to 'prove' the existence of the external world, his action seems to bypass the philosophical problem rather than solve it. In such cases, the power of the philosophical question seems to lie in the way it takes the obvious and renders it bafflingly problematic; the question mesmerizes us, revealing a mental blind spot precisely where we would least have expected it. That the external world exists seems beyond question, but when the philosopher does question this, the attempt to reply only seems to generate further difficulties.

According to Wittgenstein, the reason we are led into such difficulties is our failure to command an overview (*Übersicht*) of our concepts and their mutual interrelations. On his analysis, philosophical questions are not genuine questions but rather confusions felt as problems: they have the form 'I don't know my way around.' The philosopher's traditional preoccupation with the *a priori* is one indication of the special nature of his difficulties. Thus the philosopher does not concern himself with the contingent, with that which may be true or false; rather, he asks how a certain thing is possible, what sense it makes to say such-and-such. Both ways of phrasing the question are significant, for the first points to the fact that the source of the difficulties is a lack of clarity, while the second indicates that one aspect of the problem concerns language and the need to attain clarity with respect to it. If, therefore, one recognizes that these questions are the expression of confusion, the attempt to answer them by putting forward new explanations becomes redundant and indeed misguided in so far as it simply adds to the initial confusion. As Wittgenstein puts it in the *Big Typescript*, 'The answer to the question asking for an explanation of negation is really: don't you understand it? Well, if you do understand it, what else is there to explain, what else has an explanation to do?' (*BT*: 418).

Wittgenstein's analysis of philosophical problems assigns language a central role in any philosophical investigation. The origin of philosophical problems is seen to lie in the fact that the 'grammar' of our concepts lacks surveyability (*Übersichtlichkeit*), in other words, that the conceptual relations embodied in language are not presented to us in a systematic, readily comprehensible form. Thus crucial differences are hidden beneath apparent similarities, while deceptive analogies tempt us to try to apply concepts in ways which make no

3

sense. That language should create difficulties for reflection, however, is hardly surprising, for language evolves to meet our everyday practical needs and not the demands of philosophical clarity. Thus, when we learn to use the verb 'to think', nothing prepares us to give a description of the widely ramifying network of conceptual relations which constitute the grammar of this concept; it is therefore not surprising that confusions arise when we try to do so. The surface grammar of our language can also be extremely misleading; for example, we assume that nouns denote objects, and yet the questions 'What is Time?' and 'What is Goodness?' seem to get us nowhere. Similarly, we seek to understand verbs such as 'to think' and 'to mean' by analogy with verbs such as 'to speak' or 'to eat'; in this way, however, the supposed mental processes to which these verbs refer come to seem mysterious, indeed ghostly, and the more we seek to come to grips with them the more mysterious they appear.

As well as assigning language a central role, Wittgenstein's analysis of philosophical problems also throws the spotlight on the situation of doing philosophy. The philosopher is depicted as suffering from 'mental cramp' and as being in the grip of the illusions of language, 'screaming as it were in his powerlessness, for as long as he has not yet discovered the root of his confusion' (BT: 420–1). In more flattering terms, the philosopher can be seen as having a particular kind of sensitivity to language and a desire for clarity and conceptual order. From this perspective, 'a philosophical problem is a consciousness of the lack of order in our concepts' (BT: 421). In his search for order, the philosopher takes up a certain analogy which exists in the use of our language and then proceeds to extend it in a systematic but misleading fashion. In this way, 'a false analogy leads to continual strife and unrest' (BT: 410); like an annoying hair on one's tongue, it constitutes an irritation which refuses to go away.

This account still seems to leave unexplained the apparent fundamental nature of philosophical problems; for if these problems are simply grammatical confusions, why do they seem so 'deep', so fundamental? Answering this question involves seeking to understand what is at stake in the metaphysical desire to give a systematic account of the world. Such an endeavour has an important ethical dimension, and our discussion of the notion of truth in ethics will throw light on Wittgenstein's rejection of the idea that philosophy should (or could) unveil deep truths about the nature of reality. The attempt to understand this aspect of philosophical problems also throws light on our relation to language, for it reveals how much linguistic problems can mean to us and how these problems can connect up with deeper worries and feelings. Thus philosophical reflection can sometimes give rise to an almost mystical feeling of running up against the limits of language. However, the depth that is here revealed is the depth of grammar itself; and, in this sense, Wittgenstein's investigations continually underline the fact that language is not merely a medium for the representation of thoughts, but rather something that becomes second nature to us. As Wittgenstein notes in *Philosophical Investigations*, the roots of philosophical problems are 'as deep in us as the forms of our language and their significance is as great as the importance of our language' (*PI*: para. 111).[1]

Wittgenstein's analysis of philosophical problems brings to the fore the notion of an *Übersicht* (overview); for it suggests that certain intellectual difficulties are to be resolved not by adducing further information or by formulating explanatory hypotheses, but rather through the ordered presentation of what we already know. The idea is that these intellectual difficulties consist precisely in our inability to attain clarity about that which troubles us; consequently, all that is required for their elimination is the putting into order of our tangled thoughts. Here the problem lies in 'the crush of thoughts that do not get out because they all try to push forward and are wedged in the door' (*RFGB*: 3).[2] Problems of this kind differ markedly from scientific problems, for the understanding we seek and the difficulties we face in this context are quite different from their equivalents in the scientific sphere. Here our difficulties can be resolved without making any substantive claims about what is or is not the case, and hence in this sense, the problems are solved 'without saying anything new'.

However, the difficulty of ordering one's thoughts and of gaining a clear view of a familiar topic must not be underestimated. The Wittgensteinian call for clarity requires a discipline and a rigour not always easy to achieve. More particularly, in philosophy, confining oneself to the articulation of conceptual relations may require a great struggle, for putting forward explanations may seem to offer an easier solution to our difficulties than the painstaking attempt to trace these problems back to their roots in grammar and dispel them by mapping out the network of concepts in which they arise. The search for clarity also demands a fertile imagination, for gaining an *Übersicht* often involves finding an apt analogy or a fruitful organizing principle. Finally, it should also be noted that, although attaining an *Übersicht* involves no more than organizing what we already know, it can none the less bring about a fundamental change in our understanding. Presented systematically and so as to allow us to gain a clear view of it, what we know may take on a new aspect just as a puzzle-picture changes when we come to see what it represents. With philosophical problems, we possess, as it were, all the pieces of the jigsaw puzzle but experience a frustrating inability to put them together. This frustration can only be eliminated by organizing our thoughts and attaining clarity with respect to their subject matter. For example, a picture may cramp and distort our thinking; when we are mesmerized by one way of looking at the problem, gaining an understanding of it may seem impossible. By offering a different object of comparison, however, Wittgenstein gets us to see the issue in a new light and so eliminates our difficulties. Seen in context and such that we can gain a clear idea of the whole, the object of our uncertainty takes on a new aspect, and as clarity is attained the philosophical difficulties disappear.[3]

Here one might object that our eventual understanding could take a variety of conflicting forms, i.e. that the jigsaw puzzle might allow of being put together in a variety of ways. In support of this objection, one might even invoke Wittgenstein himself, for he often argues against the dogmatism of stressing one particular way of organizing the facts at the expense of all others. 'Couldn't it all be said rather differently?', he often asked, 'wouldn't comparing the facts with something else change the impression they make?' Here, however, these questions are inappropriate, for in philosophy we are not concerned with organizing a body of facts to establish a particular theory; rather, we are concerned with clarifying a network of conceptual relations so as to eliminate those problems which arise from our not knowing our way around. The objection that a different way of organizing the material might yield different conclusions is misplaced precisely because we are not seeking conclusions. Rather, our aim is to lay to rest particular confusions through the articulation of particular conceptual relations. Furthermore, to deny that these relations exist is not like denying that an empirical relation holds, for conceptual relations are constitutive of the concepts between which they hold. Thus, to deny a conceptual relation is to advance a new and fundamentally different concept, and hence it does not call into question the clarification of the original concept, but instead proposes a different network

6

of conceptual relations which can in turn be rendered perspicuous by articulating precisely what that network is.

Thus, according to Wittgenstein, the remedy for the conceptual confusions manifested in philosophy lies in attaining an *Übersicht* of the particular segment of language concerned. Puzzled by the deceptive similarities of surface grammar, we must note grammatical differences and seek to map out the network of conceptual relations involved. A clearer view of the linguistic facts will dispel the fog of confusion and undermine the temptation to extend the analogies embodied in our language in a misleading fashion. Similarly, the ordered presentation of similarities and dissimilarities between concepts and of their complex connections will relieve our mental cramp and put to rest our fears about the lack of order in ordinary language. Such an activity gets its point from the problems with which it deals, for the nature of these problems makes necessary a clarificatory activity which has value despite making no substantive claims of its own. Thus Wittgenstein's renunciation of more ambitious philosophical projects is not a reluctant second-best; rather, it reflects the adoption of the only method he considered genuinely appropriate to the nature of philosophical problems themselves.

These last points bring out certain ideas crucial to the entire Wittgensteinian approach, for the claim that there is a fundamental distinction between the empirical and the conceptual is absolutely central to it. Thus, as we have seen, Wittgenstein suggests that one can specify new concepts by altering conceptual relations without any question arising of whether these new concepts correspond to reality. Similarly, he rejects the idea that our concepts stand in need of justification, and by restricting the philosopher's work to clarification implicitly denies that our conceptual system may stand in need of correction. One might argue, however, that it is all very well articulating the network of concepts we currently possess, but that doing so only raises the further question of whether that network is correct and adequate. However, Wittgenstein rejects this question, arguing that it makes no sense to ask if grammar is correct. Instead he claims that grammar is autonomous (i.e. not answerable to reality). This claim is central to his later philosophical writings and it would be inappropriate to try to explore it in detail here; none the less it is worth outlining the general contours of Wittgenstein's position.[4]

Thus Wittgenstein argues that grammar, unlike propositions, is itself neither true nor false but rather that which enables us to formulate true and false propositions. Our concepts provide rules for the use of words to describe the world; by specifying the meaning of a description these rules give criteria for judging whether the description is accurate. We cannot, however, ask of the rules whether they too are accurate, for they are the standards of accuracy. Rather than describing the world, the rules are what make description possible by specifying what words mean. Thus it would be wrong, for example, to argue that our colour concepts do (or do not) accurately capture the real nature of colour. The concept of red is not answerable to what red 'really' is, for what red really is is only given by the linguistic rules which specify our concept red. People who used different rules would not be wrong, but would simply not mean what we mean by red (or colour etc.). If they grouped light red and blue objects together and asserted that they were similar, but held that light red and dark red were radically different, it would be misguided to conclude that they had blundered and set up erroneous rules. The statement that they treat what is similar as different, and the different as similar, covertly employs our own colour concepts and so merely underlines the fact that their rules are different. If we recognize this, however, the notion that the rules might be erroneous also falls by the wayside. Grammatical rules do not themselves represent the world but provide a framework for representation, and like the rules laying down a system of measurement, if they can be used there is no further scope for questioning their legitimacy. Thus a grammatical statement does not capture a deep truth about reality; rather, it is part of a network of purely linguistic connections and what gives that network life is the fact that we use it. The network is 'connected' with reality not through some mysterious transcendental correctness, but through our activity, through the manifold ways we use concepts to describe and to organize the world.

It might seem, however, that when Wittgenstein describes grammar as autonomous, he contravenes his own principles, for in doing so is he not advancing a thesis? To make this claim is to miss the point of his statement, for when he says that grammar is autonomous he is merely summarizing a particular philosophical investigation.[5] What his statement rejects is not a rival claim but a piece of disguised nonsense, for the idea that grammar must conform to reality is shown not to be false but to make no sense. This illuminates further the

8

non-substantive nature of Wittgenstein's philosophy, for it illustrates how he is concerned not to prove the truth of certain propositions or the falsity of others, but rather to separate sense from nonsense. What he rejects are the empty products of conceptual confusion, while what look like Wittgensteinian theses are in fact simply reminders of particular grammatical points. In this sense, Wittgenstein's investigations of the concepts of language and grammar have a certain strategic importance; they involve, one might say, gaining clarity with respect to the clarificatory project itself. Once this is done, however, it can be seen that the non-substantive nature of Wittgenstein's philosophy arises in the first instance from its subject matter, for depicting a certain set of conceptual relations does not involve saying anything about the reality those concepts are used to represent. The philosopher's neutrality is thus similar to that of someone listing the rules of chess, for in so doing he is neither advocating a particular chess strategy nor claiming that in a particular game a certain move should be played. This analogy helps also to explain Wittgenstein's willingness to give up any element of his account, should it be contested; for to reject one of the rules of chess is simply to describe another game, and to this Wittgenstein has no objection, as long as the rules of the new game are clearly stated and the difference from the old game firmly underlined. Rightly understood, the conflict between Wittgenstein and his critic would reflect not a clash between rival accounts, but the divergence of descriptions with differing objects; neither account could be said to be right or wrong, they would simply present different concepts, and for therapeutic purposes Wittgenstein is prepared to consider whatever concepts his interlocutor wishes to propose.

Against this, it might be objected that to describe existing conceptual structures is implicitly to defend the status quo; indeed, some would argue that Wittgenstein's comments on religion provide a vivid exemplification of just this danger. To draw this conclusion, however, is to misconstrue his comments. In his writing on religion, Wittgenstein's aim is not to defend religious practices but rather to call attention to their distinctive features and the particular nature of the concepts they involve. Above all, Wittgenstein underlines the differences between science and religion; for example, he criticizes the attempt to portray belief in God as the acceptance of an inadequately supported hypothesis, arguing that such a belief is not a hypothesis at all. Wittgenstein rejects this criticism of religion because it involves a misunderstanding of its object: what he objects to, however, is not that religion is criticized but that the criticism has its basis in confused thinking. Wittgenstein also argues that it is incoherent to try to disprove the claims of religion; for any rules of proof only have force as constituting a proof within the particular language-game of which they are a part. Because different language-games involve different arrays of concepts, their claims are literally incommensurable. Thus the meaning of a religious claim can only be specified in terms of religious concepts, and hence the attempt to assess it in terms of other concepts finds no purchase. For this reason, where language-games clash (and issue in different practices) it makes no sense to seek to adjudicate between them in purely conceptual terms.

The charge that Wittgenstein's approach is dangerously conservative could, however, be continued by suggesting that the language-game itself might be inherently confused; were this to be the case, a philosophical critique could indeed undermine it. However, the notion of an inherently confused language-game does not stand up to examination. Earlier, when we talked of conceptual confusion, we were referring to difficulties produced by our inability to find our way round our concepts in reflection, i.e. where confusion arose from the discrepancy between the concepts we actually used and our philosophical understanding of that use. We have also talked of confusion where the attempt is made to take concepts from one language-game and apply them to another. However, with respect to the language-game itself, there is no basis for talk of confusion. One consequence of the fact that concepts are only defined within language-games is that there is no independent basis for the attribution of conceptual confusion to the language-game itself. What is presupposed in the notion of an inherently confused language-game is the possibility of an independent assessment of grammar; this, however, would only be possible if grammar was in some sense responsible to reality, and, as we have seen, this idea makes no sense.[6] A language-game may, of course, be alien to us – the reasons and evidence that count in it may strike us as misguided – but it would make no sense to claim that our rejection of the language-game had a purely conceptual basis.

The key features of Wittgenstein's conception of philosophy can be brought into focus through a brief comparison with some ideas put forward by Derek Parfit in the preface to his book *Reasons and Persons*. There Parfit suggests that there are two types of philosophy – descriptive philosophy and revisionist philosophy. The former 'gives reasons for what we instinctively assume, and explains and justifies the unchanging central core of our beliefs about ourselves and the world we inhabit' (Parfit 1984: *x*). The latter, on the other hand, is concerned not only to interpret our beliefs, but also, when they are false, to change them. Parfit's notion of descriptive philosophy may seem to parallel Wittgenstein's; in fact, however, it expresses a radically different conception. Thus, for Wittgenstein, philosophy is not concerned with beliefs we hold or with assumptions we make; rather, it is concerned with concepts. Similarly, its aim is not justification or explanation but rather the achievement of clarity. As far as our beliefs and assumptions are concerned, these may be either true or false, and hence their investigation will typically involve the weighing-up of evidence. Any conclusions this investigation produces will consequently be provisional, in the sense that the discovery of new evidence will always remain a possibility.[7] In contrast, our concepts cannot be said either to be true or to be false, and hence a grammatical investigation involves neither the assembling of evidence nor its assessment. Rather, this type of investigation is an exercise in clarification, and what it involves is the clarification and systematic representation of the rules which define our concepts. Furthermore, for Wittgenstein the first step towards clarity is the recognition of the distinction between the conceptual and the empirical, and this distinction Parfit fails to recognize. Thus, from a Wittgensteinian perspective, there is no choice between ways of doing philosophy, for if the investigation is to be conceptual then the only coherent aim it can have is description *in the Wittgensteinian sense*. Hence it would be misleading to see Wittgenstein as putting forward a narrow conception of philosophy, for if one accepts his arguments, his conception is the broadest conception possible. It is not that he believes it to be more prudent to concentrate on 'limited objectives'; rather, he holds that no more can be done – indeed, for him it is precisely the attempt to do more that generates nonsense and confusion.

We began our account of Wittgenstein's views on philosophy by noting that for him, philosophical problems are to be resolved by attaining an *Übersicht* of the particular segment of language concerned. However, in the course of the process of conceptual clarification, it becomes apparent that behind particular grammatical confusions there lie more general intellectual tendencies. For this reason, Wittgenstein's philosophical activity becomes in part an attack on certain widespread and well-entrenched ways of thinking. This might seem to conflict with our earlier claims about the non-substantive nature of his philosophy, but the tension is more apparent than real. Thus Wittgenstein remains committed to not advancing theses and to simply rectifying confusions through the ordered presentation of that upon which we all agree; that this aim itself – the aim of clarity – is non-neutral with respect to confusion is of course something that has been true from the start. Later, however, we shall have to consider the basis for the claim that a particular piece of thinking is confused, for, as we have seen, the claim simply to be rectifying confusion is central to the non-substantive nature of a Wittgensteinian investigation.

One general source of confusion against which Wittgenstein argues is the temptation to seek for explanation where this is no longer appropriate. In philosophy, for example, vanity, ambition, and a peculiar kind of hubris continually urge us to say more than we really know. Impressed by the apparent depth of philosophical problems, we feel that when doing philosophy we are coming to grips with all that is most important, the essence of reality, as it were. 'The world is everything that is the case', we declaim, thinking we are grasping a profound truth when really all we are doing is repeating a contentless grammatical rule. Furthermore, our confused statements do not just express linguistic confusions, rather they satisfy 'a longing for the transcendent, because in so far as people think they can see the "limits of human understanding", they believe of course that they can see beyond these' (*CV*: 15). Thus the metaphysical response to philosophical problems has certain satisfactions, and these were not unknown to Wittgenstein himself. Indeed, he recognized that 'for some people it would require a heroic effort to give up this sort of writing' (*RW*: 105). Nevertheless, his account of philosophical problems shows that a metaphysical response can never provide a satisfactory solution to them, for in response to an incoherent question any potential 'answer' can at best only mirror the incoherence of the question.

The struggle to describe and not explain is thus both a struggle against a general intellectual tendency and a personal ascesis; what is required for clear thinking is the introduction into our thought of a rigour and discipline previously lacking. As Wittgenstein notes in *Culture and Value*, 'working in philosophy – like work in architecture in many respects – is really more a working on oneself. On one's own interpretation. On one's way of seeing things. (And what one demands of them)' (*CV*: 16). In this sense,

> what makes a subject hard to understand – if it's something signifi-
> cant and important – is not that before you can understand it you
> need to be specially trained in abstruse matters, but the contrast
> between understanding the subject and what most people *want* to
> see. Because of this the very things which are most obvious may
> become the hardest of all to understand. What has to be overcome
> is a difficulty having to do with the will, rather than with the
> intellect. (*CV*: 17)

The rigour which accurate description requires also imposes other demands on our thinking, for in our confusion we are easily led into making statements subtly devoid of sense. The laziness of our thinking also shows itself in an over-hasty recourse to certain pictures. Thus, primitive pictures (e.g. the notion that the meaning of a word is the object it designates) can dominate our thinking, while the comfort certain pictures offer us (e.g. the idea of finding an unquestionable foundation for our knowledge) can blind us to the most elementary and obvious of truths. Pictures can also exercise a charm or fascination which leads us into confusion by disguising the nature or basis of statements. For example, the Darwinian notion of evolution may appear to be a purely scientific hypothesis, but, as the reaction to it indicated, its importance lay in the framework it offered for thinking about certain issues. Thus Darwin's central thesis was not seen (or presented) as a tentative hypothesis requiring further evidence; rather, it was a picture immediately rejected by some and enthusias-
tically endorsed by others. The force of the picture lent the thesis a certainty (indeed, an apparent necessity) which went far beyond what the evidence accompanying it actually justified: 'in the end you forget entirely every question of verification, you are just sure it *must* have been like that' (*LA*: 26–7). Part of the attraction of such a picture is the simplification and pleasing unity it introduces into our thoughts. In this way, however, the picture encourages us to overlook certain differences; convinced by fifty cases out of a hundred, we are persuaded that the explanation must hold universally. Similarly, when presented with an analogy or connection between two markedly different things, we may be so impressed that we claim that one is 'really' just the same as the other (and here the paradoxical nature of our claim may actually

be one of its attractions). In contrast, Wittgenstein's philosophy seeks to combat the tendency to over-generalization and to the assimilation of the significantly different. Accordingly, as a motto for the *Philosophical Investigations* he considered using the Shakespearian line 'I'll teach you differences'.[8] An alternative motto he also considered was Bishop Butler's admirable dictum 'Everything is what it is and not another thing.'

One aspect of the tendency to over-generalization is what Wittgenstein called 'the philosopher's contempt for the particular case'. In his search for essence the philosopher turns away from the trivial and the everyday, and in this way his thinking can take on an abstract and indeed dehumanizing character. The stress on rationality, whether it manifests itself in theory-building or in the search for foundations, hides from view certain central features of human existence:

> the aspects of things that are most important for us are hidden because of their simplicity and familiarity. (One is unable to notice something – because it is always before one's eyes.) The real foundations of his enquiry do not strike a man at all. Unless *that* fact has at some time struck him. And this means we fail to be struck by what, once seen, is most striking and most powerful. (*PI*: para. 129)

From this perspective one might see Wittgenstein's philosophy as a return to the human, a series of reminders of the everyday truths which theorizing tends to make us overlook. Thus the task of philosophy becomes that of putting back into context that which looks mysterious when presented out of it or in a distorted and abstract form. In his writing on language, for example, Wittgenstein stresses that words occur in the context of action, that 'language is a characteristic part of a large group of activities – talking, writing, travelling on a bus, meeting a man etc' (*LA*: 2). Thus, when discussing aesthetics, he concentrates

> not on the words 'good' or 'beautiful' which are entirely uncharacteristic, generally just subject and predicate ('This is beautiful'), but on the occasions on which they are said – on the enormously complicated situation in which the aesthetic expression has a place, in which the expression itself has almost a negligible place. (*LA*: 2)

Once again, the careful presentation of points no one would deny can provide a path back from error and confusion to clarity and understanding.

A number of the tendencies Wittgenstein points to as underlying philosophical confusion come together in the adverse effects which can arise from the dominant position of science in our culture. In view of our culture's tremendous technological successes, it is easy for 'a kind of idol worship [to develop], the idol being science and the scientist' (*LA*: 27). This can influence both the content of our accounts and the kinds of account we find acceptable; for 'the fatal thing about the scientific way of thinking, which the whole world employs nowadays, is that it wants to produce an explanation in answer to each anxiety' (quoted in Kenny 1984: 43). As we have seen, in philosophy such a response is inappropriate, and hence Wittgenstein warns against 'the permanent danger of wanting to use [the word "explanation"] in logic (philosophy) in a sense taken over from physics' (*BT*: 418). The methods of science may also be inappropriate for other reasons; in particular a scientific approach is ill-suited to understanding certain aspects of human existence. The problems of ethics, art, and religion, for example, are not scientific in nature and so are not amenable to scientific resolution. Furthermore, the attempt to achieve a 'scientific' understanding of these fields often generates confusion and distortion, for the stress on explanation produces essentialism and reductionism, while the attempt at impartiality encourages the adoption of an abstract approach which can itself become a major barrier to understanding. Having made these points, however, it is important to note that Wittgenstein's objection is not to science itself, but rather to the over-extensive and inappropriate application of its particular methods and concepts: the danger of science is that

> *one* particular method elbows all the others aside. They all seem paltry by comparison, preliminary stages at best. You must go right down to the original sources in order to see them all side by side, both the neglected and the preferred. (*CV*: 60–1)

The influence which the model of science can exercise over the philosopher is illustrated in the work of Bertrand Russell. In marked contrast to Wittgenstein, Russell held that the future of philosophy lay in adopting the method of science. Similarly, for Russell the search for explanation, and the presentation of theories, was crucial, for the over-riding aim of his philosophy was to provide 'a theoretical understanding of the world' (Russell 1918: 17). The achievement of this goal involved the putting forward of philosophical theses, that is to say, hypotheses 'which systematize a vast body of facts and never lead to any consequences which there is any reason to think false' (Russell 1918: 103). Thus for him, philosophy is concerned precisely with establishing the truth or falsity of propositions, and for this reason he believed that a tentative, piecemeal approach would offer 'the possibility of successive approximations to the truth' (Russell 1918: 113). Furthermore, in order to make philosophy more scientific, he called for 'the elimination of ethical considerations from philosophy' (Russell 1918: 29), for he argued that only thus could the anthropocentric bias of previous philosophy be replaced by the impartiality of science.[9]

Wittgenstein's criticisms of the Russellian view are excellently summarized in Baker and Hacker's essay on Wittgenstein and the nature of philosophy (Baker and Hacker 1980: 457–92). For our purposes, however, it is more interesting to consider the implications Russell's approach has in the field of ethics, for here too the influence of science plays a crucial role in his thinking. Thus, Russell is concerned to explain the genesis of ethical notions; his aim is to describe 'the way in which ethical notions arise' (Russell 1918: 108). The conclusion he reaches is that 'ethics is essentially a product of the gregarious instinct, that is to say, of the instinct to co-operate with those who are to form our own group against those who belong to other groups'. In this way, the grand claims made by ethics are seen as illusory; according to him, 'when the animal has arrived at the dignity of the metaphysician it invents ethics as the embodiment of its belief in the justice of its herd'. Although

> ethics is in origin the art of recommending to others the sacrifices required for co-operation with oneself . . . by reflection, it comes, through the operation of social justice, to recommend sacrifices by oneself . . . [But] all ethics, however refined, remains more or less subjective. (Russell 1918: 108)

Russell's comments on ethics illustrate our earlier remarks about how enthusiasm for science can encourage a reductive and abstract approach to understanding human beliefs and practices; for he writes in complete abstraction from his own humanity ('when the *animal* . . .') and so produces an account that is hard to recognize as an account of *ethics*. Furthermore, his explanation of ethics in terms of its origins is both speculative (since it is unsupported by any evidence, it is literally pure speculation) and irrelevant (for it offers no insight into the meaning or significance of contemporary ethical practices).

16

Russell's theory offers no remedy for our uncertainties about ethics: someone wracked with uncertainty in the face of a moral dilemma will not be helped by it to gain a better understanding of the nature of his difficulties. More generally, Russell's account offers no insight into why ethics might matter to people. Ironically, the weakness of his account is revealed in the difficulty he himself had in accepting it. Thus in his *Reply to Criticisms* he writes:

> certainly there seems to be something more [to ethics]. Suppose, for example, that someone were to advocate the introduction of bull-fighting in this country. In opposing this proposal, I should *feel*, not only that I was expressing my desires, but that my desires in the matter were right, whatever that may mean. As a matter of argument, I can, I think, show that I am not guilty of any logical inconsistency in holding to the above interpretation of ethics and at the same time expressing strong ethical preferences. But in feeling I am not satisfied. (quoted in Mackie 1977: 40)

The clash between Russell's account of ethics and his own moral convictions is an indication of confusion, for, as he admits, he is unclear as to the meaning of the ethical claims he himself wants to make. Thus, rather than providing a satisfactory philosophical account of ethics, his remarks in fact constitute excellent raw material for a philosophical investigation, and we shall explore the attitude they express in Chapters 6 and 7.

In contrast to Russell's investigation, our investigation of ethics will not seek to explain ethics (e.g. by advancing hypotheses about its origin), nor will it seek to prove its validity. Instead, the aim of our investigation is to help us attain a clear view of this area of our lives by offering an accurate account of the concepts it involves and so dissolving the uncertainties about the nature of ethics which give rise to our philosophical difficulties. To understand ethics, however, we need to gain a firm grasp of its specificity, and one of the tendencies we shall fight against is the tendency to assimilate ethics and its problems to those which arise in other areas of our lives. In particular, there is a great temptation to transfer notions of proof and objectivity from other language-games and seek to apply them in ethics. However, when we remind ourselves of certain obvious features of human action, the inapplicability of demonstration in ethics becomes apparent, and this in turn illuminates the nature of the problems we encounter in this area.

17

A Wittgensteinian investigation of ethics will, however, differ from Wittgensteinian investigations of concepts such as that of a rule or of language. In the first place, the character of the investigation will be less obviously linguistic. Although the treatment of specific issues (e.g. the subjective–objective question) will parallel that adopted by Wittgenstein in other areas, overall, certain differences will arise, largely from the fact that, in the one case, we are investigating a whole area of our lives and, in the other, the grammatical relations of specific concepts. In the latter case, the sources of confusion are most immediately linguistic, whereas in the former our confusions may in part reflect certain general intellectual tendencies. Here the reminders that need to be assembled are restatements of obvious truths designed to restrain the philosopher's tendency to rationalistic abstraction. These points are illustrated by Wittgenstein's own lectures on aesthetics and religious belief, for there the main thrust of his discussions is to criticize the attempt to import scientific notions into aesthetic and religious debate. None the less, the aim of a Wittgensteinian investigation in ethics remains exactly the same as that in general philosophy: in both cases the goal is to achieve the clarity derived from gaining an *Übersicht*, and what this involves is not the putting forward of new answers but the ordered presentation of what we already know.

At this stage, it is worth reconsidering Wittgenstein's claim that his philosophy is non-substantive, for as he himself admitted in the lectures on aesthetics, he is 'in a sense making propaganda for one style of thinking as opposed to another' (*LA*: 28). The apparent contradiction here vanishes if one reconsiders the basis of Wittgenstein's claims. Thus Wittgenstein's argument is that certain intellectual difficulties can be resolved simply by eliminating confusions in our thinking. The method of resolving these difficulties will therefore not involve the advancing of substantive theses, but rather the clear presentation of conceptual relations. However, since the confusions which bedevil our thinking are often the product of certain general intellectual and cultural trends, the struggle for clarity will involve combating these trends.[10]

The notion of philosophy as therapeutic and as a struggle against confused thinking can, however, be given a slightly broader application. Here the product of confused thinking will be not literal nonsense, but a position which might not have been advanced were it not

18

for confusion. In this case, the position itself might be coherent, but it would have been adopted on the basis of misunderstanding or failure to perceive what the alternatives to it were. To give an example, in his lectures on aesthetics Wittgenstein discusses the claim that the pleasure of poetry lies in the associations it produces in us. He points out that this is an inappropriate characterization of our attitude to poetry, for we don't say 'this poem is just as good as that one, for it gives me the same associations.' Here what Wittgenstein does is to remind us of the obvious, i.e. he underlines certain differences we have been led to neglect.

> If someone talks bosh imagine a case in which it is not bosh. The moment you imagine it, you see at once it is not like that in our case. We *don't* read poetry to get associations. We don't happen to, but we might. (*LA*: 34)

In such situations, the presentation of a clear picture of the topic at issue may be of important therapeutic value. Once again, however, it would not involve making substantive claims, for there would be no attempt to question the validity of the other position as such.

Here the question arises as to how one can substantiate the claim that a certain piece of thinking is confused. Wittgenstein suggests two kinds of cases where someone can be said to be confused in his thinking: first, where there is a discrepancy between an individual's practice and the description he offers of that practice, and second, when it is clear that someone would not make a certain statement if he were aware of certain grammatical differences. In both cases, an understanding of the other person's practice is presupposed, and this presupposition is authenticated by *the other person's* acceptance of the account offered to remedy his confusion. Here it is crucial to note that the clarification is only shown to be such if it is accepted. This is of course important on therapeutic grounds, but it has a much more fundamental justification, for the proffered description is only established to be a description of the other person's practice, an articulation of his concepts, when it is accepted by him. Furthermore, where the confusion produces nonsense, only acceptance of the therapy indicates that the particular grammatical dissatisfaction in question has been alleviated; in this case, 'what the other recognizes is the [misleading] analogy which I point out to him as the source of his thoughts' (*BT*: 410).

Thus Wittgenstein's *grammatical* investigations differ markedly from the presentation of a substantive view. In the first place, the aim is different, for Wittgenstein's aim is not to advance his own personal views, but rather through description to eliminate confusion and so achieve clarity. The second and related difference lies in the notion of agreement, for that Wittgenstein's remarks simply describe a practice by articulating the concepts involved in it (and that the description is accurate) is shown by its acceptance by the participants in the practice whose concepts it purports to articulate. Furthermore, since Wittgenstein believed that any conceptual investigation could only be descriptive, he seeks neither to prove the validity of a certain position, nor to call into question the conceptual coherence of others. On Wittgenstein's account neither enterprise makes sense, for given that grammar is autonomous there is no scope for conceptual adjudication between rival practices and alternative grammars. Reality cannot justify one set of concepts as opposed to another; and any attempt to use canons of consistency or coherence to adjudicate would also be misguided, for the status of such canons would be identical to that of the grammars over which they were intended to adjudicate. Thus if someone rejects Wittgenstein's account of a practice (or concept), then his basis for so doing must either be the claim that it is not simply a description or the claim that what it describes is not the practice (or concept) of that individual. In either case, Wittgenstein's concern would be to come up with a description that was accurate and appropriate; having done that, there would be no scope for him, as a philosopher, to say more.

The existence of moral controversy might seem to pose a further problem for the non-substantive nature of a Wittgensteinian investigation of ethics, for it might be argued that such an investigation would either have implicitly to validate one side of the debate or be forced into an unhelpful silence. To take the subjective–objective debate as an example, it seems that the only alternative to arguing one side of the question is to be reduced to the banal claim that some believe one thing, some the other. Obviously more than this needs to be said and our analysis of the problem will be in two stages. First, we shall seek to clarify the nature of the question at issue. Here it is important to note that one cannot define objectivity in one context and then use this term 'in the same sense' in another; in the new context what constitutes the *same* sense may be unclear, or rather, since the context is new, there may be no such thing as the same sense. Hence it is crucial to establish what objectivity and subjectivity might mean specifically in the sphere of ethics. Second, we shall seek to explore the nature of the claims made by the two parties to the debate: what is it, for example, that is expressed in the claim that ethics is objective? Against what background can we understand this claim and the one that opposes it? The two stages of our investigation represent the attempt to separate philosophical issues from the particular claims of specific moral positions. The confusions surrounding the objective-subjective question can be dissolved; but when this is done what is revealed is the rivalry of particular moral positions, whose claims we can hope to clarify but not, as philosophers, assess. However, by bringing out the context of these claims, a purely clarificatory activity can none the less play a vital role in illuminating the significance of the issues at stake.

Having outlined Wittgenstein's views on philosophy and how we intend to extend this approach to ethics, one major issue remains, for, whatever the virtues of description, it would seem hard to deny that the great metaphysical systems of the past possess an ethical depth lacking in Wittgenstein's own writings. Ironically, Wittgenstein's account of traditional philosophy might seem to exemplify the kind of reductive account against which he inveighed. Thus he criticized Freud for analysing a 'beautiful' dream in exclusively bawdy terms, asking '*Wasn't* the dream beautiful then?'; and yet, against an account of metaphysics as the expression of linguistic confusion, one might similarly ask 'Isn't metaphysics deep?' This criticism, however, fails to do justice to the complexity and subtlety of Wittgenstein's account of previous philosophy, for Wittgenstein claimed to regard 'some of the great philosophical systems of the past as among the noblest productions of the human mind' (*RW*: 105). This prompts several questions, for how can philosophical systems have this exalted status if the problems which occasioned them simply reflect lack of clarity about grammar? Furthermore, what account can Wittgenstein offer of the transition from previous ways of doing philosophy to his own?

In the *Blue Book*, Wittgenstein demonstrates his awareness of these issues when he says that his activity might be seen as 'one of the heirs of the subject that used to be called Philosophy' (*BB*: 28). In his lectures of this period, he expands this comment:

> Why do I wish to call our present activity philosophy, when we also call Plato's activity philosophy? Perhaps because of a certain

analogy between them, or perhaps because of the continuous development of the subject. Or the new activity may take the place of the old because it removes mental discomforts the old was supposed to. (*AWL*: 28)

Thus Wittgenstein recognizes that his activity is different from Plato's, though none the less related to it. To make clear the nature of this relation, he offers a number of comparisons, for example, he describes it as similar to our relation to those mathematicians of former times who sought to trisect an angle with ruler and compasses. Here the point is that accepting a proof that this is impossible gives us a new idea of trisection, one we didn't have before the proof was constructed. 'The proof led us a road *which we were inclined to go* but it led us away from where we were, and didn't just show us clearly the place where we had been all the time' (*BB*: 41). Similarly, Wittgenstein's construal of philosophical problems as grammatical confusions changes the nature of philosophy and hence offers a solution to philosophy's previous quest only in so far as it shows a way to find rest for the intellectual dissatisfaction that previously motivated that quest.

Elsewhere Wittgenstein claims that his aim in philosophy is to show the fly the way out of the fly-bottle, and this metaphor itself is illuminated by the context of a parallel comment in the *Remarks on the Foundation of Mathematics*. Here Wittgenstein is discussing the popular puzzles in which a number of geometrical shapes have to be arranged to form a particular shape such as a rectangle. Our difficulties in solving such a puzzle reflect an intellectual 'blind-spot' – it is as though 'a demon [had] cast a spell round this position [the solution] and excluded it from our space' (*RFM*: 56). Showing someone the solution removes the blindness by showing them a new way of seeing the problem – 'as if a fly were shown the way out of the fly-bottle' (*RFM*: 56). In another illuminating comparison, Wittgenstein compares the philosopher to the would-be thumb-catcher, who holds out his thumb and snatches at it, only to find that the object of his snatching disappears in the act of snatching. Here 'there is a conflict between the aim of a person who wants to catch his thumb and the fact that he would not be satisfied had he done it' (*AWL*: 166). Similarly, on Wittgenstein's account, the philosopher's dissatisfactions are such as will never be relieved through the giving of answers to his questions, for although a particular system may give temporary relief it will itself become the subject of questioning, and in this way the original sources of grammatical unease will again re-emerge. Wittgenstein therefore proposes that we look at these questions in a different way, and by altering our conception of philosophy find the means to give philosophy peace. The search for profound answers gives way to the quiet weighing of linguistic facts.

> The old idea – roughly that of the (great) western philosophers – was that there were two kinds of problem in the scientific sense: essential, big, universal problems and inessential, as it were accidental, ones. According to our conception on the other hand we cannot speak in science of a *great* essential problem. (*CV*: 10)

The need for the completeness of a system (the giving of *all* the essential answers) also disappears; 'instead, we now demonstrate a method, by examples, and the series of examples can be broken off. – Problems are solved (difficulties eliminated), not a *single* problem' (*PI*: para. 133).

Wittgenstein's activity is thus very different from Plato's. What is it, however, that gives the latter's philosophy its profundity? Here we can take up another of Wittgenstein's comparisons, for in the manuscript of the 'Remarks on Frazer's Golden Bough' Wittgenstein compares metaphysics to magic. One effect of this comparison is to bring out the central role of language in both, for 'magic is always based on the idea of symbolism and language' (*RFGB*: 64). The reference to magic brings out the power of words, what they can mean to us and the ritualistic function they can fulfil. Taking his own earlier work the *Tractatus* as an example, Wittgenstein asks 'When I began in my earlier book to talk about the "world" (and not about this tree or this table) was I trying to do anything except conjure up something higher by my words?' (*MS*: 178). Wittgenstein's intention here is not to pour scorn on this tendency, but rather to illustrate how preoccupation with grammatical problems can come to partake of something of a more lofty nature. As Waismann noted, the puzzles about time (about the grammar of this concept) reflected in Augustine's question 'What is Time?' link up with 'deeper levels of uneasiness – terror of the inevitability of time's passage, with all the reflections upon life that this forces upon us' (Waismann 1971: 5).

Thus the attempt to answer the questions of philosophy can give expression to genuinely profound responses to the human condition: the meditation on time may yield a new way of seeing the world, a new way of making sense of human life. Nietzsche makes this point in his lectures on the early Greek thinkers, for he stresses that their greatness lies not in their contribution to our knowledge of the world, but rather in the new possibilities of life they opened up, i.e. in the grandeur and dignity of the ethical vision their works convey. The contrast here between Russell and Nietzsche could hardly be greater; for where Russell argues that the ethical element is a flaw in philosophy to be replaced with the scientific, Nietzsche sees it as philosophy's greatest virtue, treating the scientific element as essentially irrelevant. That Wittgenstein too was aware of this crucial, ethical dimension to metaphysics is hardly surprising, for the transcendental idealism of his own *Tractatus* illustrates this very point by the way in which he seeks to express the dignity of the human individual through a stress on the radical heterogeneity of the world and the will. Wittgenstein's analysis of philosophical problems, however, eliminates the possibility of philosophy continuing to fulfil this function; as Wittgenstein himself noted, one effect of this is to transform philosophy into a skill, i.e. an activity no longer requiring profundity in its exercise. Thus, for Wittgenstein, the work of the philosopher in ethics does not involve presenting particular moral insights (or would-be insights), but rather consists in clarifying the area of ethics in general. Such a clarification is made all the more necessary by the fact that the failure to separate conceptual issues (where clarity is needed and unanimity possible) and particular moral claims (about which there may be disagreement) is itself an important obstacle to attaining a clear view of the domain of ethics.

The impossibility of 'progress' in philosophy, which was the starting point of our discussion, can therefore be seen to have two sources. On the one hand, in so far as philosophical problems reflect the lack of conceptual clarity, their solution cannot consist in the gradual discovery of a body of truths which will definitively answer philosophy's questions. On the other hand, in so far as these problems give rise to ethical conceptions of the world and Man's role in it, the idea of progress (in an unambiguous and not itself ethically loaded sense) is inappropriate. Wittgenstein therefore proposes a conception of philosophy which separates the ethical and the conceptual. The possibility of such a separation, however, might itself be questioned and hence in this sense a Wittgensteinian investigation of ethics has a special necessity, for by clarifying the possibility (and importance) of this separation it throws light both on ethics itself and on the value of the shift from traditional conceptions of philosophy to that advocated by Wittgenstein.

Thus a Wittgensteinian investigation of ethics will not have the ethical character of the great Western metaphysical systems, for its aim is not profundity but clarity. For this reason, it will be non-substantive in the sense of simply describing our concepts and practices without seeking to justify them; the value of such a description will lie in its dispelling certain confusions which dominate our attempts to gain a philosophical understanding of ethics. Furthermore, in so far as some of these confusions reflect particular cultural or intellectual trends, our attempt to achieve clarity will involve struggling against these trends. Impressed by this point and by Wittgenstein's personal respect for man's tendency towards ethics, M.O'C. Drury has claimed that there is a neglected ethical dimension to Wittgenstein's own thought. Thus Drury claims that the *Tractatus*'s attempt 'to draw the limits to the ethical from the inside as it were . . . to put everything firmly into place by being silent about it' (Drury 1981: 81-2) is continued in the later philosophy. From our discussion, however, it should be clear that this misses the point; in so far as Wittgenstein's later work does impose an ethical demand, it does this not because it draws the limits to what can be said, but rather because it imposes that process of self-discipline needed to restrict oneself to 'mere' description.[11] Furthermore, the struggle for clarity might also be said to force us, as *non-philosophers*, to face up to those real moral problems from which the lazy thinking and comfortable pictures of philosophy would protect us. Thus, if Wittgenstein's philosophy has profundity of a kind, this lies in its struggle to eliminate superficiality and reveal the genuine problems which philosophy's pseudo-questions prevent us from appreciating.

MISUNDERSTANDING HUMAN ACTION (I)

His discussion of Aesthetics [and Ethics], however, was mingled in a curious way with criticisms of assumptions which he said were constantly made by Frazer in the *Golden Bough*, and also with criticism of Freud.

(Moore, in *M*: 312)

In Chapter 1 (p. 14), we quoted Wittgenstein's remark to the effect that the real foundations of a man's enquiry do not strike him at all; this remark comes from the same notebook as Wittgenstein's comments on Frazer, and the significance of this is underlined by a bracketed reference to Frazer with which the remark originally ended. This suggests that Wittgenstein saw a parallel between the errors made by Frazer and those that occur in philosophy, and in the next two chapters it is this parallel that we shall seek to explore. Our motivation for so doing lies in the common origin of Frazer's problems and the problems of moral philosophy, for in both cases confusions and distortions arise from the difficulty of giving an accurate and convincing account of human action. After examining Wittgenstein's critique of Frazer in this chapter, we shall move on in the next to consider how similar criticisms can be made of much contemporary moral philosophy.

Frazer's major work, and the one with which Wittgenstein was familiar, is *The Golden Bough* – an elaborate and fascinating exploration of early myth and ritual. Opening with a description of one particular institution (the King of the Wood at Nemi), he presents a vast body of anthropological data, grouping his material together into broad themes and families. His attitude to earlier times, however, is a strange mixture of tolerance and condescension: discussing what he calls the 'errors' of our ancestors, he suggests that these 'were not wilful extravagances or the ravings of insanity, but simply hypotheses, justifiable at the time when they were propounded, but which fuller experience has proved to be inadequate' (Frazer 1922: 264, quoted in the notes to *RFGB*: 62). Thus, earlier peoples are taken to have had a false idea of the course of nature; their beliefs, although grotesquely primitive, are taken to be proto-scientific, that is to say, of essentially the same kind as our own scientific knowledge. Although this may make earlier peoples seem stupid, such an impression recedes (he argues) when one comes to realize how widespread (and primitive) primitive thinking was; according to him, what seems stupid today was at the time quite plausible. None the less, if correct, his work would yield a number of surprising results; for example, it would demonstrate that 'human pretenders to divinity have been far commoner and their credulous supporters far more numerous than hitherto suspected' (Frazer 1911: ix).

The gulf between us and primitive peoples is explicitly underlined by Frazer; indeed, it fits well with his wider project, for he sees himself as contributing to a mental (or social) anthropology that would chart the course of Man's mental development. Impressed by Darwin's account of how the human body has evolved, Frazer held that the human mind 'has undergone a parallel evolution, gradually improving from perhaps bare sensation to the comparatively high level of intelligence to which the civilized races have at present attained' (Frazer 1931: 237). His accumulation of facts is thus intended to provide the basis for theories laying bare the general principles or laws of this development and hence of human action in general. Such theories would be psychological and reductive in nature; for example, he claims that the most powerful force in the making of primitive religion was probably fear of the human dead (Frazer 1922: 7). His scientific aims are also evident in his accounts of how ritual practices arose. For example, popular peasant ceremonies in spring, at midsummer, and at harvest are explained on the hypothesis that they 'were originally magic rites intended to cause plants to grow, cattle to thrive, rain to fall and the sun to shine' (Frazer 1911: xviii). The same approach is evident in his account of his central example. He summarizes his conclusions thus:

> I explained the priest of Aricia – the King of the Wood – as an embodiment of a tree spirit, and inferred from a variety of

27

considerations that in an earlier period one of these priests had probably been slain every year in his character of an incarnate deity. (Frazer 1911: xviii)

Wittgenstein's criticism of Frazer focuses precisely on this attempt to explain ritual practice in scientific terms; indeed, the first move in Wittgenstein's critique is to deny that Frazer has explained ritual practices at all. Instead, Wittgenstein argues that all Frazer has done is to make such practices plausible to people of the same background as himself. By claiming that ritual practices rest on mistaken scientific hypotheses, he offers an easy way of understanding them, but one whose persuasiveness is undermined by the fact that it presents ritual practices 'as, so to speak, pieces of stupidity' (*RFGB*: 61). The practices, however, only come to seem stupid because Frazer fails to recognize the specific features which set them apart from other types of activity. Thus he takes no account of the fact that magic and ritual play a special role in the lives of those who practise them, and yet one of the most striking features of ritual is that only on certain occasions do people act in this way. As Wittgenstein puts it, 'the same savage, who stabs the picture of his enemy in order to kill him, really builds his hut out of wood and carves his arrows skillfully and not in effigy' (*RFGB*: 64). Similarly, Wittgenstein notes, primitive peoples celebrate rites invoking the sun towards morning, when the sun is about to rise, but not at night when they simply burn lamps.

This simple reminder already points to the distinctive nature of ritual practice, for it suggests that in contrast with other activities there is no clear distinction within a ritual between the means and the end. Thus what is at issue is not an independently specifiable goal but the performance of a highly specific set of actions. For this reason it is misguided to see rituals as superseded by later technological advances or as resting on primitive scientific hypotheses subsequently shown to be false. Indeed, one might say that what is distinctive about a ritual is that showing that the ritual does not have a particular effect is *not* sufficient to undermine it. Thus the distinguishing features of rituals point to a connection with a fundamentally different sphere of human life, one more connected with the ethical and the religious than with the practical or the efficient. Hence one could say that Frazer shows himself to be 'more savage than most of his savages, for they are not as far removed from the understanding of a spiritual matter as a twentieth century Englishman. *His* explanations are much cruder than the meaning of the practices themselves' (*RFGB*: 68-9).

The criticisms Wittgenstein makes do not simply point to minor blemishes in Frazer's work; rather, they reveal confusions endemic in his very approach. Frazer's aim is to explain ritual practices with scientific impartiality; because of his aim, however, he abstracts from the human significance of rituals and so misses their point. Similarly, in order to provide a unified framework for his 'explanations' he adopts a reductive and grossly simplified picture of human action, implicitly construing all action in means-end terms and as aiming at want-satisfaction. However, this picture not only misrepresents the actions of earlier peoples, but also ignores certain features of our own actions, for we too sometimes perform acts that are not simply means to an end. As Wittgenstein points out, when someone kisses the picture of his beloved 'that is *obviously not* based on the belief that it will have some specific effect on the object which the picture represents' (*RFGB*: 64). The existence of a similarity between some of our acts and ritualistic actions also raises other questions concerning Frazer's account, for it suggests that he has mistaken the very nature of our interest in ritual practices. If these practices are not as alien to us as Frazer makes them appear, then the condescension and lofty impartiality of his approach may turn out to be inappropriate.

A further point emerges if one considers the terms which Frazer uses to describe ritual practices, for it is significant that when he comes to describe the views of these people he has to hand words as familiar to himself, and to us, as 'ghost' or 'shade'. As Wittgenstein points out, without words of this kind, Frazer's descriptions would be impossible. This, however, further underlines the kinship between ourselves and earlier peoples; indeed, this kinship is thus shown to be crucial to Frazer's enterprise, for without it the practices he describes would be literally unintelligible to us. This kinship is therefore the basis of his account and yet it is something he completely ignores: as Wittgenstein notes,

> much too little is made of the fact that we count the words 'soul' and 'spirit' as part of our educated vocabulary. Compared with this, the fact that we do not believe that our soul eats and drinks is a trifling matter. (*RFGB*: 70)

Our kinship with Frazer's so-called savages is evident in the direct and striking impact which his descriptions make upon us. They do not strike us as simply peculiar, but rather as imbued with a mysterious significance, and it is this that arouses in us the desire to understand them: the practices seem impressive, and our difficulty is specifying why this is so.

As we have seen, Frazer's response to our perplexity is to seek to explain these practices in terms of their origin. Wittgenstein, however, sees this as misguided; indeed, he claims that 'the very idea of wanting to explain a practice – for example, the killing of the priest-king – seems wrong' (*RFGB*: 61). One reason for this is that such actions, like any genuinely religious actions of today, in a certain sense allow of no explanation. If we can understand why people act in this way it is not because we can explain their action, but because we can see its significance. Wittgenstein illustrates this point with reference to Frazer's central example, for he notes that

> if one compares the phrase 'the majesty of death' with the tale of the priest-king of Nemi, one sees that they are the same. The life of the priest-king shows what is meant by that phrase. Someone who is affected by the majesty of death can also give expression to this through such a life. – This, of course, is also no explanation, but merely substitutes one symbol for another. Or: one ceremony for another. (*RFGB*: 63–4)

As this quotation indicates, the nature of the understanding we seek in this context is totally different from the understanding of a natural process provided by a scientific explanation. For this reason, however, Frazer's hypotheses (and his scientific approach) are misplaced and redundant. To understand ritual practices 'one must only correctly piece together what one *knows*, without adding anything, and the satisfaction being sought through the explanation follows of itself' (*RFGB*: 62–3). Our incomprehension in the face of the practice is eliminated by organizing our knowledge of the practice so as to clarify its significance. In so doing we come to understand both the practice and our reaction to it.

Wittgenstein's rejection of the attempt to explain ritual practice may initially seem puzzling, but as we have seen it does not entail a rejection of the attempt to understand. Rather, the word 'explanation' is here being used in a more limited sense, with the intention of underlining the fundamental difference between understanding human action and understanding a mechanical or natural process. The latter type of understanding is achieved by tracing a mechanism or a pattern of causes, by seeking to present the process as the outcome of a set of natural laws. Understanding the process enables us to predict its occurrence and also in many cases to manipulate it. In understanding human action, however, prediction and manipulation are typically not the key issues. Similarly, our aim is not to discover a mechanism which produced the action nor to subsume the action under universal laws of the kind 'Whenever X occurs in circumstances Y, Z will ensue'.[1] Rather, what we seek is the ability to understand a piece of behaviour as a *human* action, as the action of a conscious being. Thus we seek to fit it into a context of intentions, desires, and emotions. For example, we may come to understand an appeasement ritual by connecting it up with occasions when we too feel actions of appeasement would be appropriate. Why people should perform such acts at all, however, is left unexplained, and someone to whom the notion of appeasement means nothing is simply left with the fact that human beings act in this way.

Frazer's work itself both in its form and in its content involuntarily underlines the points we have been making and so brings out the differences between understanding human action and understanding natural phenomena. Thus in the preface to *The Golden Bough*, Frazer makes a strange admission, for he writes:

> by discarding the austere form, without I hope the substance, of a scientific treatise, I thought to cast my material into a more artistic mould and so perhaps to attract readers who might have been repelled by a more strictly logical and systematic arrangement of the facts. (Frazer 1911: viii)

Ironically, what he does not realize is that in so far as he does this, he adopts precisely the form appropriate to his material, for the fascination of his own book underlines the fact that our interest in ritual is precisely not scientific.[2]

> That a man's shadow which looks like a man, or that his mirror image, or that rain, thunderstorms, the phases of the moon, the change of seasons, the likenesses and differences of animals to one another and to human beings, the phenomenon of death, of birth and of sexual life, in short everything a man perceives year in, year out, connected together in any variety of ways – that all this should play a part in his thinking (his philosophy) and his practices, is obvious, or in other words this is what we really know and find interesting. (*RFGB*: 66–7)

The further irony here is Frazer's blindness to the value of his own work, for what he writes illustrates Wittgenstein's claims. Thus

> when Frazer begins by telling us the story of the King of the Wood of Nemi, he does this in a tone which shows that he feels, and wants us to feel, that something strange and dreadful is happening. But the question 'Why does this happen?' is properly answered by saying: Because it is dreadful. In other words, what strikes us in this course of events as dreadful, magnificent, horrible, tragic, etc anything but trivial and insignificant, *that* is what called this incident into being. (*RFGB*: 63)

Thus the real foundations of Frazer's enquiry do not strike him at all; the most important aspects of what he describes are hidden from him precisely because of their simplicity and familiarity. Seeking to explain with scientific impartiality, he is led to abstract from the human significance of ritual and so advances an account whose inaccuracy is manifest. Rather than constituting a laudable rejection of anthropocentricism, his scientific approach is itself a source of distortion: as this indicates, the choice here is not between prejudice and impartiality, but rather between understanding and not understanding, for to ignore the human significance of these practices is precisely to eliminate the possibility of achieving the understanding of them which we seek. What Frazer ignores is the fact that our understanding of the actions of the King of the Wood differs in kind from the physicist's understanding of the 'behaviour' of atomic particles, for we understand it not by discovering the general law under which it can be subsumed, but by coming to see its significance. To recognize this difference is not to capitulate to anthropocentric prejudice; rather it is to fit one's approach to the subject matter at hand.[3]

Wittgenstein's criticisms of Frazer can best be illustrated by considering a particular example, and one case which Wittgenstein discusses in some detail is Frazer's account of the Beltane Fire Festival, a ceremony practised in Europe as recently as the eighteenth century. Interestingly this case seems to contradict Wittgenstein's central claims, for here Frazer's explanation does indeed seem important. Frazer describes the festival as follows:

> the person who officiated as master of the festival produced a large cake baked with eggs and scalloped round the edge, called the

am bonnach beal-tine, i.e. the Beltane cake. It was divided into a number of pieces, and distributed in great form to the company. There was one particular piece which whoever got was called cailleach beal-tine, i.e. the Beltane carline, a term of great reproach. Upon his being known, part of the company laid hold of him and made a show of putting him into the fire . . . And while the feast was fresh in people's memories they affected to speak of the cailleach beal-tine as dead.

(Frazer 1922: 618, quoted in notes to *RFGB*: 75)

Frazer explains this practice as a survival from the times of human sacrifice, and here his hypothesis seems to crystallize all that seems sinister about the practice. However, on closer examination, the role of his hypothesis is not what it seems, for 'what gives this practice depth is the *connection* with the burning of a man' (*RFGB*: 75). Compared with the impression which the description makes on us, his explanation is too uncertain, for it offers a mere hypothesis, whereas the festival as described is striking and disturbing *whatever* its origin. Thus 'it is not simply the thought of the possible origin of the Beltane Festival that carries with it the [sinister] impression, but rather what is called the enormous *probability* of this thought' (*RFGB*: 79). Independently of any empirical research, the practice strikes us as age-old and something other than a mere fortuitous survival. The hypothetical nature of Frazer's explanation is thus inappropriate, while what lends it support and plausibility has nothing to do with empirical evidence about how the practice arose. Indeed, as a factual claim, his explanation is speculative and of little interest; its real merit lies in illuminating the inner nature of the ritual (its significance) and thereby enabling us to understand why description of the practice makes such an impact upon us.[4]

Thus

the deep, the sinister, do not depend on the history of the practice having been like this, for perhaps, it was not like this at all; nor on the fact that it was perhaps or probably like this, but rather on that which gives me grounds for assuming this. (*RFGB*: 77)

The ceremony acquires its sinister character 'through the thoughts of man and his past, through all the strange things I see, and have seen and heard about, in myself and others' (*RFGB*: 79). The connection with human sacrifice renders explicit what is sinister about the Fire

Festival, for what we find so disturbing is that people should want to take part in a ceremony modelled on such an act: indeed, the 'spirit' of the festival is such that were it to be re-enacted one could easily imagine it getting out of hand. Although the notion of human sacrifice may be appalling, we can understand the complex of feelings that might go with it; the idea that in certain situations only a human death can appease the gods may be at odds with contemporary culture, but, as Frazer's descriptions and our response to them illustrate, the idea is less alien to us than we might hope or pretend.[5] The function of Frazer's 'hypothesis' therefore is not to provide a scientific explanation of why the practice arose, but rather to point to the reason for its being performed in distant times just as much as recently.

Against Wittgenstein's account of the Beltane Fire Festival, one might object that his interpretation is purely speculative and that it is impossible to be certain that the ritual had the same meaning for its original participants as it has for us. The first point to be made in response to this objection, however, is to note that regardless of whether Wittgenstein's account captures the original meaning of the practice, it still allows us to understand better our own response to it. It should also be noted that when we attribute a meaning to a ritual we are in a similar position to when attributing motives in general. Evidence about the circumstances and manner of the action and the utterances before, during, and after it on the part of the agent or agents are crucial to the judgement we make, but, in the absence of confirmation from the agent, the attribution of motive ultimately rests on the necessarily indemonstrable claim to insight, the conviction that one has grasped why the person acted as he did. Thus reference to the fact that it is impossible to prove an interpretation of a ritual to be correct does not count against any particular interpretation, for the bare claim that an interpretation might be wrong simply underlines the theoretical possibility of error. Finally, one might also note that the question of whether Wittgenstein is right about specific rituals is irrelevant to his fundamental aim which is to illuminate the nature of ritual in general. When we understand better why rituals of any kind should be performed, the existence of such ceremonies among earlier peoples appears not as a strange folly but as something that is readily comprehensible.

Having outlined Wittgenstein's criticisms of Frazer, let us consider the alternative account of ritual which Wittgenstein puts forward. In contrast to Frazer, when seeking to clarify the nature of ritual Wittgenstein confines himself to description. Thus he notes that

> one could begin a book on anthropology by saying: When one examines the life and behaviour of mankind throughout the world, one sees that except for what might be called animal activities, such as ingestion etc, etc, etc, men also perform actions which bear a characteristic peculiar to themselves, and these could be called ritualistic actions. (*RFGB*: 67)

Wittgenstein's aim is to bring out the specific nature of these actions and he stresses that one of their main characteristics is that they are *not* done as a means to an end. The ritual 'aims at satisfaction and achieves it. Or rather it aims at nothing at all; we just behave this way and then feel satisfied' (*RFGB*: 64). When we are confronted with a ritual action, it is a mistake to try to get beyond or behind the actions it involves; rather, what must be understood is the action itself which in one sense can be seen as a gesture. To illuminate this point, Wittgenstein compares ritualistic action with more everyday gestures such as beating the ground with one's feet to vent one's anger. Here it is clear that the action is not based on the belief that beating the ground will in some sense help one's situation. Furthermore, 'an historical explanation, say, that I or my ancestors previously believed that beating the ground does help is shadow-boxing, for it is a superfluous assumption that explains *nothing*' (*RFGB*: 72). In contrast, the connection with punishment is important because it illuminates the significance of this particular action by relating it to others, for when an individual stamps his feet in anger it is as if he wished to punish the earth itself for the wrongs he has suffered. Here if we can understand this action it is not because we can explain it. Understanding does not derive from possession of the correct theory but reflects a certain kinship or affinity with the other person: where we cannot understand our difficulty is not that we cannot predict the other person's action but that we find what he does irredeemably alien.

If, therefore, we recognize that rituals present what can be seen as a highly developed gesture-language (*RFGB*: 70), it also becomes clear why it would make no sense to talk of improving the ritual or to claim that subsequent discoveries have shown it to be erroneous. The essence of the ritual is that precisely these actions be performed, and hence there is no external yardstick against which the ritual can be judged to be deficient. It would be equally wrong, however, to conclude

35

that the ritual simply serves to give expression to certain feelings. Such a claim misleadingly suggests that what is expressed could be distinguished from the means of expression, as if the ritual might equally well be replaced by some other set of actions. Furthermore, to talk of feelings is inappropriate, for it ignores the ethical dimension to ritual action, a dimension which manifests itself in the claim that a particular set of actions is uniquely appropriate or fitting and that to fail to perform them (or to perform them in the wrong spirit) would be an act of hubris or in some cases sacrilege.

The fundamental differences between ritual action and other more everyday activities can be further illustrated by considering the role of belief in this context. Thus, in contrast to Frazer, Wittgenstein argues that 'the characteristic feature of ritualistic actions is in no sense a view, an opinion whether true or false, although an opinion – a belief – can itself be ritualistic or part of a rite' (*RFGB*: 68). Were the practices based on the belief that they were the most efficient means of attaining a certain end, then to show this belief to be false would be sufficient to alter the practice, 'but this is not the case with the religious practices of a people' (*RFGB*: 62). Although a ritual may involve beliefs, these beliefs are not its foundation:

> when, for example, [Frazer] explains to us that the king must be killed in his prime, because the savages believe that otherwise his soul would not be kept fresh all one can say is: where that practice and these views go together, the practice does not spring from the views but they are both just there. (*RFGB*: 62)

The word 'belief' is in fact as misleading in this context as it is in the phrase 'belief in God', for what is at issue is not so much an opinion which may be straightforwardly true or false, but rather a distinctive outlook or way of understanding the world. The belief is not the expression of a particular empirical claim which can be resolved by a straightforward appeal to the facts; rather, it draws its support from a much wider field, in a sense from the entirety of the individual's experience. For precisely this reason, however, it is absurd to abstract such beliefs from their contexts and treat them as mistakes or massive blunders. For example, when it is said that Attila the Hun undertook his military campaigns because he believed he possessed the sword of the god of thunder, it would be ridiculous to understand his actions as based on a misapprehension as to the provenance of his sword. Rather, the belief is simply 'the last result – in which a number of ways of thinking and acting crystallize and come together' (*LA*: 56). The basis of such a belief, and the role it plays in the life of an individual, is totally different from that of an opinion, and, as Wittgenstein notes elsewhere, it is for this reason that in the context of religion we use words such as dogma. To understand such beliefs we must consider them in context and against the background of the way of thinking of which they are a part; only then can we recognize their significance and understand why people should have come to hold them. If, on the contrary, we assimilate them to empirical beliefs and consider them in abstraction from their context, then it is little wonder that they come to seem absurd and stupid.

Here understanding involves coming to understand the meaning a person's action has for him and this is achieved by examining the context of his action, the background against which it has its meaning. The distinctive features of a ritual can be brought out by comparing and contrasting it with others, and hence if Frazer's explanations fulfil a positive function, it is because they connect one practice with others, more particularly with other practices or actions which themselves cannot be explained, but which we already (or more easily) understand. However, the hypothetical and historical nature of his 'explanations' is thereby revealed to be superfluous to their function:

> the historical explanation, the explanation, as an hypothesis of development is only *one* way of assembling the data – of their synopsis. It is just as possible to see the data in their relation to one another and to embrace them in a general picture without putting it in the form of an hypothesis about temporal development. (*RFGB*: 69)

What is important is the perspicuous representation of the data, i.e. the arrangement of the material such that we attain an *Übersicht* (or overview) with respect to it. The practice initially puzzles us through the striking but sinister impression it makes; what is being described seems deeply significant, but its exact meaning escapes us. However, when the material is organized and connected up with the rest of our experience (e.g. when the phrase 'the majesty of death' is put together with the tale of the priest-king of Nemi) its significance becomes clear. In this way, we come to understand the practice; it would be misleading, however, to claim that we had explained it. Similarly, there is a danger of misunderstanding the role any hypotheses may have played in our account, for in this case a hypothetical connecting link does

> nothing but direct our understanding to the similarity, the relatedness of the *facts*. As one might illustrate an internal relation of a circle to an ellipse by gradually converting an ellipse into a circle; but not in order to assert that a certain ellipse actually, historically, had originated from a circle (evolutionary hypothesis), but only in order to sharpen our eye for a formal connection. (*RFGB*: 69)

Wittgenstein's criticism of Frazer raises wider issues, for Wittgenstein stresses the specific type of understanding involved in understanding human action, and yet the suggestion that understanding human behaviour involves a distinctive set of concepts is highly controversial. As we have seen with Frazer, the pre-eminent position assigned to science within our culture encourages the attempt to extend the methods and concepts of science to all fields, and this in turn can generate conceptual confusion. Thus, within the sphere of philosophy, it has become a part of established orthodoxy that when an individual states the reason for his action he is in fact making a disguised causal claim. Wittgenstein considered this claim to be an important confusion, and why he thought this, should in part already be clear from our account of his critique of Frazer. However, since the controversy about reasons and causes is an important one, it is worth considering it separately and in some detail.[6]

Wittgenstein's first move when considering reasons and causes is to point to the different ways in which each is established. Thus while a cause is established by experiment, through statistics, or by tracing a mechanism, the reason for an individual's action is typically established simply by asking the agent. The statement that such-and-such was the cause is an inductively justified hypothesis, but 'in order to know the reason which you had for making a certain statement, for acting in a particular way, etc, no number of agreeing experiences is necessary, and the statement of your reason is not a hypothesis' (*BB*: 15). Furthermore, just as reasons and causes are established in different ways, so too the nature of our interest in each is different. Thus, reasons for action often function as a justification for the action concerned, providing as they do an important criterion according to which we judge actions. On the other hand, with respect to causes there is nothing like this.

Against this one might argue that all this shows is that reasons are a special kind of cause, one in which we take a particular kind of interest. The certainty with which reasons are known might then be explained by claiming that reasons are 'causes seen from the inside'. The first difficulty raised by this claim is that it fails to explain the certainty with which reasons are known. Even if the agent were a privileged observer of the cause of his action, this would not endow his reports with certainty, but would merely increase the probability that his reports were accurate. Furthermore, it is significant that our reason-giving statements do not have the form or the grammar of genuine reports. Thus, no scope is left for the possibility that the individual might have misdescribed his inner processes or that he might have difficulty in observing them. More fundamentally, reason-giving statements cannot be reports of inner processes, for if they were, some independent means of access to these processes would be necessary to give meaning to the claim that a particular process had taken place.[7] Without such a means of access, however, it is in principle impossible to distinguish between the agent reporting correctly and his reporting incorrectly, and hence the question of correctness, and with it the reference to inner processes, falls away as irrelevant. To put it another way, since the supposed processes do not connect up with anything other than the agent's report, the only difference between a certain process having occurred and its not having occurred is that the corresponding 'report' is true! This, however, makes a nonsense of the idea that the processes are something independent on which the statement reports, for it reveals that the reference to inner processes is a misleading paraphrase of the reason-giving statement rather than an explanation of what it means.

The agent's statement, therefore, cannot be seen as a report; but what account of its meaning can we give? If we simply describe the language-game, it would seem that without any evidence the agent makes a statement purporting to offer the reason for his action and that this statement is then typically accepted by others as fulfilling precisely that function. Such an account of our language-game has a deliberate air of paradox but also reveals why the language-game is felt to be in such desperate need of explanation. Faced with the apparent absurdity of our language-game, even an unconvincing explanation can seem attractive, for while it may bring problems in its wake at least it lends the language-game some temporary plausibility. Wittgenstein, however, argues that explanation is both unnecessary and misguided; instead, he claims that what is needed is a better understanding of the language-game itself. As we saw, the claim that a reason is a cause seen from the inside is offered as an explanation of why the agent's sincere statement of his reason is treated as necessarily correct. On Wittgenstein's account, however, this necessity, like all necessity, is grammatical: that an agent should know his reason for action is part of what we mean by this term, for our interest in reasons is precisely an interest in the agent's own account of his action. The reason fulfils its function not by reporting something that occurred but by making the action intelligible as the action of a conscious individual. Someone whose account makes no sense is treated as abnormal, but *not* because his account fails to correspond to 'what really went on inside him'. Thus our language-game with reasons rests on the presupposition that in general an individual will be able to offer a reasonably coherent account of why he acted as he did. If things were such that this were no longer the case, then our language-game with reasons would lose its point. As things are, however, 'when you ask: "why did you do it?" in an enormous number of cases people give an answer – apodictic – and are unshakable about it, and in an enormous number of cases we accept the answer given' (*LA*: 22).

The background to our language-game with reasons can be clarified by considering a remark by Wittgenstein in the *Philosophical Investigations* where he stresses the distinctive nature of our interest in *Äusserungen* (avowals). Thus Wittgenstein notes that

> the criteria for the truth of the *confession* that I thought such-and-such are not the criteria for the true *description* of a process. And the importance of the true confession does not reside in its being a correct report of a process. It resides rather in the special consequences which can be drawn from a confession whose truth is guaranteed by the special criteria of *truthfulness*. (*PI*: 222)

This quotation underlines the special role that reasons and other *Äusserungen* (avowals) play in our lives, for the shift from truth to truthfulness (sincerity) brings out the key point that avowals are not reports on inner processes but have a distinctive role as *expressions* of the individual's inner life. Thus that an individual thought such-and-such is not demonstrated by advancing evidence that a certain process took place at that particular time but rather by the individual sincerely stating that at that time he had such-and-such a thought. The individual's statements about present thoughts and past thoughts thus have a very similar grammatical status; in both cases, if the statement is sincere, it makes no sense to ask if it is accurate.

Similar points apply with respect to the individual's statements about past and present intentions; and this is particularly germane to our earlier discussion, for reasons and intentions are closely connected – one might almost say, different sides of the same coin. Thus when a person acts we typically assume that he is acting with some intention, and the correlate of this assumption is the presupposition that if asked he will be able to tell us why he acted as he did. The attribution of a reason or intention goes together with understanding the action of the other person as a voluntary action, and in this sense, the postulation of intentionality and the ability to give reasons characterizes our relation to other human beings. To ask how people know their reasons or intentions (or to suggest that they might be liable to extensive error in this area) would be to undermine our concept of the individual as an agent and would be like asking how the individual knows what he is thinking. (And the answer to that question is not that the individual has special access to the processes of thought – sees them from the inside – but rather that he *says* what he is thinking, i.e. that his sincere statement that he was thinking such-and-such is sufficient to establish that he *was* thinking such-and- such.)[8]

Thus the background to our relation to others is the assumption that their behaviour will manifest a certain coherence and that they will be able to offer an account in terms of reasons, intentions, desires, etc. which will make that coherence apparent. Where this assumption breaks down, our relation to the individual concerned alters, and we can no longer treat him as a normal adult.

> Not all that I do, do I do with some intention. (I whistle as I go along etc. etc.). But if I were now to stand up and go out of the house, and then come back inside, and to the question 'Why did you do that?' I answered: 'For no particular reason' or 'I just did', this would be found queer, and someone who often did this with nothing particular in mind would deviate very much from the norm. (*RPP1*: para. 224)

To approach the language-game from the opposite end, one might note that with respect to our reason- or intention-giving statements the question is not 'What happens within you?' but 'rather: "Why should what happens within you interest me?'' (His soul may boil or freeze, turn blue or red: what do I care?)' (*RPP1*: para. 215). The response to this question is that our interest is not in putative processes but in the thoughts, feelings, desires, etc. of a person. Thus the bedrock of the language-game is simply the fact that we *do* take an interest in an individual's utterances about what he thinks, feels, wants, etc., just as we take an interest in his statements about how he will act and about why he acted as he did.[9]

Another way of bringing out the difference between reasons and causes is to note that causal explanations could not fulfil the role we assign to reasons. An account in terms of causes operates in a different dimension from one in terms of reasons and hence offers no scope for the concepts of intentional action. Causal explanation clashes, for example, with the notion of rationality, for rational action is charac- terized by the fact that it is determined by the merits of the situation rather than by the prior state of the agent. Similarly, an account in terms of causation cannot capture the notions of decision and choice, both of which are central to our talk about human action.[10] Further- more, our reasons, intentions, beliefs, etc. are related to each other and to our actions, not in terms of their causal efficacy but in terms of their content. Thus if an individual offers a reason for doing one action which could equally well have applied to another course of action open to him, he will normally be called upon to point to a differ- ence between the alternatives which led him to favour one over the other. Of course, he may reply that he was indifferent between the two actions and that he could just as well have done one as the other, but where the chosen action involved more effort etc. such an answer would be unacceptable and if the individual were then to say 'Well, the causal connections just *were* such as to make me act in that way' we should have to treat this either as a joke or as a plea not to treat his action as voluntary.

The claim that a belief caused the individual's action also brings together dissonant elements, for a belief has grounds and leads the individual to act by convincing him that a certain course of action is appropriate. The belief must therefore be relevant to the action, and out of the multitude of considerations which could possibly have led someone to perform the action, it is shown to be the decisive one by the individual's sincere statement of precisely that. In contrast, the efficacy of a cause is established by demonstrating the mechanism through which it operated or by proving a correlation between states of one kind and those of another. Furthermore, the relation between cause and effect excludes choice, so that if one treats the individual's action as caused, any decision on his part can only be seen as an epiphenomenal illusion. Finally, if the individual is seen as acting because of a certain belief, it would make sense to seek to alter the way he is acting by trying to convince him that the belief was false. However, asking the agent for the grounds of his belief and seeking to convince him that the belief is false involves treating his action not as caused, but as the result of reflection and so modifiable in the face of cogent argument or a more accurate perception of the facts.[11]

To underline the different dimensions in which reasons and causes operate, we can return to Wittgenstein's critique of Frazer, for, as we noted there, the difference between reasons and causes is correlated with a difference between the type of understanding which each furthers. Thus to know that one state always leads to another would not constitute what we call understanding a human action, for in this context we want not just to know that there is a transition but, as it were, to understand the connection itself. What interests us is not the predictable connection of two states but the thoughts and emotions which lead a person to act in a certain way and which culminate in an action we may find abhorrent or edifying, futile or worthwhile. Thus our aim is neither an increased ability to manipulate the world nor a more complete theoretical description of it; rather, it is to understand another *person* and why he acted as he did.

Before ending this section, one further point remains to be made, for having described the basic structure of our language-game with reasons, it is important to note that this structure can be modified to give rise to ever more sophisticated games. The grammar of these more complex games may allow not only for sincere and insincere avowals but also for self-deception. Thus in certain types of situation the individual may be treated as blind to his own motivation, or again in other contexts it may make sense for him to say he is uncertain as to why he acted as he did. Even in these more complex language-games, however, questions about what did or did not occur inside the agent remain irrelevant. Furthermore, such games only make sense against the background of a certain complexity (e.g. amid the complications of interpersonal relations) and can occur only as special cases, for if all reasons were insincere or the product of self-deception, the notion of a reason would collapse and our language-game with reasons would come to an end. Hence, although there are more sophisticated games these presuppose the basic language-game in which the agent is able to offer a reason and in which his sincere statement is treated as necessarily correct.

In his essay 'Actions, Reasons and Causes', Donald Davidson rejects the Wittgensteinian ideas we have outlined. He accepts that an agent's statement of his reasons is not based on induction, but argues that the explanatory function of a reason can only be accounted for on the assumption that reasons are causes. Davidson notes that 'central to the relation between a reason and an action it explains is the idea that the agent performed the action *because* he had the reason' (Davidson 1980: 9): however, he finds it hard to pin down the nature of this 'because'. Thus he recognizes that citing a reason places an action within a wider pattern, but argues that this is insufficient to explain it.

> One way we can explain an event is by placing it in the context of its cause; cause and effect form the sort of pattern that explains the effect, in a sense of 'explain' which we understand as well as any. If reason and action illustrate a different pattern of explanation, that pattern must be identified. (Davidson 1980: 10)

According to Davidson, no such pattern is forthcoming and hence reasons must be assumed to be causes; if not, their connection with action would be thoroughly mysterious.

Taking up an example from A.I. Melden's book *Free Action*, Davidson considers the case of a man driving a car who raises his arm in order to signal. What pattern, Davidson asks, explains this action? One possibility he considers is the following: 'the man is driving, he is approaching a turn; he knows he ought to signal; he knows how to signal, by raising his arm. And now, in this context, he raises his arm' (Davidson 1980: 11). This account Davidson rejects as inadequate: the man

> had a reason to raise his arm, but this has not been shown to be the reason why he did it. If the description 'signalling' explains his action by giving his reason, then the signalling must be intentional; but, on the account just given, it may not be. (Davidson 1980: 11)

44

From this, Davidson concludes that if we are to explain the man's signalling we must assume a causal connection between some pro-attitude on his part and the subsequent action of signalling; only in this way can we make sense of the claim that he acted as he did because of the reason.

Davidson's argument stresses the distinction between there being a reason for someone to do X and someone actually doing X for a particular reason. According to Davidson, the claim that someone acted for a particular reason should be taken as asserting that out of a number of possible causal processes one particular process occurred. However, such an account fails to mesh with our actual language-game with reasons. Thus when we say that someone has a reason to do something we are not asserting that a certain causal process might take place. Rather, we are pointing to a consideration which could lead the individual to choose to act in a certain way. Correspondingly, after the individual has acted, we find out what his motivation was by asking him and not by an empirical investigation into what occurred before or while he was acting. The connection between a consideration which might have led the individual to act in a particular way and the individual's actual behaviour is forged by the individual citing that consideration as his reason for acting. Such a statement by the agent characterizes his action as trying to do such-and-such or as acting thus-and-so for such-and-such a reason. Part of what is involved in understanding his action as voluntary is the presupposition that he will be able to offer a reason for it, and to this presupposition corresponds an acceptance of the agent's sincere statement of his reason as necessarily correct. The individual is treated not as a site of causal processes but as an agent, and *qua* agent he is attributed a privileged role, for by citing a consideration he authoritatively locates his action in the wider network of aims and intentions which gave it its sense.

To return to the example Davidson considers, if we wished to find out why the man raised his arm the appropriate way to do so would be to ask him. His statement would demonstrate that not only did he have a reason to raise his arm but that that was his reason for so doing. Here Davidson would accept that the agent has a privileged role in stating his reasons for action, but would argue that the statement 'He acted because . . .' can only have content if it is seen as backed up by a causal claim. We have seen that this is not so, but it is important also to note that the two claims which Davidson makes here cannot be harmonized; for if a causal claim is involved, then prior to a thorough empirical investigation the agent's opinion is as unfounded as anyone else's. Similarly, if one takes seriously the claim that reasons are causes, the question 'Why did you do X?' must be construed as meaning 'What happened prior to X to cause you to do it?' To that question, however, the individual may have no answer, or if he can mention something that happened this will generally be irrelevant. Thus he may remember an image flitting through his mind or having a certain sensation, but in general such things are neither what lead him to act nor are they of any particular interest to those trying to understand his action. Here once again the reference to 'what happened' is irrelevant. If this is so, however, there is no scope for the application of the notion of causation, and hence one is forced back to a recognition of the distinctness of reasons and causes.

A more consistent, and consequently more extreme, position than Davidson's is contained in an article by two psychologists, Richard Nisbett and Timothy Wilson. Nisbett and Wilson assume that reasons are causes and draw from this the logical conclusion that we are wrong to pay any attention to an agent's reason-giving statement. Thus they claim that 'the accuracy of subjective reports is so poor as to suggest that any introspective access that may exist is not sufficient to produce generally correct/reliable reports' (Nisbett and Wilson 1977: 233). Later, rejecting the claim to introspection, they argue that the reasons people offer are in fact based on implicit causal theories. Thus they claim that when

> subjects were asked about their cognitive processes . . . they did something which may have felt like introspection, but which in fact may have been only a simple judgement of the extent to which the input was a representative or plausible cause of output. (Nisbett and Wilson 1977: 249)

The type of basis on which Nisbett and Wilson make these claims can be illustrated by briefly describing one of the experiments which they quote. Thus in one experiment (conducted by Latane and Darley) groups of various sizes were allowed to overhear an individual in another room having what sounded like an epileptic seizure. The statistics gathered in this experiment showed that people were increasingly less likely to help others in distress as the number of witnesses or bystanders increases. However, when asked in whatever way (subtly, directly, tactfully, bluntly, etc.) subjects denied that the number of other people present affected their behaviour. Nisbett and Wilson take this experiment to show that people may put forward reasons which are in fact wrong; while the subjects in the experiment claim not to be influenced by the presence of others, the statistical data assembled seems to prove the opposite.

The argument which Nisbett and Wilson advance is interesting, but only gradually does it become clear just how radical its implications are. For example, when they consider the case of someone who is in a bad mood and explains that he is always in a bad mood when he fails to break 100 in golf, they argue that this statement presents an empirical hypothesis correlating stimuli of a general type and responses of a general type. Consequently, they hold that the statement may turn out to be wrong, i.e. that the reason/cause of the individual's bad mood may turn out to be quite other than he suspects. Another example Nisbett and Wilson consider is the case of someone who is asked whether he enjoyed a certain party. When the subject responds affirmatively and adds that he liked the people at the party, Nisbett and Wilson treat his statement as the product of a 'Why People Enjoy Parties' theory supplemented by a quick check that, say, his six worst enemies were not there. On their account therefore the subject may have enjoyed the party for some reason of which he was quite unaware. If, however, the agent may be wrong in stating his reason for liking the party maybe he is wrong in saying he liked it at all! For the sake of consistency, this statement too must surely be treated as the application to his own case of the causal theory that phenomena such as parties generally have a positive effect on human beings.

By this stage, it is clear that something is awry with Nisbett and Wilson's account. Extension of their argument increasingly undermines our concept of agency. Attention to the reasons people offer is supplanted by the attempt to explain human action on the basis of statistical correlations between behaviour of a certain kind and stimuli of a certain kind. This shift, however, serves only to highlight the divergence from what we usually mean when we talk of trying to understand human action. Thus normally when we ask someone why he is in a bad mood we are not asking him to advance a hypothesis, while if someone says that he enjoyed a party we do not expect him to arrive at his answer through recourse to a theory. The grammatical relations involved here are best illustrated by considering the case of expressing a liking or preference, for it is part of our concept of liking that the individual is the authoritative enunciator of what he likes and that when he supplements this statement with the reason for his liking something this latter statement has precisely the same grammatical status as the original one, for it is simply an amplification of it. It would, of course, be possible to define a set of exclusively behavioural criteria for liking, but this would be to propose a new concept of liking and for this reason it would make no sense to treat our earlier expressions of liking as wrong. The new concept would introduce a new game, and if the king moves one way in draughts and another way in chess this does not imply that in one of them it moves incorrectly!

Thus Nisbett and Wilson can be seen as proposing a new approach to human behaviour, one in which the concept of a reason has been abolished. On their approach, only the individual's behaviour is important, and the asking for reasons is replaced by the attempt to find statistically supported generalizations which will describe the individual's behaviour. This constitutes a radical break with the past, for the proposed new way of looking at human behaviour bears little or no resemblance to what we previously called understanding why someone acted as he did. For this reason, however, it makes no sense to see the new game as a correction of the old; rather, we have two language-games, two types of 'explanation', and since these explanations are established in different ways and have a different function both explanations may be correct at the same time.[12] The experimental data reviewed by Nisbett and Wilson therefore only seems to call reasons into question, and it only does this if one starts from the mistaken assumption that the statement of a reason involves a claim to privileged access to causal processes; as we have seen, this is not the case, and hence, *pace* Nisbett and Wilson, the offering of reasons is not simply a superstition which must disappear in the face of scientific progress. If there is error and confusion here it lies in Nisbett and Wilson's account rather than in our language-game, for Nisbett and Wilson mistakenly see themselves as making a discovery rather than a proposal, and erroneously believe themselves to have shown our language-game with reasons to be incorrect.[13] Furthermore, one might query how far one could actually get on their approach; in particular, it is hard to see how one could treat one's own behaviour as they suggest we should treat that of others, and yet if one accepts one's own reason-giving statements why should one not accept those of other people?

As our response to Nisbett and Wilson has indicated, the Wittgensteinian stress on the grammatical distinction between reasons and causes does not involve rejecting the possibility of trying to analyse human behaviour in causal terms. Rather, what is rejected is the conceptual confusion which arises when our language-game with reasons is misunderstood and reasons are treated as implicit causal claims. In a culture where science has gained a certain intellectual dominance and where causal concepts have correspondingly been thrust to the fore, it is important to remember that in general when we talk of coming to understand human behaviour we are not concerned with the discovery of causes, but with the attempt to understand the deed as the action of a thinking being, i.e. as an action chosen in the light of particular beliefs, desires, and intentions.

The peculiarly modern confusions which can arise in relation to human action can be further illustrated by considering Freud, whose work contains many of the reductive features we noted in Frazer. As with Nisbett and Wilson, much of the fascination of Freud's work lies in the way he seems to overthrow our language-game with reasons, for he seems to demonstrate that an individual's actions are often determined by forces of which he is not consciously aware. Wittgenstein was impressed by the power of this idea and by the sophistication with which Freud elaborated it; indeed, according to Rush Rhees, he would even refer to himself as a 'follower of Freud' (*LA*: 41).

However, Wittgenstein maintained that Freud was often confused about the status and indeed the nature of his own work. Thus while Freud often sees himself as having made a scientific discovery about the true causes of human action, his writings are better seen as offering a new perspective on human action rather than the correct one. Furthermore, it is not always clear what rules Freud is proposing for the new language-game he introduces; the stress on the patient's having to recognize and accept a dream interpretation as correct suggests he is proposing a modification of our game with reasons, but the emphasis on certain theories or guidelines for interpretation points in the opposite direction. Similarly, he proposes new concepts such as that of unconscious thought or intention, but since he believes himself to be making empirical discoveries, he often fails to specify clear rules for the use of these concepts. For example, it is not clear what the decisive criterion is for the fact that a dream expresses a particular unconscious thought: sometimes the analyst (and the complex theoretical apparatus of Freudianism) is treated as crucial, while at other times the vital factor is the patient's endorsement of the interpretation presented by the analyst.

One example of Freud's work which Wittgenstein discussed in

some detail was his investigation of the nature of a joke. Here Freud sees his aim as that of explaining laughter and so establishing its cause. The method he adopts, however, is not the experimental method of science; furthermore, his argument, while amply illustrated, persuades rather than offers proof of his claims. What he in fact does is to present jokes in a new light, and the value of his work does not lie in its having been empirically verified (for this Freud does not do), but rather in the illuminating comparisons it offers. Here it is also important that in particular cases the correctness of Freud's interpretation is shown by his patient's agreeing to it; and yet, as Wittgenstein notes, there is nothing corresponding to this in physics (*AWL*: 40). 'What the patient agrees to can't be a *hypothesis* as to the *cause* of his laughter, but only that so-and-so was the *reason* why he laughed' (M: 317). For a scientific investigation of the cause of his laughter, the patient's agreement or disagreement is irrelevant; however, if we seek the reason for his laughter, then his agreement is essential, for only his acceptance establishes that the proffered explanation was the reason.

Here Freud's failure to distinguish between reasons and causes not only renders the nature of his enquiry ambiguous, but also introduces a distorting element into the account he offers. Thus, failing to recognize the nature of the understanding here at issue, he seeks for explanations of a scientific type; in this way, however, his account becomes reductive and essentialist, for he seeks to discover *the* nature of a joke rather than recognizing that in different contexts jokes may be made for different reasons. Similarly, the nature of Freud's achievement is other than he himself imagines, for his investigation does not explain why people make jokes; rather, it offers one way of looking at jokes which throws an interesting light on their relation to other pieces of human behaviour. Thus both Frazer and Freud seek to offer explanations in contexts where Wittgenstein holds that what is required is not an explanation, but that clarification embodied in the attainment of an *Übersicht*. Ironically, the value of both Frazer and Freud's work lies in their contribution to that end.[14]

As the example of Freud illustrates, the errors made by Frazer are the reflection of a more general tendency, and in this sense Wittgenstein's criticisms of Frazer can be seen to isolate a set of distinctively modern confusions. Thus what dominates the investigations of both Frazer and Freud is the model of science; as a consequence of this each seeks for (causal) explanations in a context where this is inappropriate. Here the attempt to be scientific encourages the assimilation of reasons and causes and so leads to a reductive account of human action. Similarly, the misguided attempt to maintain a scientific impartiality in the investigation of human practices itself becomes an obstacle to understanding, for the rationalistic spirit it promotes encourages a blindness to certain aspects of human life (what might be called a blindness to the spiritual). In the next chapter, we shall consider how these same confusions manifest themselves in the attempt to understand ethics.

3

MISUNDERSTANDING HUMAN ACTION (II)

> When we do philosophy we are like savages, primitive people, who hear the expressions of civilized men, put a false interpretation on them, and then draw the queerest of conclusions.
>
> (Wittgenstein, *PI*: para. 194)

In the last chapter we considered Wittgenstein's critique of Frazer and noted how Frazer's scientific aims led him to offer a distorted account of ritual practice. As we saw, Frazer's errors are the product both of difficulties in understanding human action and of certain distinctively modern intellectual trends. In this chapter, we shall argue that similar errors arise in contemporary moral philosophy: our aim will be to show that much which has recently been written on ethics embodies a startling failure to understand the nature of the moral practices and concepts we actually possess.

An appropriate starting point for our investigation is utilitarianism, for this distinctively modern doctrine has been widely influential both inside and outside philosophy. The account we shall consider is that outlined by J.C. Smart in the book he wrote with Bernard Williams entitled *Utilitarianism: For and Against*. Smart presents his views with commendable frankness and clarity; unfortunately, however, his desire to be hard-headed and businesslike leads him to highly paradoxical conclusions. Thus from the start it is clear that he finds it hard to understand how any reasonably clear-minded person could possibly reject utilitarianism. The reason for this is that he sees utilitarianism as the systematic code of conduct implied by generalized benevolence; hence he holds that only the hard-hearted (or the confused) could reject it. Despite its evident sincerity, this claim is slightly disturbing, for that there are a wide variety of intelligible, indeed plausible, moral systems seems clear. Consequently, Smart's denial of this truism raises doubts about the basis of his own views, for it suggests that his advocacy of utilitarianism may rest on philosophical difficulties in understanding the alternatives to it.[1]

As with Frazer, one index of the weakness of Smart's account is the fact that all other ethical systems are presented as pieces of stupidity. For example, when discussing our reluctance to view praise and blame merely as social tools for utility-maximization, Smart claims that often

> when a man says that another is wicked he may even be saying something of a partly metaphysical or superstitious connotation. He may be saying that there is something like a yellow stain on the other man's soul. Of course, he would not think this quite literally. If you asked him whether souls could be coloured, he would of course laugh at you. His views about sin and wickedness may be left in comfortable obscurity. Nevertheless the things he *does* say may indeed entail something *like* a yellow stain view. (Smart and Williams 1973: 52)

Here the suspicion that Smart has failed to do complete justice to the view he describes is overwhelming; indeed, as we shall see later, his own rationalistic superstitions, like Frazer's, are far greater than any to which he points in others. The above quotation also illustrates a different parallel between Smart and Frazer, for just as Frazer sees rituals as resting on errors, so too Smart suggests that ethical practices may rely on erroneous metaphysical beliefs. Thus, in another example, he claims that natural-law ethics depend on quasi-Aristotelian metaphysics. Such a claim, however, is misguided: first, because it suggests that practices may depend on assumptions which play no part in them or which like the yellow-stain view might be rejected by those who purportedly hold them (see below); and second, because it takes the practice to rest on the belief as on something that could be true or false. However, as in Frazer's account of ritual, this involves a failure to recognize the nature of belief in this context. Construed as empirical beliefs, the yellow-stain view and the notion of a natural law make no sense; what their real significance and meaning is, however, Smart leaves completely unexplored.

In line with his desire to be hard-headed, Smart asks what the purpose of morality is, and the only plausible answer he can find is 'to subserve the general happiness'(Smart and Williams 1973: 68). The question itself, however, is somewhat odd, for who is to say that all moral systems serve the same purpose or, indeed, that talk of purposes is here appropriate? Already in his question Smart treats morality as if it were a social institution (a special kind of National Health Service, as it were), and this in part determines his later conclusions about its content. However, if one considers our actual moral practices what is most striking is that they are *not* a social institution; that is to say, they are not something set up by a particular group of people with a certain purpose. Thus if moral concepts play a role in our lives, it is not because a determinate group of people put them forward with the intention that they should fulfil this role. For this reason, however, the question as to morality's purpose, approaches our moral practices from the wrong angle, for as they stand our moral practices involve no reference to purposes, and hence, although it may be argued that they fulfil certain purposes, *that* is not our reason for engaging in them.[2]

The question as to the purpose of morality is, of course, in harmony with Smart's wider assumption that human action can always be understood in means-end terms. This assumption goes together with his stress on utility, and yet, as we saw with Frazer, adopting such an approach involves not just simplification but distortion; by stressing one aspect of human behaviour it leads us to ignore others that are at least as important. As the case of ritual action illustrates, it is not always true that the reason something is done is because it is useful: '[the] destruction of an effigy may have its own complex of feelings without being connected with an ancient practice or with usefulness' (*AWL*: 33–4). In such contexts, it may be impossible to separate the reason for action from the specific action performed: the deed may be done not as a means to an end or because it produces a certain amount of utility, but simply because of the deed it is. Thus an individual may decide to visit a friend not because this is the utility-maximizing expenditure of time and energy (who can say what that would be?), but simply because the other person is a *friend* and because he wants to see *him*. The attempt to understand this action in abstraction from the particular circumstances in which it occurs misfires, for it leaves out of consideration precisely the factors which led the individual to act as he did.

A further source of confusion embodied in the notion of utility is the suggestion that pleasure can be quantified, for this suggests that pleasures differ in quantity, whereas they are better seen as differing in kind. Usually in making a choice, our decision is between objects which are of different kinds and hence have different attractions; for example, in choosing between going to the cinema and going to a party, we face a choice between highly different pleasures, not between different quantities of the same thing. Even in choosing which film to see, the idea that our aim is simply to maximize pleasure may be a distortion, for one may of course go to the cinema not just for entertainment but also for instruction, edification, or some mixture of all three. A further drawback to the idea that pleasure is quantifiable is that in treating pleasure and pain as belonging to one scale, it assimilates all human decision-making to a weighing-up, the calculation of a sum. However, to use one of Wittgenstein's examples, 'when a man jumps out of the window rather than meet the police he is not choosing the more agreeable' (AWL: 37). Perhaps he simply couldn't face capture or perhaps he acted from despair or wished to make a last heroic gesture of defiance. In any event, the notion of calculation is inappropriate, while to say he chose the lesser of two evils is to say nothing if the only basis for this statement is that he acted as he did. As Wittgenstein concludes, 'it happens only sometimes that when we do not choose the lesser pain or the greater pleasure we choose what will produce these in the long run' (AWL: 37).

Thus, in general, the notion of utility can easily become an obstacle to understanding human action. This point can be further illustrated with respect to ethics if we consider the account of moral reasoning put forward by Smart. Although there are numerous technical difficulties about the mechanics of actually applying the utilitarian calculus, for our purposes what is more interesting is the radically new way in which calculation is introduced into morality. For example, Smart considers the case of a Frenchman living in England in wartime conditions, where the government has requested that households save energy by only heating their homes to a maximum temperature of 50°F. As a utilitarian, the Frenchman argues that disobeying this request will have a negligible impact on general utility while considerably increasing his own; consequently, he disregards the government's request. This, Smart believes, is the rational thing to do, and he defends himself against the claim that it would be disastrous if everyone acted thus by arguing that in a rational society every individual would adopt what game-theorists call a 'mixed strategy'. This would maximize social utility on the assumption that all adopted the same rational strategy, for each individual would 'give himself a certain probability of not obeying the government's request, e.g. by deciding to throw dice, and disobey the government's request if and only if he got a certain number of successive sixes' (Smart and Williams 1973: 59). That anyone would seriously go through with this charade is hard to believe, and yet Smart presents this as an account of how we would all act if fully rational. What is even more striking, however, is the total absence of any similarity with the reasoning we actually adopt in such situations. The obvious missing element is an awareness that considerations other than utility-maximization might be at stake; although an individual might well decide to disobey any such government request, few would want to deny the relevance of questions as to his right to disobey it and the fairness of his doing so.

Thus Smart ignores an important aspect of the situation; indeed, one is tempted to say he ignores its moral aspect. Justice, however, is only one of the moral concepts of which his utilitarianism can offer no account. The concepts of loyalty and betrayal, for example, can also play no role in utilitarian thinking, for the individual's relations with friends and relatives is governed by the same utilitarian calculus as relations with strangers, and the same weight is assigned to both groups in determining how the individual ought to act. Similarly, for Smart a good agent is 'one who acts more nearly in a generally optimific way than does the average one' (Smart and Williams 1973: 48). Normally, however, what is more important to us is the sincerity of the agent's actions, the spirit in which he acts, and other such considerations. These aspects Smart ignores; instead, as Williams notes, he 'abstracts from the identity of the agent, leaving just a locus of causal intervention in the world' (Smart and Williams 1973: 96). Treating the agent as a means, he defines the best agent as that agent who contributes most efficiently towards the end of utility-maximization. The inappropriateness of approaching ethics in this way is highlighted when Smart suggests that it is superstitious to have an abhorrence for an evil man that is in any way different from 'the natural abhorrence one has for a dangerous natural object such as a typhoon or an octopus' (Smart and Williams 1973: 53). Again, he finds it hard to understand why anyone should disagree with this claim, and yet only within the context of an abstract philosophical account does it have a moment's plausibility. Our attitude to other human beings does differ from our attitude to natural objects, and a whole range of reactions which are appropriate in the one case are not in the other. If one denies this, it is no wonder that it becomes difficult to understand our everyday moral views and reactions.

The reductive nature of Smart's view of man is clear from the sequel to the above remarks, for Smart continues by claiming that 'a man is the result of heredity and environment' (Smart and Williams 1973: 53). In a similar fashion, he elsewhere treats our moral views as conditioned reflexes, arguing for instance that an *intrinsic* abhorrence of sadism, i.e. an abhorrence of it independently of its consequences for other people, is only comprehensible as the product of conditioning. However, the fact that he adopts this position stands in the way of his understanding ethics, for it encourages him to ignore the question as to why sadism might be held to be intrinsically abhorrent, and in ignoring such a question, he might almost be said to give up on the attempt to understand ethics even before he starts. Preoccupied with science, Smart seeks to adopt a scientific approach to ethics without realizing that such an approach is here entirely inappropriate – not because ethics is 'subjective', but because the issues it raises have little or nothing in common with those treated by science. The gap this creates between his account of ethics and our actual moral practices becomes apparent in the problems his view encounters, e.g. in its difficulty in accounting for the superiority of the life of Socrates over that of the fool, or in the elaborate and somewhat jesuitical arguments it requires in order to 'justify' poetry as against pushpin. Such problems arise only because the abstract notion of utility is mistakenly placed at the heart of human affairs: whatever the value of wisdom and poetry, this does not lie in their 'utility', and if one takes this notion as one's guiding star then it is small wonder that the search for understanding becomes an arduous one.

Replying to Smart, Bernard Williams raises various objections and the most important of these centres on the claim that utilitarianism offers no account of one's actions as distinctively one's own. Thus, according to Williams, there may be some projects with which the individual is so deeply and extensively involved and identified that it would be impossible for him to apply the utilitarian calculus to them. This objection rightly focuses on the way utilitarianism privileges states of affairs over actions; however, it misleadingly makes the difficulty seem a contingent psychological one. In fact, the point is not that we happen to be unable to think in this way, but rather that to think in this way would neglect much that we consider important. Like Frazer's discussion of ritual, Smart's account of ethics shows no awareness of the fact that an action can have value simply because of the action it is, i.e. that my reason for lending money to my brother may be precisely that he is my brother. Since for Smart all rational action must be comprehensible in means–end terms, actions of this kind (and much else) look irrational and superstitious. In particular, deontological views are held to derive from confusions such as 'rule worship', but to believe that it is never permissible to kill an innocent man is neither superstition nor rule-fetishism. It may indicate what one might call respect for the sanctity of human life, and although as an individual one may not share this respect, it takes a rare spiritual blindness to label it a confusion.

Smart's utilitarianism also has problems in accounting for other moral principles; for example, his account of promising betrays no recognition that our respect for the bonds of trust and friendship reflects more than the fact that the existence of such bonds is socially useful.[3] When someone decides to fulfil the trust placed in him, his decision to do so will rarely involve reflecting on the fact that the existence of such behaviour is socially useful; what is more important is the fact that failure to do so would constitute a betrayal of trust, and on many occasions this in itself may be sufficient to determine the way an individual acts. The inappropriateness of treating all actions as means to an end is further underlined by Smart's remarks on praise and blame; for, according to Smart, praise and blame are mere tools for utility-maximization. Consequently,

> a utilitarian must . . . learn to control his acts of praise and dispraise, thus perhaps concealing his approval of an action when he thinks that the expression of such approval might have bad effects, and perhaps even praising actions of which he does not really approve. (Smart and Williams 1973: 50)

Here the divergence from our actual moral practices could hardly be more extreme, and even the most ardent rationalist is likely to find something distasteful in the notion of insincere praise and blame. Smart himself occasionally seems aware of the tremendous gulf between the views he is led to embrace and more conventional views. Indeed, he sometimes draws back in the face of this gulf, admitting, for instance, to sympathy with a non-utilitarian attachment to justice, even though on his own account such sentiments are irrational (Smart and Williams 1973: 72). What our account of utilitarianism has been designed to show is that Smart finds himself in this position because of the philosophical preconceptions with which he approaches ethics. Like Frazer, he adopts a limited and distorting perspective on human action, and so finds himself unable to give a philosophically satisfactory account of why justice, for example, should be valuable. In this way, not only do his arguments betray a failure to understand the alternatives to utilitarianism, but they also suggest that his own view is adopted precisely on the basis of this failure.

———————

It might seem that in criticizing utilitarianism we have chosen too easy a target, but the features of Smart's account we have criticized are not exclusive to utilitarianism but reflect more general confusions. Thus, as Richard Norman points out in his book *Reasons for Actions*, many recent ethical philosophers 'while not explicitly accepting the label ['utilitarian'] have employed certain fundamental assumptions of a broadly utilitarian character' (Norman 1971: 3). What unites such accounts is their reductive treatment of human action and their distortion of the notion of a reason. Norman therefore uses the term 'utilitarian' to refer to any theory which claims that 'all reasons for performing actions must ultimately be derivable from statements of human wants or desires or satisfactions' (Norman 1971: 3). His intention in using the term 'utilitarianism' in such a broad way is to highlight a picture of human action which has dominated the work of a wide range of recent moral philosophers. According to this picture, human action is the product of desire, while reasons for action are seen as derived from a psychological state that gives them their force. This state is then treated as the ultimate or 'real' reason for action and therefore as the basis for moral argument; in this way, however, the reasons we actually offer are played down and the specific nature of moral reasons ignored.

Some of the attractions of this picture should be clear from our discussion of reasons and causes in the preceding chapter, for as we saw there our language-game with reasons can easily seem impossibly paradoxical. By contrast, postulating a 'real' reason lying behind the reason actually offered seems to fulfil several useful functions. First, it seems to provide human action with an unambiguous foundation and allow all action to be seen in basically the same pseudo-causal terms. Second, it seems to offer an explanation of human action, for some external phenomenon is seen as causing the psychological state, and this state is then seen as causing the action. Third, it seems to hold out the possibility of proving (or disproving) the validity of moral claims. If, for example, it could be shown that morality has effects which we must all desire, then it would seem that morality's claims would at last receive a cast-iron justification. The presentation of desires or wants as the foundation for human action has in turn two important considerations to recommend it: first, desires or wants have a transparent connection with action, so that there are no problems about how having a particular desire gives the agent a reason for action; and second, desires or wants seem to provide a foundation which is unquestionable, for the question 'How do you know that you desire or want X?' makes no sense. The attempt, however, to avoid the grammar of our language-game with reasons is misguided. These last two points, for example, simply reflect the grammar of the words concerned, and hence do not establish that desires or wants have a privileged 'foundational' status. As reasons for action, 'I did X because I wanted to' and 'I did X because it was the just thing to do' have the same status, and either may constitute an adequate reason for action. To seek to found the second in terms of the first is not only unnecessary, but also somewhat paradoxical, for the one is typically contrasted with the other, and hence the gulf between the two seems unbridgeable. Consequently, as Norman argues, acceptance of the utilitarian position leads one to doubt the very possibility of altruism, and yet such action only seems problematic within the rarefied atmosphere of philosophy. Outside the study, we apply the concept without hesitation, and confronted with non-altruistic behaviour we do not console ourselves with the philosophical reflection that any other form of action would have been conceptually impossible.

As with utilitarianism proper, the force of utilitarian accounts is to assimilate human action to the mechanical product of causally interacting forces. In this way, however, an abstract and reductive account, adopted out of what is seen as philosophical necessity, comes to stand between us and a clear view of the facts. The diversity of reasons we actually offer and their significance (what might be thought the very subject-matter of ethics) is passed over in favour of a psychological state taken to be the 'real' basis of our action. Thus if I insist on paying my debts, claiming this is the just thing to do, my action is explained as arising from a desire to pay my debts. The reason I actually offer is ignored, and the notion of justice – what it means and why I think it here appropriate – is simply bracketed off. Furthermore, the specifically moral aspects of my action are obscured, for here it is significant that paying my debts may be the last thing I desire to do.

One way of rebutting this criticism would be to argue that to act in a certain way definitionally implies having a desire to act in that way. However, it is important to note that this is a definitional move, altering the meaning of the term 'desire'. Furthermore, it is a move which brings with it many dangers, for one is encouraged to see all action as the product of desire, where desires are taken as private and just given. The picture of the mind here invoked is highly dubious[4] and the account of human action it leads to highly misleading, for having extended the meaning of the term 'desire' (or 'want'), one is encouraged to overlook the fact that in the normal sense *not* all human action arises from desire. Furthermore, since ethical motivation is typically characterized precisely by distinction from such motivation, this has the effect of encouraging one to overlook the specific nature of ethical action. The thrust of this definitional move therefore is to promote a terminology which, while in itself unobjectionable, distorts our view of the facts by encouraging us to overlook certain distinctions.

The distortion this involves can also be seen in the way in which utilitarian accounts encourage us to see all action in teleological terms; for with the view that action is always desired goes the notion that what is desired is always desired either as a means or as an end. The plausibility of this claim rests on the fact that, in judging an action, consideration of the consequences always seems appropriate. This is only so, however, to the extent that consideration of the consequences is essential to characterizing the action. As Norman notes, the more objectionable teleological claim is 'that the appraisal of an action *consists simply in* the weighing of its consequences'(Norman 1971: 87). This simply rules out by fiat those moral positions which hold that in some circumstances an action may be morally imperative whatever its effects.

This criticism can again be countered by a definitional move, for such positions may be construed as invoking special kinds of ends, e.g. justice or fairness, as ends in themselves. Such a move, however, has the same sort of pernicious consequences as its predecessor. Thus it groups together under one heading all that is not valued as a means, despite the fact that this conceals enormous differences. Furthermore, it gives primacy to the idea of a state of affairs brought about by the action involved, so encouraging an ethics of achievement rather than an ethics of action. This has the further consequence of implicitly favouring ethics of a certain kind, for states of affairs are para-digmatically materialistic. Norman summarizes these points with respect to the concept of fairness:

> To assert that an action is to be evaluated in terms of means and ends is to suggest that it should be evaluated by reference to the state of affairs which it will bring about. The point here is not just that to see the man's acting fairly in teleological terms is liable to be misleading. What is important is rather that, although we can if we wish apply to the man's actions the categories of ends and means, nevertheless in order to bring out what is significant and distinctive in his action it is necessary precisely to *contrast* it with actions performed from a teleological point of view. (Norman 1971: 90)

As Norman's remark suggests the utilitarian account, like utilitarianism in the strict sense, has the greatest of difficulties in handling a broad range of fundamental ethical concepts. The problem here lies in the stress on desire, for a desire-based account hides from view precisely that dimension which is the ethical. Thus notions of integrity, justice, and obligation come to seem odd or incomprehensible. Similarly, the notion of guilt is obscured, for it becomes difficult to distinguish regret over an imprudent action from remorse at having done wrong. The grounds for the latter are not that one's desires have been thwarted or that a sub-optimal situation has been produced: 'what is really constitutive of [one's grief] is not the thought that evil has occurred, but that it has become part of oneself. It has entered into one's soul, as it were' (Norman 1971: 95). As these points suggest, there are a large number of ethical positions which the utilitarian account encourages us to ignore. Thus, within certain ethical perspectives, particular actions may be assigned an absolute value, e.g. it may be considered morally imperative that the truth be told regardless of the suffering this may cause, or the taking of human life may be considered wrong, whatever the circumstances. Such views are neither irrational nor superstitious; like any other ethical position, what they express is a distinctive way of understanding the world. Thus they may involve the notion that life is sacred or the idea that one's action should reflect a proper sense of one's role in the wider order.

Such lofty conceptions may seem exceptional, but to object that ethics of this kind are far from typical misses the point, for the utilitarian approach encounters the very same problems with the notion of obligation itself. Thus it can accept neither that the existence of an obligation can be a sufficient reason for action, nor that obligations can be prior to interests, desires, etc. However, to deny the first is simply dogmatism; while, as Norman notes, to deny the second is to rule out a variety of ethical positions, viz. those which hold that 'the relations in which a man stands to other human beings can themselves only be described in terms of the concept of obligation' (Norman 1971: 107). Why this might be so or what it might mean we shall discuss later. Here, however, it should be noted that the process of coming to understand such views is similar to that of coming to understand a ritual practice. In both cases, it is a question of coming to see why acting in a certain way should have the importance and significance it does for the individual concerned. In this sense, the abstract nature of utilitarian accounts is a reflection of their misrepresentation of the nature of the understanding here at issue; for the treatment of reasons as desires mistakenly takes understanding human action to consist simply in identifying the desire which was supposedly its cause.

The attractions of utilitarian accounts, and more particularly of the stress on desires or wants, is evident in the influence such accounts exercise even on philosophers whose starting point is quite different. R.M. Hare, for example, bases his original account of ethics on the idea that moral judgements are universal principles of conduct. In his first book, *The Language of Morals*, however, why anyone should adopt principles, and moreover universal principles, is left entirely unclear. Later, however, when Hare amplifies his account in *Freedom and Reason*, investigation of this question immediately brings desires and interests to the fore. Thus Hare seems to see moral decision-making as a two-fold process in which the first stage, and the fundamental one, is captured by the question 'What do I want?', and the second stage by the question 'What ought I to do?'. Given the structure of this model, the only candidate for consideration at the second stage is the wants of other people, and hence the function of morality becomes simply to co-ordinate the wants of society's members. Any other conception of morality is then treated as fanaticism, an irrational attachment to mysterious ideals – why anyone should adopt these ideals is itself again left entirely unclear.

Here as elsewhere an important factor which distorts the attempt to understand ethics is the search for proof, and yet, paradoxically, one might almost take the desperation with which proof is sought as itself an indirect testimony of the impossibility of proof in this context. In any event, the attempt to prove morality generally has to begin by purging it of all its most distinctive features, for only then does the search for proof seem even remotely possible. Thus in utilitarian accounts the desire to prove moral claims (e.g. that one ought to be honest or just) takes the form of an attempt to show moral action to be in the individual's interests. As we saw, however, such a project is doomed to failure, for moral action is often precisely not in the individual's interest. More sophisticated accounts such as those of G. Warnock and J.L. Mackie seek to prove moral claims by focusing on their social value. Thus, according to Warnock, morality is a social device and its proper object is 'to make us more rational in the judicious pursuit of our interests and ends . . . to expand our sympathies, or, better, to reduce the liability to damage inherent in their natural tendency to be narrowly restricted' (Warnock 1971: 26). Similarly, for Mackie, morality's aim is 'to help to constitute a reliably responsive human environment for the freely variable purposive actions of [human agents]' (Mackie 1977: 157).

The stress on society which is evident here has radical consequences for morality's content; indeed, on Mackie's account, morality becomes much more a matter of choice than had previously been supposed. Thus, according to Mackie, the only constraint upon it is the pragmatic consideration that it must be capable of being 'adopted socially by a group of people in their dealings with one another' (Mackie 1977: 147). This emphasis on choice, however, clashes with other aspects of his account, for elsewhere he emphasizes that our actions and attitudes are often the product of social conditioning, so that when we think we are nobly choosing to act as we ought we are often doing no more than acting as programmed. Thus conscience, for example, is seen as 'moulded by evolutionary forces', while when discussing justice Mackie suggests that it is social conditioning which accounts for the widespread acceptance of this notion (Mackie 1977: 124). One effect of this reference to social conditioning is to undermine traditional moral concepts at least in their 'naive' forms. This, however, creates a fundamental difficulty both for Mackie and for other philosophers who invoke social conditioning, for it introduces two levels of account (that from inside and that from outside our dispositions), and yet once this split is introduced holding the two levels of account together becomes almost impossible.

This can be illustrated with respect to the position of the philosopher himself, for the reference to social conditioning together with the stress on morality as a social tool has the effect of placing the philosopher outside society, as it were, looking down upon it. Raised above the human condition, he is asked to propose ways of ameliorating it. In this way, however, the philosopher's relations to others becomes implicitly manipulative, for his role is to exploit their socially conditioned nature and selfish motivation to produce the best possible society. A further problem here lies in the question of the philosopher's own motivation, for if he is not acting selfishly then concepts such as altruism or justice will have entered by the back door, and Mackie's account would therefore rest on moral concepts of precisely the type which he claims do not stand up to reflection. One might also note that the philosopher finds himself in the difficult situation of having to induce people to act justly precisely because, having failed to explore the human significance of justice, he has rejected this concept out of hand.

One apparent way out of this dilemma is to argue that, although reflection about the social necessity of morality initially involves the suspension of moral concepts, these concepts can subsequently be readopted once we have seen their social advantages. The attempt, however, to drive a wedge between the concepts and their justification is unsuccessful, for to believe in the social necessity of dispositions to just actions is not to believe in justice. Furthermore, the split between oneself and others again manifests itself, for it is certainly not socially necessary that everyone without exception act justly, and so a recognition of the social necessity of just dispositions is quite compatible with the readiness to act unjustly oneself. Ironically, to avoid such difficulties Mackie himself is forced back onto the 'naïve' employment of moral concepts. For example, he notes that an individual's action presupposes that others act in certain ways and then argues that 'the demands that I thus make on others are not *unfair* if there are other transactions in which I am content that other people should treat me as a means' (Mackie 1977: 156-emphasis added). Thus, even on his account of morality, straightforward (as it were, unreformed) moral concepts end up playing a central role.

To admit this, however, would be to focus on certain features of human action which Mackie ignores, for he treats man's basic motivation as an egotism supplemented only by the dispositions wisely instilled by social necessity. Thus, according to Mackie, while rationality recommends flight to soldiers, 'military traditions of honour and loyalty to comrades can serve as invisible chains' (Mackie 1977: 116) to keep them at their posts. His account of how these chains function makes clear the reductive nature of his approach, for on his account the point is that 'the stigma of cowardice, with the disgrace and shame associated with it, can be as effective as external penalties' (Mackie 1977: 116). Here the notion that an individual might act loyally for loyalty's sake is simply disregarded. One might even argue that it is implicitly treated as an illusion; for while the individual believes that he ought to remain at his post because to do so is right, on Mackie's account his believing this is simply a product of social conditioning. To put it another way, if he attained rationality and full self-consciousness, the chains of morality would simply fall away. Mackie's blindness to the attractions (and significance) of traditional values is also evident in his review of the ethical systems of the past, for the great ethical and religious ideals that have moved people for centuries are simply rejected as 'fantasy moralities'. The biblical injunction 'Love thy neighbour as thyself', for example, is dismissed as simply 'impracticable'. In a Frazer-like manner, Mackie seems unable to understand what gave these systems their force, and hence he can only see them as illusions of extraordinary longevity. However, since concepts from this tradition still infuse our everyday moral thinking and practices, Mackie's speedy dismissal of such ideas is simply a further indication of just how far his concept of morality diverges from what we would normally call moral.

This point is underlined by an alarming section of Mackie's book entitled 'Extensions of Morality'. Here he explains that 'morality . . . is concerned with the well-being of active, intelligent participants in a partly competitive life' (Mackie 1977: 193). Strictly speaking therefore those who fall outside such a description also fall outside morality, and these include 'young children, the unborn, members of future generations, the aged, the sick, the infirm, the insane, the mentally defective and non-human animals' (Mackie 1977: 193).[5] Morality can, however, be extended, and Mackie justifies its 'extension' to children on the grounds that they are essential to society's continuation, while the aged and the sick are supposedly treated morally because we recognize that we too may one day be unable to compete. As far as those who are mentally or physically ill from birth are concerned, 'we could afford to ill-treat [them]', and hence if we do extend morality to them, the extension is 'gratuitous' and simply reflects the usefulness of cultivating humane dispositions (Mackie 1977: 193). The primacy here assigned to society is striking, as is the radical divergence from what would normally be considered moral. Indeed, Mackie's philosophy leads him so far from the everyday that, *mirabile dictu*, the truest teachers of moral philosophy [turn out to be] the outlaws and thieves who, as Locke says, keep faith and rules of justice with one another, but practise these as rules of convenience without which they cannot hold together, with no pretense of receiving them as innate laws of nature. (Mackie 1977: 10–11)

As a personal expression of his own ethical beliefs, Mackie's account may perhaps be correct;[6] as a contribution to an understanding of what is generally meant by morality, however, it is radically misleading.

The reference to society in Mackie's account fulfils the same role as that assigned to desires in the utilitarian account, for both serve to simplify morality in the attempt to make it amenable to proof. Thus, in order to adjudicate between rival accounts of the virtues, Philippa Foot argues that for something to be a virtue it must be possible to prove that its possession is to the advantage of the individual, i.e. in his self- interest.[7] Similarly, if morality is seen as having a social purpose, then there seems to be a possibility of establishing at least certain features of morality as necessary. The idea, however, that one can prove the claims of morality is itself misguided; for how can logic or mere conceptual considerations force upon the individual a particular moral viewpoint and the way of acting that goes with it? What would it mean to demonstrate that one had to act in a certain way? All that could be shown is that within a particular viewpoint a certain action is wrong; however, there is no way that such a 'proof' can be advanced independently of the proof system in which it is arrived at, i.e. independently of the particular moral viewpoint of which it is a part. If, none the less, one seeks to prove the claims of morality, then one's account necessarily becomes reductive, for only by construing it as a means to an independent end is it possible for the idea of proof to gain a purchase. Thus a basis for proof is sought by presenting morality as a vehicle for self-interest or as a device with a certain social function. Such moves, however, are reductive and offer a distorted picture of morality, for if one wishes to claim that morality has a point or purpose, then this point is no less controversial than morality itself.[8]

Here it is also important to note that such attempts at justification are necessarily irrelevant to understanding our existing moral practices; for when someone states that he acted in a certain way because to do so was just, he does not (usually) go on to say that his respect for the claims of justice is based on a regard for self-interest or the interests of society. If, however, references to such ends play no role in the moral justifications which the individual actually offers, then (as a point of grammar) they cannot be said to be part of his reasons for acting. Although the effect of his action may be to increase social utility, this cannot be the motivation or justification for his action unless the individual endorses it as such. Just as one cannot be said to be following a rule unless one knows the rule and justifies one's conduct by reference to it, so too the reason for an agent's action is the justification he offers for it; and it makes no sense to claim that the 'real' justification for an action may be unknown to him. To say that the action is justified and to offer some independent justification as its 'real' justification can only mean that we, for reasons of our own, endorse the individual's actions; and although this may be true, it does not constitute a special insight into his reason for action and certainly does not reveal what the 'real' reason must have been.

The attempt to prove the claims of morality is thus doubly misguided: first, because the notion of proof is here inappropriate; and second, because the elements from which a proof is to be constructed are drawn from outside morality, and hence any practices they might justify would not be the moral practices we actually engage in. Furthermore, as we noted, the search for proof becomes reductive because a distorting simplification of morality is required if proof is even to seem plausible. Here the virtue of the notions of self-interest and, to a lesser extent, social utility is that both are readily comprehensible and sufficiently vague to seem uncontroversial foundations. Indeed, it might seem that the two can be unified, for one might argue that the force of arguments based on social utility lies in an indirect appeal to self-interest. One might argue, for example, that without truth-telling life in society would be impossible; that social life is immeasurably advantageous to the individual; and that therefore individuals ought to tell the truth. Such an argument, however, is deceptive, for as an appeal to self-interest it has little or no force. While the individual might accept that the prevalence of truth-telling is to his advantage, it does not follow that truth-telling must begin at home; indeed, on this account the best of all possible worlds might well be one in which everyone was truthful except the individual himself. As we saw in the case of Mackie, if such arguments have any force it is via other moral concepts such as fairness, viz. given that you wish others to tell the truth, it is unfair of you not to do so yourself. Thus, although the notion of self-interest may be more readily comprehensible than the notion of justice, this is no reason for rejecting justice in favour of self-interest or, indeed, for seeking to base one on the other. In fact, what the comparison brings out are the differences between the two notions, and it is these which require philosophical investigation.

———————————

Bernard Williams's recent book, *Ethics and the Limits of Philosophy*, may seem to offer a contrast with the accounts we have previously discussed, for Williams's opposition to utilitarianism is well-known, and the explicit aim of much of his work is to bring moral philosophy closer to our everyday concerns. As should become clear, however, he has more in common with other contemporary moral philosophers than may at first be apparent. Thus he too takes as central to moral philosophy the attempt to justify morality and accordingly opens his book by considering two different attempts to provide morality with foundations. Although ultimately he is sceptical about these projects, it is significant that he sees morality as standing in need of philosophical justification. Indeed his scepticism about the possible success of foundational projects generates the problems the rest of the book is intended to resolve. As we shall see, his approach to these foundational projects exhibits similar confusions to those we have already discussed, and these confusions later undermine the plausibility of his whole account.

Thus Williams too sees justification as something at least in principle separable from the practice, for he suggests that the practice may be engaged in and its justification discovered only later. As we have already noted, this is an important confusion, for something can be a reason for action only if known to the agent and endorsed by him as his reason. The justification of the practice therefore is not something that can be 'discovered'; rather, it is manifest in the practice as it already exists. Hence if we wish to understand our present practices we need to consider the justifications which they already possess, for to propose a new justification would be to inaugurate a new practice. Williams, however, pursues the fiction of an 'external' justification, rejecting as subjective or otherwise inadequate the justifications we actually offer. Thus, like Frazer, he does not consider the human significance (and justifications) of our practices, but instead insists on a more abstract, independent justification. He is wrong, however, to believe that such a justification is needed, for, as we have emphasized, the philosophical task is to understand our moral practices, not to provide them with so-called foundations. Furthermore, the demands he places on what might count as a justification are impossible to meet, for it must simultaneously belong to the practice and not belong to it. If it belongs to or is part of the practice, then he will treat it as merely internal, and yet if it does not, then he would be wrong to treat it as a justification of *that* practice.[9]

Williams's restrictiveness in his approach to what might 'justify' morality goes together with a more general attitude to human action; for here too he adopts an 'external' viewpoint, holding this to be in some sense more objective. The effect of adopting this viewpoint, however, is to promote an abstract picture in which egotism (the reference to the self as essential for all action) is misleadingly foregrounded. Consider, for example, Williams's account of the sympathetic response to someone in trouble:

> Confronted with someone in a dire emergency, I will, if I am a humane person, acquire an overriding preference to help him if I can. That operates through consideration of what it is like for him, a consideration in which some part is played by thoughts of what this or something like it would be like for me. My knowledge of what someone wants (let us say, that I should help him out of the fire) sets off in me, granted a humane disposition, a desire to help him out of the fire. So there are four relevant truths about me in this situation. First, I know how it is for him and that he wants to be helped. Second, I know that if I were in that situation I should want to be helped. Third, I have a preference now, in my own person, for being helped in such situations. Fourth, being of humane disposition, I want to help him. (Williams 1985a: 90–1)

Here two points are worth noting: first, the pseudo-scientific, pseudo-causal nature of Williams's description (*given* a humane disposition, this *sets off* in me a desire etc.); and second, its inaccuracy, for when I move to help someone I do *not* necessarily think of what it would be like for me to be in his situation, and to say that I 'acquire an overwhelming preference to help him if I can' is not to describe some inner process with which science has yet to come fully to grips, but simply to paraphrase the claim that I want to help him as best I can. As with Frazer, it is ironic that the account which is presented as the more 'objective', the more 'correct', is in fact simply an abstract and *in*accurate one.

70

The abstraction from the human has a further important consequence for Williams's account; for having assumed that morality is
essentially a matter of dispositions, he is faced with the (insuperable)
problem of reconciling the internal and the external viewpoints. One
place where this problem becomes apparent is in Williams's remarks
on the basis of moral value:

> The difference between the inside point of view, the view from
> one's dispositions, and the outside view of those dispositions shows
> how it is that in the most obvious sense it is not true that all ethical
> value rests in the dispositions of the self, and yet, in another way, it
> is true. It is not true from the point of view constituted by the ethical
> dispositions – the internal perspective – that the only thing of
> value are people's dispositions . . . If we take up the other perspec-
> tive, however, we may ask the question 'what has to exist in the
> world for that ethical point of view to exist?' The answer can only
> be 'people's dispositions'. There is a sense in which they are the
> ultimate supports of ethical value. (Williams 1985a: 51)

The consequences of this claim and the tensions it generates fill the rest
of Williams's book; the claim itself, however, is based on an ambiguity. Thus, believing that murder is wrong might be said to
involve having a disposition to say certain things and to act in certain
ways; this does not imply, however, that believing murder to be wrong
simply *is* having this disposition. The point here is that in treating the
belief exclusively as a disposition, Williams abstracts from its content
and hence implicitly treats the question as to whether or not murder is
wrong as empty or irrelevant. His claim is thus inherently reductive
and itself implies a particular viewpoint, viz. one which treats traditional moral claims as empty. This, of course, is a point of view like
any other, but it is misguidedly presented as in some sense objectively
superior to other points of view. Here Williams's attitude is again
similar to Frazer's, for a particular modern position is taken to be
unproblematically superior to those which have gone before. Thus
with respect to ethics, Williams takes reflection to undermine traditional moral values by enabling us to recognize that acceptance of
them simply reflects the fact that individuals have come to be disposed
in a certain way.[10] Williams, however, is too quick in his rejection of
traditional values, for he fails to explore the claim which is constitutive
of traditional moral views, viz. the claim that moral judgements are
not simply the product of conditioning but are the uniquely correct

expression of the standards which ought to govern human behaviour.

The suspicion that Williams has failed to comprehend the nature of the questions at issue here is strengthened by a consideration of his comments on religion, for once again his critique is hasty and confused. Thus, from the fact that we consider certain religious ethics crude, he concludes that religion is non-'truth- tracking'; for 'if religion is ultimately a matter of what the world is like, why should the world *not* be that crude?' (Williams 1985a: 33). Here he mistakes the nature of the issue in question; for while a religious position (or a non-religious one, for instance, that of Williams himself) may be judged a crude response to the human condition, an oversimplified way of understanding the world, this does not imply that there is nothing at stake other than our reactions, nor that a more sophisticated response will necessarily exclude a reference to God.[11] Rather, what this points to is the special nature of these propositions; and yet this Williams fails to consider.

A further consequence of Williams's belief that moral values have to be seen as essentially dispositions which the individual possesses is that the nature of ethical problems changes. Thus the central questions of ethics are transformed from questions as to right or wrong into what might be called social questions. For example, according to Williams, the central question of ethics is 'granted that human beings need to share a social world, is there anything to be known about their needs and their motivations that will show what this world would best be?' (Williams 1985a: 153). Having abstracted from the content of human dispositions, however, Williams finds it difficult to find a satisfactory answer to this question and so provide morality with some content. The reason for this is the gap which his view creates between the agent's perspective and the outside view. According to Williams, 'we understand . . . that the agent's perspective is only one of many that are equally compatible with human nature, all open to various conflicts within themselves and with other cultural aims' (Williams 1985a: 52). The gap this reveals cannot, it seems, be plugged, and hence the key element becomes not so much the validity of one's beliefs as one's confidence in them. Given Williams's perspective there is little way of choosing between various possible dispositions; all he is able to say is that whatever dispositions we do adopt we will be happiest if we, as a community, do so confidently.

The emphasis which this places on the social is also evident in his comments on praise and blame; for, like Smart, Williams cuts these notions free from their usual context and treats them as a piece of social 'machinery', the optimal functioning of which then becomes one of his central concerns. In fact, he seems to suggest that the good citizen should operate a self-policing policy; for, according to him, in adopting his moral views he ought in reflection to abstract from their content and ask 'How useful is it that I think and feel like this?' (Williams 1985a: 191). Here what is held to be important is not the content of the individual's views, but rather the usefulness (to society) of someone thinking and feeling in a particular way. Thus, starting from the claim that ethics is a matter of dispositions, Williams is led to propose a radical revision of our moral thinking – indeed, it might be less misleading to say that he proposes the abolition of ethical thinking and its replacement with something new.[12] Here two aspects of Williams's account are particularly noteworthy; first, his reductive treatment of the human; and second, his attitude to ethics as traditionally understood, for his discussions of such ethics suggest a failure to understand either its basis or its nature. Ironically, Williams starts with the Socratic question 'How should one lead one's life?' and ends with the optimal social planning of dispositions – what one might call ethics as social self-conditioning.

Thus Williams's account reflects the same tendencies as the work of the other contemporary moral philosophers we have considered. Viewed as a whole, what is most striking about these accounts is, first, the reductive account of the human which they involve, and second, the corresponding failure to understand the nature and significance of moral concepts. As with Frazer, the adoption of an abstract approach leads to a failure to understand, for the stress on explanation and 'objectivity' involves a refusal to consider the human significance of the practices concerned. Consequently, just as in Frazer's work the distinctiveness of ritual action is ignored, so too in the work of many contemporary moral philosophers the distinctively moral dimension seems to disappear. Central moral concepts such as justice, integrity, and guilt are marginalized or rendered opaque, while the very notion of obligation comes to seem highly problematic. Thus the existence of a specifically moral sense of obligation is denied by some (Williams, Anscombe, MacIntyre, Foot, etc.) or explained away by others (Stevenson, Ayer, Hare, etc.). In contrast, our aim in the next three chapters will be to clarify the concept of obligation and, in the course of so doing, bring out those aspects of our moral practices which are distinctively moral.

4

THE INEFFABILITY OF VALUE

The sense of the world must lie outside the world. In the world, everything is as it is and happens as it does happen. *In* it there is no value – and if there were it would be of no value.

If there is a value which is of value, it must lie outside all happening and being-so. For all happening and being-so is accidental.

What makes it non-accidental cannot lie *in* the world, for otherwise this would again be accidental.

It must lie outside the world.

(Wittgenstein, *TLP*: 6.41)

As we saw in the last chapter, many of the difficulties in understanding our moral practices arise from the fact that the attempt to understand them is made from the 'outside'; the problem here is that from the perspective of the external viewpoint the concerns of ethics are, as it were, invisible. However, the attempt to understand ethics from the inside also runs into difficulties, as we can see if we consider the account of ethics put forward by Wittgenstein in his *Tractatus* period. Particularly important for understanding Wittgenstein's position is the lecture on ethics which he gave sometime between September 1929 and December 1930. In this lecture it becomes clear that the unusual, indeed mystical, claims of the *Tractatus* have their origin in an attempt to come to terms with everyday moral experience. Thus one of his central concerns is to do justice to our respect for the ethical, our sense of its profundity.[1] None the less, in pursuing this goal Wittgenstein seems to encounter insuperable obstacles; indeed, the philosophical difficulties are such that he is led to the conclusion that ethical propositions are literally nonsensical – futile attempts to say what cannot be said. Despite his respect for the impulse which lies behind such attempts, Wittgenstein's verdict upon them is unequivocal: ethics, he claims, is a running-up against the boundaries of language and 'this running up against the walls of our cage is perfectly, absolutely hopeless'.[2]

From this perspective, the philosophical attempt to understand ethics seems equally hopeless; indeed, far from yielding a clearer view of its subject, Wittgenstein's lecture serves only to heighten our sense of its inexplicability. Unlike contemporary philosophers, however, Wittgenstein responds to this difficulty not by condemning ethics as illusory, but by embracing a mysticism which he expounds more fully in the *Tractatus* and the *Notebooks*. Since this mysticism is largely motivated by philosophical considerations, the attempt to understand it is philosophically revealing. Indeed, coming to understand how he was led to embrace mysticism throws light on the philosophical problems of ethics and thereby reveals a way of overcoming them. As we shall see, Wittgenstein's later philosophy provides the basis on which to develop a new account of ethics, one which incorporates the insights of his lecture without invoking its mystical and metaphysical theses. Let us begin, however, by considering the lecture itself.

Wittgenstein begins his lecture by trying to give his audience a general idea of what he means by ethics. Here he invokes the definition offered by Moore, viz. that ethics is 'the general enquiry into what is good'. He adds, however, that he will be using the word 'ethics' in a broader sense than Moore, using it, in fact, so that 'it includes the most essential part of what is generally called Aesthetics' (*LE*: 4). He then goes on to offer a number of other definitions, hoping in this way 'to produce the same sort of effect which Galton produced when he took a number of photos of different faces on the same photographic plate in order to get the picture of the typical features they all had in common' (*LE*: 4). Thus he describes ethics as the enquiry into what is valuable, or really important, claiming also that it could be said to deal with the meaning of life, what makes life worth living or the right way of life.

The next step in the lecture is again indebted to Moore, for Wittgenstein notes that each of expressions he mentions ('good', 'important', 'valuable', etc.) can be used in two very different senses – a relative sense and an absolute sense. The relative sense of these terms is unproblematic: a good chair is one which fulfils a predetermined purpose, while to say that a certain road is the right road is to say that it is the right road relative to a particular destination. The word 'ought' can also be used in this way. Thus the statement 'You ought to take this road' can be replaced by a factual statement ('This is the quickest route to X') or by one conditional on a certain goal ('You ought to take this road, if you want to get to X in the shortest amount of time'). 'Used in this way, these expressions don't present any difficult or deep problems. But this is not how Ethics uses them' (*LE*: 5). In ethics, we say that something is good without specifying a particular purpose for which it is good; and when we say that something is the right thing to do, we seem to want to say that it is absolutely right, independently of any goal. Similarly, in ethical contexts, 'You ought to do X' cannot be paraphrased in factual terms, nor is its force merely conditional. Used in this way, however, the meaning of these terms becomes obscure. The questions 'Why is that the right thing to do?' and 'Why ought I to do X?' seem unanswerable, and hence the attempt to use these terms 'absolutely' itself comes to seem incoherent. The conclusion Wittgenstein draws from this is that the absolute use of such terms involves an attempt to say the unsayable. On very similar grounds, other philosophers have concluded either that no specifically ethical use of such terms exists or that the attempt to use such terms absolutely is confused.[3]

However, the attempt to deny that these words can properly be used with an absolute sense is unconvincing, for it is the absolute use of these terms that seems distinctively ethical. Indeed, it is here that the mysteriousness of value comes most obviously to the fore. The essence of the problem here seems to lie in the contrast between the concrete reality of fact and the ineffability of value, for while judgements of relative value can be treated as disguised factual statements, 'no statement of fact can ever be, or imply, a judgement of absolute value' (*LE*: 6). Similarly, all facts stand on the same level; as facts, none are in themselves sublime, important, or trivial. The fact that someone is hungry or in pain is simply a fact like any other. One consequence of this is that it would not make sense to try to establish ethical propositions scientifically, for 'we cannot write a scientific book, the subject of which could be intrinsically sublime and above all other subject matters' (*LE*: 7). Furthermore, with respect to ethics all theories and explanations seem beside the point – indeed, one might almost say that the ethical begins where all theories and explanations come to an end. As Wittgenstein puts it, 'ethics in so far as it springs from the desire to say something about the ultimate meaning of life, the absolute good, the absolutely valuable, can be no science' (*LE*: 12). If this is so, however, and if scientific investigation cannot reveal the ethical, what can? Indeed, if value cannot be derived from the factual, from where does it arise?

The linguistic investigation of ethics runs into similar difficulties. Thus, according to the *Tractatus*, propositions have meaning in virtue of depicting states of affairs; however, the propositions of ethics certainly do not do this, and consequently according to this account they are meaningless and hence strictly speaking not propositions at all. Furthermore, since they do not depict states of affairs, ethical statements cannot be verified, nor therefore can they be said to be true or false. One consequence of this is that the status of ethical statements comes to seem fundamentally obscure. The continued comparison of fact and value serves only to darken this obscurity further. Thus, since every fact is independent of other facts and contingent, each can be imagined otherwise; with values, however, this is not the case, for how could the good be the bad or vice versa? What would it mean to say that this could be imagined? Here values seem not just interdependent, but also somehow non-contingent; one would hardly say, for example, that murder just *happens* to be wrong. In this respect, the status of ethics seems similar to that of logic, for both seem concerned with the world as a whole and thereby gain a strange profundity which sets them apart from those truths which are merely contingent. Each seems, as it were, to transcend the world and yet simultaneously to constitute its innermost order.

As Wittgenstein recognized, the heart of the problem here is the action-guiding nature of value terms, for it is this which makes them seem so mysterious. Thus Wittgenstein notes that the absolutely right road would be one

> which *everybody* on seeing it would, *with logical necessity* have to go, or be ashamed of not going. And similarly the absolute good, if it is a describable state of affairs, would be one which everybody, independent of his tastes and inclinations, would *necessarily* bring about or feel guilty for not bringing about. (*LE*: 7)

The problem, however, is that 'such a state of affairs is a chimera. No state of affairs has, in itself, what I would like to call the coercive power of an absolute judge' ibid. Here Wittgenstein's investigation comes to a dead-end; unable to discover the basis of action in the facts, he is forced to look elsewhere. Thus in the *Notebooks* he considers the notion of the will and treats this as the origin of our actions. However, since the world is motivationally inert he transposes the will to *beyond* the world. Only through this transcendental will, Wittgenstein argued, do things acquire significance (*N*: 84) and hence a relation to action. Thus, ethically speaking, what our actions are taken to reflect is the transcendental relation of world and will – something of which one literally cannot speak. As we can see here, it is the connection with action which makes value seem deeper, more significant than fact, and yet, by the same token, intangible and elusive. For Wittgenstein, however, what this reflects is the limits of language: 'propositions', he concludes, 'can express nothing higher. Ethics cannot be put into words' (*TLP*: 6.42–421).

Wittgenstein's conclusion is not easy to accept, but the alternatives to it are far from obvious; more particularly, if one wishes to take the claims of ethics seriously, the issues it raises seem inescapable. The difficulties here can be dramatized by considering the picture to which Wittgenstein's account is a response. Thus the contrast of fact and value conjures up a picture of the agent stranded in a motivationally inert universe. The world in which he finds himself is a world devoid of significance – a world of facts and causes and hence one which offers no foothold for considerations which might guide his actions, no purchase for reflection on what he should do. In such a world, value is nowhere to be found, for in it 'everything is as it is and happens as it happens'. The impact of this picture is both alarming and confusing; what it seems to show is that in our actions the world leaves us frighteningly in the lurch. While we say that such-and-such is the right thing to do and while we act thus-and-so, our doing so seems to have no real basis, or if it does this basis must somehow be outside the world of facts. Against the background of this picture, human action itself comes to seem deeply mysterious; for *why* do we act? *How* do we know what is right? To talk of a transcendental will in relation to which things acquire significance may be unpalatable, but what alternative to it is there?

One possibility here would be to follow Moore and appeal to intuition as the source of moral truth. Such an explanation, however, is of little assistance, for the posited intuition seems no less mysterious than that which it was intended to explain. Whatever such a faculty might tell us, the basis of its authority remains obscure. Furthermore, the original difficulty re-emerges, for whatever the information may be, there seems no reason why it should have a necessary action-guiding force; since no information of any kind can compel us to act, the gulf between inaction and action seems as unbridgeable as ever. At this stage, to invoke perception would be equally futile, for to claim that we perceive values is not to explain how we know what is right, but rather to affirm that we do know. In this respect, Wittgenstein's account is at least straightforward, for in situating the will beyond the world it states clearly that such matters allow of no real explanation. Somehow, it seems, we move from inaction to action, despite the seemingly unbridgeable gulf between them. Although we cannot say what, something makes us act. On all such matters, nothing can be said: the inexplicability of human action seems complete.

Impatient with this inexplicability and sceptical of the ineffability attributed to value, the only alternative seems to be to dismiss value as illusory. Thus one might explain value as a 'projection' of human concerns onto the world of facts. The symmetry of this response with the previous one is striking, for the same picture plays a crucial role in both. On this occasion, however, values are not the ghostly light cast by a transcendental realm, but rather a superficial gilding of the world conjured up by an overactive human imagination. By itself, however, the notion of projection is not sufficient to explain human action, for even if we do project qualities onto the world, a projected quality is no better than a non-natural quality as an explanation of our action. Thus, since no quality can have its action-guiding nature built into it, the account in terms of projection must be supplemented by one based on causation. Here human action, like any other form of action, is explained as the product of causal factors. The difficulty, however, is that the shift to causation involves a change in dimension and therefore seems to avoid the problem rather than resolve it. The reflection and deliberation involved in human action are ignored, and hence the ethical sphere seems to disappear. Rather than explaining how an individual knows that something is right, the causal account suggests that such notions are irrelevant, epiphenomenal to the real causal mechanism.

Thus we are left facing a radical dichotomy, a dichotomy according to which ethics is either ineffable or illusory. Neither option is attractive, for where the one seems mystificatory, the other is straightforwardly reductive. However, that we should reach such an impasse suggests that we have gone awry. Indeed far from clarifying the nature of ethics we have succeeded only in rendering human action itself deeply mysterious. The difficulty we face, however, is typically philosophical, for the source of our perplexity is not the inadequacy of our information, but the difficulty of making sense of what we know, the difficulty of putting our knowledge into a coherent form. In this respect, our investigations have at least revealed the real problem, for, as we have seen, the fundamental difficulty lies in understanding human action itself. Once this problem has been overcome, understanding ethics should be correspondingly easier. To achieve this goal, however, we need a fresh start: 'the axis of our examination must be rotated about the fixed point of our real need' (*PI*: para. 108). Thus, rather than starting from the contrast between fact and value, we shall take as our central theme the notion of human action itself.

As we saw in Chapter 2, understanding human action involves a distinctive type of understanding, for it involves a consideration not of causes but of reasons. Here to understand is not to grasp a mechanism lying behind the action; rather, it is to see the action's significance – what it meant to the agent, what considerations made him choose to act as he did. Understanding the action thus takes place within the same dimension as the action itself, for the considerations which we offer as reasons are of the same kind as those which may precede an action. These considerations, however, do not force us to act, rather they offer us grounds for acting in a certain way, and we show the importance we attach to a particular consideration by *acting* according to it. Hence in understanding human action one eventually reaches the bedrock of a reaction, for at some point the giving of reasons comes to an end, and we are faced with the fact that the individual acted as he did. The reasons the individual offers for his action tell us why he acted and so offer us a way of understanding his action, but they do not show that his action was the only one logically possible nor do they demonstrate that everyone faced with such considerations would necessarily have acted as he did. Neither of these demands is coherent, for the transition from reasons and action necessarily involves a substantive reaction on the part of the individual: ultimately, the way he expresses his commitment to a certain way of assessing a situation is by acting according to that assessment.

Recognizing these points, one might talk of two levels on which an action can be understood. On the one hand, one may see an action as voluntary and know that it was done for such-and-such a reason and so understand it, but still find it strange or alien as a way of acting; on the other hand, one might find an action (and the reasons for it) easily comprehensible, perhaps (but not necessarily) thinking that it is precisely how one would have acted oneself in the same situation. In this second sense, understanding the action manifests a kinship with the agent, an ability to see why such things should matter to him; conversely, where such a kinship is absent one is simply faced with the fact that others act differently from oneself.[4] The demand for explanation or justification therefore eventually becomes inappropriate. Tautologically, where reasons run out, the demand for further reasons cannot be met. Asked why we act as we do, we can give our reasons for acting, but where these are rejected nothing remains to be said (but *not* because what remains to be said is unsayable). Here we reach bedrock, and all we can do is describe: this is how we act, and these are reasons we offer for so doing; someone to whom these reasons mean nothing is simply left with the fact that we act in this way. Similarly, to ask why we find things significant is to ask a question whose sense is unclear. The fact is that we do find things significant, and our doing so manifests itself in our actions. The reasons we offer can elucidate the nature of this significance, but it makes no sense to attempt to give the reaction itself some further basis. In answer to the question 'Why do you find things significant?' we can only reiterate our reaction and say that it is because they *are* significant.[5]

Another way of making the point that reasons come to an end is to note that the gap between reasons and action is a logical gap. Thus it is bridged not by a special kind of reason, but by our acting according to reasons; in this sense, the relation between reasons and action is always contingent. However many links one may add to the chain of reasons the need for this transition cannot be eliminated; eventually, the agent himself must act, and no number of reasons can make the transition to action for him. Our earlier sense of the unbridgeable gap between inaction and action reflects the existence of this logical gap, for our reasons do not compel us to act; rather, we show what considerations count for us by acting according to them. Here it becomes clear that what leads us to deny that reasons come to an end is precisely the tendency to assimilate reasons and causes. Thus questions such as 'What makes us act?' point us in the direction of a causal explanation where this is misleading. The apparent inexplicability of human action is thus a reflection of our own confusion, and the remedy for this confusion is a recognition of the differences between reasons and causes and hence of the inappropriateness of our original questions. In the sense in which we have reasons for action, these do not make us act, nor are the reasons according to which we act peculiar entities which cause us to move from inaction to action.

Bearing these grammatical points in mind, let us reconsider the fact-value contrast. The first point to be noted here is that just as the question 'What makes us act?' encourages us to assimilate reasons and causes, so too there is a temptation to take the factual as a model to which value is forced to conform. Not surprisingly, the consequence of this is that value comes to seem mysterious, for it is presented either as a weird kind of fact or as an unworthy aspirant to facthood. Such a train of thought is at its worst when values are presented as phantastic objects. Mackie, for example, writes that objective values would have to be entities with their 'to-be-pursuedness' built into them; since this is impossible, he concludes that values are not objective, not part of the 'furniture' of the universe. This argument, however, is confused; like the early Wittgenstein's claim that values are not in the world, it misleadingly takes the heterogeneity of fact and value to have metaphysical and ontological implications. What this heterogeneity reflects, however, is simply the fundamentally different roles fact and value play in our lives. The search for value in the world of facts is thus a search in the wrong dimension, for the very idea that values might be in the world is confused. Indeed, since the distinction between fact and value is grammatical in nature, one might almost say that the world of facts is by definition value-free.[6]

Consider, for example, the apparent truism that no fact is in itself good, bad, significant, or whatever. Already, the universal nature of this claim suggests that it has a logical rather than an empirical basis. Thus, even if we were sure that knowing a certain fact always led people to act in a certain way, we should still maintain that there was a gap between the fact and the ensuing action, i.e. that the reaction to the fact was contingent. The reference here to a reaction is important, for the crucial point is that to claim that a fact is significant is to react to it, to assign to it a certain role in one's thinking and action. Hence what is incoherent about the idea of a fact being intrinsically significant is the notion that this reaction could somehow be built into the fact itself. The same point can be made in slightly different terms, if we note that for a fact to be significant in itself the reaction to it would have to be a *necessary* one. The point here, however, is that this reference to necessity cannot be substantiated. On the one hand, it could not be causal, since a causal connection would at most establish that a certain state of affairs always caused (e.g.) humans to act in a certain way; and, on the other hand, it could not be logical, since the suggestion that logic might compel us to act makes no sense. Thus the attempt to discover a necessary connection between fact and action is misguided; what it reflects is a failure to recognize that reasons come to an end, i.e. that in understanding human action one eventually reaches the bedrock of a reaction.

The logical gap between fact and action parallels that between reasons and action. Just as the connection between reasons and action is forged not by a super-reason but by our acting according to reasons, so too the claim that a fact is significant (or important, etc.) is manifested in our reaction to it, in the role we give it in our thoughts and actions. Furthermore, since such claims involve a reaction on the part of the individual, a fact is always significant for someone. Precisely because the claim manifests a reaction, it is always logically possible for someone else to reject the claim and correspondingly act differently. This logical point, however, does not rule out the possibility of someone claiming that there is a 'right' and a 'wrong' reaction. What has to be clarified is what this means, for the nature of moral claims differs from that of empirical claims, and correspondingly the grammar of moral disagreement is different from that of empirical disagreement. Thus to believe (incorrectly) that Manchester lies nearer to London than Birmingham does is to make an error about something which can be independently assessed. Someone who did not accept a measurement of the distances involved as being relevant would not mean what we mean by the word 'nearer', etc. However, if someone claims that a certain action is right and someone else that it is wrong, their dispute cannot be solved by reference to some universally agreed procedure nor does it necessarily imply linguistic confusion. Rather, in the dispute we are confronted with two different ways of judging and acting, and each party to the dispute may claim that his perspective is uniquely correct. Here the claim that the position one adopts is uniquely valid is itself part of one's reaction, and hence one's position itself involves a reference to the fact that others may react differently. It would be a mistake therefore to move from the logical point that value judgements have their basis in an individual's reacting in a certain way, to the claim that value judgements merely reflect an individual's subjective reaction. The second claim is no longer purely logical, for it involves assessing the reaction and rules out a certain type of moral position; as such, it is a substantive claim which itself expresses a distinctive position.

The contrast between fact and value which earlier seemed so mysterious is thus revealed to be grammatical in nature; correspondingly, it becomes clear that the failure to discover a necessary connection between fact and value demonstrates neither that value is transcendental nor that it is illusory. Instead, this failure illustrates the nature of value's connection with action, underlining the point that facts are connected with our actions through our invoking them in our reasons, i.e. through our finding them significant, important, etc., through our reacting to them in particular ways. This grammatical point also enables us to see why science can make no direct contribution to ethics, for there is always a logical gap between the discoveries of science and the judgements and actions one may derive from them. Thus science could not discover that something is important; at most, it might discover something we all agree to be important. It could, for example, discover that with current rates of pollution the earth will shortly be uninhabitable. If this were a fact, it would not compel action but for many it would constitute a good reason for doing something. Although the fact would be a fact like any other, we might none the less assign it a certain importance.[7]

These considerations bring to the fore certain obvious facets of human action – facets, however, which were ignored (or implicitly denied) in the preceding discussion. Thus the search for a mysterious non-causal link between fact and value (and between fact and action) is replaced by the recognition that we act and offer reasons for our action, i.e. that we relate the facts to our actions by citing them in our reasons. For example, if someone is in pain, I may move to comfort him, and the connection between the fact of his being in pain and my action is that I cite the former as my reason for acting. If I am asked why someone's being in pain constitutes a reason for action, then I have no answer – it is things of that kind that matter to me, that is how I act. Similarly, it is equally inappropriate to ask what *made* me act, for in one sense nothing made me act; his being in pain gave me a reason for acting, but in Wittgenstein's phrase this fact did not have 'the coercive power of an absolute judge'. On another occasion, I might respond to it differently. Here there are no conceptual or logical grounds for claiming that everyone must respond to this fact in the same way, while the claim that everyone ought to do so is itself the expression of a substantive reaction and hence not something which logic could force us all to accept. This does not imply, of course, that what counts as a reason for me may not also count as a reason for others; nor does it undermine the substantive moral claim that certain considerations ought to weigh with everyone. The point here is that if others act differently the *logical* status of their action is the same as that of my own. If one wishes to criticize their action one can only do so on moral and not logical or conceptual grounds; if they 'go wrong', they go wrong morally not logically.

The logical points contained in the notion of bedrock may seem obvious, and indeed our discussion so far has been intended simply to assemble a number of 'reminders' about the nature of human action. Despite this, however, there is a perennial temptation not to recognize bedrock and instead to wish for something more. As we saw in Chapter 1 when we were discussing Wittgenstein's claim that grammar is autonomous, there is a desire to claim that our concepts and our practices reflect reality or are justified by it; incoherently, we want to claim that what we do is dictated by what is the case, as if our actions themselves could be based on truth. In ethics, this temptation is particularly strong, since within the moral sphere our deepest convictions may be called into play. What would it mean, however, for something to lie behind our actions? In what sense could truth be the foundation of action? As we saw earlier, that something is true cannot of itself logically imply action of a certain kind; the transition from the facts to action is a logical step which cannot be eliminated and one which the agent must make for himself. It is for this reason that value judgements cannot simply be derived from the facts themselves; given their connection with action, values are always the values of someone – what they reflect is always a particular way of acting. This logical point would hold even if we all acted in exactly the same way. Although in such a case no one would dispute the move from the facts to action, the logical gap would none the less remain. If we all agreed in our moral judgements (or possessed an agreed decision-procedure for resolving disagreements) this would increase the apparent similarity between moral and empirical judgements but would not eliminate the fundamental logical differences between them. The existence of moral agreement would remain contingent, for although our response to what is the case would *ex hypothesi* be unanimous, it would remain one logical possibility among others.

The attempt to deny this logical point reflects an exaggerated fear of disagreement; indeed, the search for value in the world can be seen as an attempt to rule out the very possibility of disagreement. A similar wish manifests itself in the desire for proof in ethics, indeed for 'presuppositionless' proof. Such proof, however, is no more available in ethics than elsewhere. Even in those areas where we do have proofs, the proofs are not presuppositionless but function within a particular context, within a particular game. Within Euclidean geometry, for example, one can prove that the sum of the angles of a triangle is 180°, but in non-Euclidean geometries this may no longer be the case. The point here is that a proof is only a proof within a certain context, within a game we play; outside that game, or for people to whom such a game is alien, the proof has neither meaning nor significance. Thus, even if we recognized proofs in ethics, this would not achieve what the philosopher demands, for it would still be possible for others not to recognize such proofs. If they rejected our 'proofs' and acted differently from us, what would be achieved by confronting them with these 'proofs'? One might reply that the proofs would enable us to say that they acted wrongly; but this we can say even without 'proofs'! If one now says 'Well, we would be justified in saying so', then one can only ask, 'Aren't we justified already, as things stand?' The difference between a situation where we had proofs and the actual situation would simply be the greater cohesion within our community, since *ex hypothesi* we would all recognize certain moral arguments as proofs. The logical status of our moral judgements, however, would be unchanged, and the possibility of disagreement would remain. Paradoxically, it is the incoherence of the demand for proof which reveals part of its attraction, for by eliminating the possibility of disagreement, proofs would, as it were, take over responsibility for our actions. Not only would everyone necessarily assent to our views, but we too would be spared the possibility of doubt. Although this dream is incoherent, it exercises a powerful but subtle influence over our moral thinking.

The inappropriateness of the demand for proof can be further illustrated by considering the context of moral judgements, for when we do so the possibility of disagreement appears in a very different light. Imagine, for instance, a world where there was unanimity over what was and what was not significant, where in every case the members of society did agree on how the individual should act. One striking aspect of such a world is that it would offer little or no scope for maturity, wisdom, or personality; one could talk neither of an individual coming to understand the world better, nor of his coming to perceive more clearly what was really important, nor indeed of his having a particular outlook of his own. In this respect, diversity – the fact that we react differently from each other – is of such importance that it seems paradigmatically human: a people whose actions and outlooks were absolutely uniform would seem more like automata than conscious individuals. Seen in this light, that we agree with respect to facts and disagree about values seems not mysterious but eminently comprehensible; what is perhaps most striking is not disagreement, but the extent of agreement. The possibility of dispute about value therefore arises not from its ghostly nature, but from the differences in our reactions, from the obvious point that the values by which one person lives may mean nothing to another.[8] The logical possibility of disagreement (of people acting differently from ourselves) cannot be eliminated; while, given the nature of the questions at issue, the actual existence of disagreement is itself unsurprising.

To illustrate the way in which disagreement can dominate (and distort) the philosopher's perspective on ethics let us consider Alasdair MacIntyre's account of moral argument. Like several other philosophers, he considers present-day morality to be in a state of grave disorder. According to him,

> the most striking feature of contemporary moral utterance is that so much of it is used to express disagreements; and the most striking feature of the debates in which these disagreements are expressed is their interminable character. I do not mean by this just that such debates go on and on and on – although they do – but also that they apparently find no terminus. There seems to be no rational way of securing moral agreement in our culture. (MacIntyre 1981: 6)

MacIntyre diagnoses this state of affairs as the product of conceptual disorder. Thus he stresses the conceptual incommensurability of the various types of reasons offered, underlining the point that while each set of reasons is internally coherent, there is no independent way of adjudicating between them. According to him, the problems this poses are more than just interpersonal:

> if we possess no unassailable criteria, no set of compelling reasons by means of which we may convince our opponents, it follows that

in the process of making up our minds we can have made no appeal to such criteria or such reasons. If I lack any good reasons to invoke against you, it must seem that underlying my position there must be some non-rational decision to adopt that position. Corresponding to the interminableness of public argument, there is at least the appearance of a disquietening private arbitrariness. It is small wonder we become defensive and shrill. (MacIntyre 1981: 6)

MacIntyre's picture of moral argument is an alarming one; however, the features which MacIntyre treats as symptoms of conceptual disorder are in fact grammatical points presented in a misleading way. Thus the 'conceptual incommensurability' of reasons simply reflects the logical possibility of a difference in reactions; while, as we have seen, the impossibility of independent adjudication follows not from some contingent feature of contemporary morality, but from the nature of a reason. According to MacIntyre, we lack a rational way of securing moral agreement, but in what sense could this be otherwise? In what sense could the criteria for a moral judgement be 'unassailable'? Like the notion of proof in ethics, such ideas are chimerical; since approving an action involves a commitment to acting in a certain way rather than just the application of a linguistic rule, the possibility of disagreement can never be ruled out. Whatever criteria we use for assessing whether a deed should be done, our judgement could never be unassailable, for given the nature of such judgements the logical possibility of others rejecting them can never be eliminated. MacIntyre, however, takes this logical point to reflect a blemish in contemporary morality. Furthermore, he takes it to imply that our moral judgements are in some sense arbitrary. In making this claim, however, he moves from a necessary truth, viz. that we do not have proof ('compelling reasons', sense 1) to a manifest falsehood, viz. that we lack good reasons altogether ('compelling reasons', sense 2). On the one hand, that our reasons do not compel us (that they are not such that everyone must act on them) is a grammatical point, while on the other that there are reasons which convince us (considerations we find 'compelling') is a truism. *Pace* MacIntyre, we do have reasons for making our moral judgements, although of course these reasons do not fulfil the incoherent requirement of it being logically impossible to reject them. Thus the absence of proof is no reflection on the state of contemporary morality. If disagreement does constitute a problem, it is a social not a philosophical one, for the extent of disagreement reflects not conceptual confusion, but social and cultural fragmentation; if this is taken to be a problem, it is not one to whose solution the philosopher *qua* philosopher can make a special contribution.

MacIntyre continues his discussion of moral argument by claiming that the reasons we offer for our actions cannot be all they claim to be. Thus when we offer reasons we do so with the implication that 'the reason given for the action either is or is not a good reason for performing the action in question independently of who utters it or even whether it is uttered at all' (MacIntyre 1981: 9). He takes this implication to be undermined by the feature of moral argument discussed above; however, this again is confused. The logical possibility of others rejecting the reasons I offer does not imply that these reasons are purely personal. If I say that a certain act is just, then of course it is I who am making this claim, but this does not mean that the claim itself involves a necessary reference to me. I may add that whoever denies that the act is just is wrong, and that I too would have been wrong had I denied it. In this sense, my reason may be 'impersonal' even if I advance it alone against a hostile world. Similarly, the fact that *ex hypothesi* no one would have advanced the claim had I not done so does not affect the content of my claim; in making the claim, I am reacting in a particular way, but the content of my claim is precisely a denial that this merely reflects a reaction on my part. The logic of my claim may be complex, but it is certainly not contradictory.[9]

The obvious objection to the claims that we have made is to deny that understanding human action does involve a distinctive form of understanding. If everything else is to be explained causally, why not human action as well? This objection requires detailed consideration; for the moment, however, we shall simply make two points. The first involves noting that a distinction between these types of understanding does exist and indeed plays a crucial part in our lives. When acting ourselves we reflect, come to decisions, etc., and in our mutual interaction ask for and offer reasons for what we do. Thus the dimension in which we act and in terms of which we seek to understand the actions of others simply is distinctive and (more specifically) non-causal in nature. Second, since ethics is concerned precisely with these reasons, it is only within the context of this type of understanding that our moral practices can be understood. Thus to suggest that all action should be understood in causal terms is to move outside the moral sphere and hence to make understanding ethics impossible. The particular attitude towards ethics which this implies we shall explore later (cf. pp. 129–39).

A very different objection to what has been said is the claim that to invoke the notion of bedrock is to treat all moral conviction as arbitrary. Thus Wittgenstein has often been accused of advocating a new form of irrationalism. Such a claim, however, is based on a misunderstanding of his argument; in fact, it embodies the very confusions Wittgenstein condemns. Since there must necessarily be an unmediated transition from reasons to action, the fact that moral conviction involves such a transition does not imply that it is arbitrary. On the contrary, moral conviction is a paradigm of what we call non-arbitrary belief, and it only comes to seem arbitrary if we have a confused and incoherent idea of what a non-arbitrary conviction would have to be.[10] To put it another way, Wittgenstein is not claiming that we should resignedly accept the fact that our moral practices lack foundations; rather, he is arguing that both the demand for foundations and the claim that they are lacking are equally the product of philosophical confusion. The one demands the impossible (or more accurately, the incoherent), while the other bemoans our inability to achieve it. In both cases, what is needed is recognition of the fact that it is of the nature of a practice that in investigating it we eventually reach bedrock, that is to say, a way of acting for which no further reasons can be given. The demand for further reasons involves a failure to recognize the infinite regress inherent in such a demand; for even 'if they are given you, you will once more be facing a terminus. [And hence additional reasons] cannot get you any further than you are at present' (Z: para. 315).

The belief that further reasons are required also involves a failure to recognize the nature of a reason (RPP2: para. 314); for to offer a reason is not to establish that in a certain situation only one action is possible or correct; rather, it puts forward one way of seeing the situation within which a particular action is appropriate. Similarly, the further reasons which are offered for acting in this particular way do not provide the original reason with 'foundations'; rather, they expand upon it, indicating the wider outlook of which the original reason is a part. Thus the further reasons that are offered are of the same logical status as the original reason, i.e. the logical gap between reasons and the way of acting that goes with them remains unchanged. To reject the reasons we offer as inadequate because they fail to establish a necessary connection with action is therefore simply confused, for the notion that they might do so makes no sense.

Thus Wittgenstein's only concern is to 'remind' us of certain grammatical features of human action, and in so far as he attempts to undermine certain ways of thinking, his target is a rationalism which is confused and incoherent. As we have seen, the thrust of this rationalism is to disguise or deny the gap between reasons and action, and one adverse consequence this can have is to privilege certain kinds of reason over others. Part of utilitarianism's attraction, for example, is its rational form, the impression it gives of putting ethics on a scientific footing. Ultimately, however, the reasons offered by any ethical system come to an end; however rational its form and however articulate and sophisticated it may be, ultimately the system has to convince us – we have to take it to heart and act on it. The elaborateness of the chain of reasons can conceal the need for an unmediated transition to action, but it cannot eliminate it. The apparent simplicity of a system such as utilitarianism can also be somewhat misleading. Smart, for example, claims that utilitarianism is implied by the principle of benevolence, so that once the individual embraces benevolence the rest is, as it were, done for him. This, however, is misguided, for the specific injunctions of utilitarianism will define what benevolence here means, and hence the invoked principle of benevolence has the same logical complexity as utilitarianism itself. Thus in embracing utilitarianism (or a specific form of it) one's decision is of the same kind as that involved in embracing any other complex moral system: both decisions embody precisely the same logical step.

Here one might also note that the stress which Smart and other contemporary philosophers place on certain types of consideration (in particular social and psychological considerations) does seem to reflect an attempt to deny certain grammatical points. Williams, for example, seems to think that sociology or psychology might have provided the kind of justification moral beliefs ideally require. Whatever such sciences might discover, however, the transition from their findings to moral belief (and action) would remain a further step.[11] If one recognizes this point, however, there is less reason to reject more spontaneous and non-systematic ethical reactions. As a reason for action, the belief that a particular act is socially necessary is no different in kind from the belief that to act in a certain way would be noble, just, fitting, or whatever. In both cases, one shows that the consideration in question matters to one by acting according to it – hence in logical terms their status is the same. Furthermore, the one just as much as the other throws light on why the agent acts as he does. Thus to claim that the latter type of reason is inadequate is merely to express a rationalistic prejudice. Against this, Wittgenstein stresses the spontaneous character of much moral action. As he puts it, 'a man reacts *like this*: he says "No, I *won't* tolerate that!" and resists it. . . . [Here] if you fight, you fight. If you hope, you hope. [And] you can fight, hope and even believe without believing scientifically' (*CV*: 66). At the most fundamental level, an ethical belief involves a rejection of certain types of action and an acceptance of others, and from a logical point of view the extent to which one's response is systematic is beside the point.

Having made these grammatical points about the notion of a reason, it is worth re-considering Wittgenstein's lecture on ethics, for much of what is said there can be seen to embody a confused recognition of precisely those grammatical points which we have been stressing.[12] The claim, for example, that ethics is ineffable can be seen as a distorted representation of the fact that reasons come to an end, for the effect of this claim is to reject precisely those questions which from the perspective of Wittgenstein's later philosophy can be seen to be inappropriate or incoherent. Thus since no words (reasons) can bridge the gap between reasons and action, it is almost correct to say that our actions show what our words cannot; what this reflects, however, is not the ineffability of value, but the grammatical point that the offering of reasons must eventually give way to action. Here the reference to ineffability also underlines the sense in which bedrock, as the basis of our actions, is at once totally secure and yet totally unsupported. Thus, when faced with disagreement or when we reflect upon the fact that there are alternative possibilities, we feel strangely disconcerted; that a certain act is wrong, we feel, can hardly be denied and yet, of course, it can. Here the strength of our conviction comes up against the frustrating impossibility of proof, and the difficulties we experience gain expression in the paradoxical claim that ethics while real is ineffable.

Here it is also interesting to note the way in which our difficulties manifest themselves in a condemnation of language. One reason for this is that we take the inability of language to meet our incoherent demands as reflecting on language and not on those demands themselves. Also interesting, however, is the way in which our reaction makes it seem as if it were our conviction that filled our words with meaning. Thus when someone rejects our claim that a certain deed is noble we feel that he has not grasped what we mean by noble, what nobility really is. Here it is only of someone who responds as we do that we are prepared to say he understands what we mean. Anyone else misses, as it were, the 'essence' of our utterance, and is left with the mere husk of the words themselves; what we want to say seems ineffable, our words seem to hint at it without ever quite being able to express it.[13] The existence of this reaction manifests, on the one hand, our sense of the profundity of ethics, and, on the other, the grammatical differences between ethical and non-ethical language-games. Thus in communicating a piece of information, I state what I believe to be the facts, and if I am understood the communication is successful. If, however, I claim that a certain act is morally obnoxious someone may understand the content of my claim without in any way participating in the reaction it expresses; consequently, the most important part of what I want to say seems to get left out. Faced with a disagreement in reactions, there may be little more that can be said; and hence where reasons run out, we may end up asking 'Don't you see?' in the final hope that the other will see what we mean – , and here that means understand things as we do and therefore *act* as we do.

The confused recognition of bedrock detectable in the claim that ethics is ineffable also manifests itself in other comments Wittgenstein made at about the time of his lecture. Consider, for example, some comments he made in 1930 on Schlick's ethics. Here Wittgenstein contradicts Schlick's claim that, of the two theological conceptions of the Good, that which holds that the Good is good because God wills it is less profound than that which holds that God wills the Good because it is good. According to Wittgenstein, the first conception is the deeper, 'for this cuts off the path to any and every explanation "why" it is good, while the second conception is precisely the superficial, the rationalistic one, which proceeds as if what is good could be given some foundation' (*WWK*: 115). As these comments illustrate, Wittgenstein's attack on the attempt to explain ethics (what he refers to as 'all the chatter about ethics') reflects a recognition that reasons come to an end, a recognition that ultimately ethical commitment reflects not something derivable from the facts but a distinctive reaction on the part of the individual. Similarly, as he himself noted at the time, the fact that he ended his lecture in the first person is quite essential; for when one has noted the ethical tendency in Man, nothing more can be established without taking up an attitude towards it and at this stage the philosopher can only appear as a person speaking for himself (*WWK*: 116). Thus the grammatical points which in the lecture are seen through a glass darkly can be seen in full clarity from the perspective of Wittgenstein's later philosophy. Furthermore, on the basis of a recognition of these points it becomes possible to offer an account of ethics which is neither mystificatory nor reductive.

5

ETHICS AND HUMAN ACTION

And once when I mentioned Goering's 'Recht ist das, was uns gefällt',[1] Wittgenstein said that 'even that was a kind of ethics. It is helpful in silencing objections to a certain attitude. And it should be considered along with other ethical judgements and discussions, in the anthropological study of ethical discussions which we may have to conduct.'

(Rush Rhees, conversation with Wittgenstein, in Rhees 1970: 101–2)

As our investigation of the fact-value distinction has shown, the key distinctive feature of value judgements is their grammatical connection with action. This connection is of fundamental importance and has crucial implications for the nature of value concepts. Thus notions such as belief, truth, and objectivity have a fundamentally different meaning in this context and elsewhere. Here surface similarities are deceptive, for despite apparent similarities, statements such as 'That is red' and 'That is good' are of fundamentally different kinds. In this chapter, we shall seek to bring out these grammatical differences by considering the use of the word 'good'; before we do this, however, we shall quickly sketch the grammatical differences between descriptive and evaluative terms in general.

Here the first point to note is that our use of terms such as 'good', 'noble', etc. is not governed by agreed procedures for their application; rather, applying them involves reacting in a certain way. For this reason the notion of bedrock is of crucial importance here, for the fact that they express a reaction means that disagreement (a difference in reactions) is always possible.[2] With descriptive terms, however, the criteria for their application are fixed; empirical judgements therefore occur in the context of agreed procedures for verification, i.e. in a situation where we share a complicated game of evidence used in the application of these concepts. For the same reason, there is no connection between making a judgement and acting in a particular way. In contrast, believing an action to be wrong (ignoble, unjust, or whatever) does involve acting in certain ways, e.g. trying to avoid doing the action, discouraging others from doing it, regretting it if one does it, etc. Furthermore, while one may offer reasons why a certain action is wrong (e.g. that it causes unnecessary suffering), others may reject these reasons and hence deny the original judgement. In this case, however, the disagreement is not open to independent resolution, nor can one appeal to agreed procedures. None the less, the disagreement is not merely verbal but very real – it reflects the conflict between two ways of understanding the world and correspondingly two different ways of acting.

Another way of making these points is to note that different types of language-game are involved in the two cases. Thus we make empirical judgements (use descriptive terms) within the context of a shared language-game. The language-game as a whole rests on an agreement in reactions, for such an agreement is presupposed in our having been able to learn its rules. Furthermore, the language-game also presupposes a large degree of agreement in judgements, for only when this is so is it clear that we are playing the same game, i.e. using the same rules. Our use of words such as 'good', however, is quite different, for in this case our use of the word does not occur in the context of agreed procedures for its application. Here the language-game does not consist in rules which we learn; rather, it extends and develops certain natural reactions (viz. expressions of approval, condemnation, etc.). In this way scope is created for reactions of a new sophistication and complexity; however, what underlies the language-game (the bedrock of the language-game) is the reaction itself. Here agreement in reactions is presupposed in the sense that our being able to use words such as 'good' involves our reacting in ways mutually recognizable as reactions of approval, etc. On the other hand, however, agreement in judgements is not essential to the language-game; indeed, the function of the language-game may be to give expression to differences of reaction within the context of an underlying kinship. Thus we may recognize the reaction as a reaction of approval, even though it may be that of judging to be good something of which we disapprove.[3]

The importance of these points and their implications for ethics can be brought out by a detailed consideration of the use of the word 'good'. In considering a word of this kind, the first problem we encounter is our inclination to move from the fact that it is an adjective to the idea that it denotes a quality. However, this move creates difficulties, for having made it we are immediately struck by major disanalogies between the use of this word and that of other quality-denoting terms. The most obvious of these is the extent and nature of disagreement in its application. Equally puzzling, however, is the fact that the goodness of an object (or action)[4] cannot be said to lie in any one of its specific features, for, having noted a specific feature of the object, it always makes sense to ask 'But is the object good?' Thus, having characterized goodness as a quality, one is none the less forced to recognize that it is fundamentally different from other qualities. In this way, however, one's original claim is rendered obscure, and one is left with the difficult task of explaining exactly what sort of quality goodness is.

This is precisely the predicament faced by G.E. Moore in *Principia Ethica*, and his response to it is to claim that goodness *is* a quality, but a non-natural and indefinable one. The significance of this claim is notoriously hard to pin down; its most striking feature, however, is the implied analogy between arriving at a value judgement and perceiving. Unfortunately, the analogy proves hard to maintain. As an analogue for the sense by which perceptual qualities are detected, Moore is forced to invoke intuition; however, he is unable to specify a vehicle for this faculty, nor does he mention any means by which one might attain agreement as to its deliverances. In this way, however, the analogy with perception is revealed as an empty metaphor, one which cannot account for disagreement and which succeeds only in rendering value judgements mysterious. Thus, while Moore recognizes differences between the use of words such as 'good' and that of others such as 'yellow', he does not investigate the grammar of these differences but instead simply concludes that good denotes a special kind of quality, viz. a non-natural one. In doing this, however, he treats a categorial difference as if it were a difference within a category ('as though the word "kind" here meant the same thing as in the context "kinds of apples" ' (*BB*: 29)). The effect of this is to conceal the differences between the categories and so generate confusion. Similarly, little is gained by simply claiming 'that the word "good" is indefinable. What we want to know, to get a bird's eye view [*Übersicht*] of, is the use of the word "good" . . .' (*RPP1*: para. 160).

One way of doing this is to consider how we learn to use the word: 'doing this on the one hand destroys a variety of misconceptions, [and] on the other hand, gives you a primitive language-game in which the word is used' (*LA*: 1). In this case, what is important is that the word 'good', unlike the word 'yellow', is not taught by reference to samples but rather as the replacement or extension of a natural reaction. Roughly speaking, the word is taught as an interjection and

> one thing that is tremendously important in [the] teaching is exag-gerated gestures and facial expressions. The word is taught as a substitute for a facial expression or gesture. The gestures, tones of voice, etc., in this case are expressions of approval. (*LA*: 2)[5]

Shared human reactions underlie the setting-up of the language-game in two ways: first, in the child's behaviour possessing aspects which we can recognize as expressions of approval; and second, in his responding to our facial expressions and gestures and thereby coming to use the word 'good' as we do. Thus, through our teaching, the child's natural expressions of approval are extended into language, and his non-verbal behaviour is supplemented by a language-game which opens up to him new possibilities of expression.

Here it might seem that our account presupposes the notion of approval, and in an important sense it does. If one asks what it is that makes the use of a word (or piece of pre-verbal behaviour) into an expression of approval, the simple answer is the game in which it appears, for the word (or gesture) only has the meaning it does within a particular context. The attempt to define the concept (to provide abstract rules specifying when and where it applies) is futile, for the concept is not taught via a definition, nor does an abstract definition underlie our use of it. Rather, a child reacts in certain ways, makes certain expressions, etc., and on this basis we teach it a more elaborate game. Thus we treat certain of the child's expressions and actions as primitive expressions of approval and seek to develop these reactions so that the child can come to play increasingly complex language-games of approval. Such games have both verbal and non-verbal components and, like the basis from which they emerge, manifest a reaction on the speaker/agent's part. The involvement of language brings with it a new dimension of complexity, and this complexity runs through and transforms the individual's whole behaviour, for within the context of a more elaborate practice, this behaviour can take on a new significance; indeed, as we shall see with ethics, it can take on a new kind of significance.

The importance of context in the language describing human reactions can be clarified by considering the parallel case of a facial expression such as a smile. Thus the word 'smile' picks out a certain (human) facial expression: it does not do so, however, in virtue of abstract rules defining what is to count as a smile. Rather, within the play of human expression, we see similarities, a pattern, and use the word 'smile' to pick out one such pattern. The context which provides the background to the word's use is crucial, for outside this context its application becomes uncertain. As Wittgenstein notes, a face which was not susceptible to gradual and subtle alteration but which snapped straight from one expression to another could not be said to smile (*RPP2*: para. 614). Unlike a smile, such an expression would mean nothing to us: we would not know how to react to it nor how to find our feet with the person whose expression it was. Similarly, if someone only ever 'smiled' at moments of extreme exertion, it would make little sense to describe this as smiling, for smiling goes together with experiencing pleasure, expressing goodwill, etc. Thus we only call something a smile within a certain context and where it has certain connections. Similarly, the word 'approval' picks out one particular strand of behaviour, which is constituted as such by its relation to the general background of human behaviour against which it appears.

Thus what makes the word 'good' an expression of approval is not something simultaneous with or lying behind the expression (e.g. a mental process); rather, expressions of such-and-such a kind in these types of context constitute that particular strand of human behaviour which we call approval. This illustrates a general point, for it brings out the importance of considering words together with their context and the actions which accompany them. Similarly, it underlines the differences between Moore's linguistic investigations and Wittgenstein's; as Wittgenstein put it in his lectures on aesthetics, 'the main mistake made by philosophers of the present generation, including Moore, is that when language is looked at, what is looked at is a form of words and not the use of the form of words' (*LA*: 2). What is important in the investigation of the word 'good' is not the adjectival form of the word, but the occasions on which it is used, the role it plays in our lives. In this case, as in general, Wittgenstein's investigations start not 'from certain words, but from certain occasions or activities' (*LA*: 3). With respect to the word 'good', this brings out the connection between using the word and acting in certain ways. Hence it under-lines the fact that the use of the word involves a reaction on the part of the individual. One consequence of this is that there are no set criteria for application of the word. Thus, if two people disagree in applying it, this does not mean that one of them does not understand it; indeed, with the word 'good', the child's going on to apply it to different objects from its teacher may be a sign not that it does not understand the use of the word, but that it does.

At this stage, we can re-consider the points we made earlier, for, as we noted, both the use of words such as 'yellow' and that of words such as 'good' presuppose agreement; each does so, however, in a signifi-cantly different way. In the former case, the use of the word forms part of a language-game whose rules we learn and where the agreement in reactions lies in our being able to learn those rules. Furthermore, if it is to be clear that we are following the same rules (that we mean 'the same thing' by yellow), a large degree of agreement in our judgements is necessary.[6] In the latter case, however, the use of the word is itself an extension of a natural reaction; opening up new possibilities of expres-sion, use of the word builds a verbal component onto our non-verbal behaviour. Use of the word does not involve the application of rules; rather, when an individual says that something is good he expresses his reaction to it, and this only makes sense where his judgement is accompanied by certain kinds of behaviour, e.g. his preferring the designated object to others. One consequence of this connection with action is that in using the term the possibility of disagreement cannot be ruled out. Thus, while our use of colour predicates is based on our all making the same judgements in the same circumstances, our use of the word 'good' has the effect of allowing scope for difference – indeed, scope for finer and more sophisticated shades of difference.

One important feature of the use of the word which enables us to do this is the possibility of supplementing a value judgement with reasons for making it. This in turn introduces the possibility of distinguishing between liking something ('feeling positive towards it') and believing it to be good.[7] Supplemented by reasons, calling something good can become part of a complex practice, and here the background to one's judgement may be an elaborate ethical system. In this way, the basis for one's judgement (and for the actions which follow from it) may be an entire ethical system, for only within that system does the particular judgement have its meaning. Here to describe what morally approving of an action consists in one would have to describe the particular practice in its entirety. As Wittgenstein notes with respect to appreciation in aesthetics, 'it is not only difficult to describe what appreciation consists in, it is impossible. To describe what it consists in we would have to describe the whole environment' (*LA*: 7). This remark underlines the complexity and variety of our evaluative language-games, for use of the word 'good' can be part of a wide spectrum of complex specific practices. The aim, however, of approaching more sophisticated cases of approving via the natural reaction in terms of which we learn to use the word 'good' is not to reduce the former to the latter. On the contrary, the latter is simply the starting point (along with much else) for our learning the more sophisticated game. As such, however, it gives us a simplified case which clarifies some of the confusions which can arise while doing philosophy. To put it another way, in the simpler game, the logical (or grammatical) structure of the language-game is easier to grasp. What is thereby highlighted is, first, the connection between using the word 'good' and acting in certain ways and, second, the corresponding sense in which using the word rests on or manifests a reaction on the part of the speaker. Thus the speaker calls certain things 'good' and in his actions shows that he approves of them.

Having outlined the grammar of the word 'good', various problems remain to be considered. For example, the relationship between the empirical features of an object and its goodness may still seem puzzling, for offering reasons for calling something 'good' involves pointing to certain features of the object, and yet as we noted earlier these in themselves do not constitute its goodness. The difficulties here parallel those arising with respect to fact and value in general, and the important point to note is that the reasons we offer do not just pick out certain features of the object, but in picking them out assign them particular importance. Thus one's sensitivity to particular aspects of an object (or action) manifests one's reaction to it, the position one takes up towards it. This point can be clarified by considering how we determine whether something is good. As we noted, Moore argued that it is wrong to identify an object's goodness with any one of its qualities, since after specifying the object's qualities it is still coherent to ask 'But is the object good?' This seems to leave the goodness of an object highly mysterious, for it seems to render unanswerable the question as to how one knows that something is good. Once again, we seem forced to appeal to the mysteries of intuition.

In the Ambrose lectures, however, Wittgenstein outlines an alternative account.[8] There he argues that in determining whether an action is good, either the features of the object must be sufficient to determine its goodness, or its goodness must be something independent, for which those features constitute inductively related symptoms. In the latter case, an independent investigation of the object's goodness would have to be possible, otherwise there would be no basis for the inductive correlation. Indeed, without the possibility of an independent investigation it would be unclear what was being correlated with what. With respect to goodness, however, no independent investigation is required (or, indeed, possible); rather, in specific cases, we apply the term 'good' on the basis of particular descriptive features. Knowing that a strawberry is juicy, well-shaped, red, etc., is sufficient to know that it is a good strawberry; while, for a Catholic, to know that someone told the truth is to have sufficient evidence to conclude that his action was good. As these examples illustrate, although it is features of the object or action which determine its goodness, these features are not in themselves good, for the object or action is called good only within a certain practice or from a certain point of view.[9] The fact that it is always possible to say 'He told the truth, but was his action good?' simply reflects the logical possibility of adopting an alternative practice or a different point of view. In doing this, one would be putting forward alternative criteria for using the word 'good', and correlated with this would be the claim that other ways of acting would be more appropriate.

Thus, while the word 'good' is used to express approval, the meaning of any particular expression of approval – its basis, implications, and significance – depends on the specific context in which it occurs. To put it another way, the criteria for applying the word are not fixed: just as the meaning of the word 'beautiful' is bound up with the object it describes, so too 'in ethics, the meaning of the word "good" is bound up with the object it modifies' (*AWL*: 35). Furthermore, in a particular context, the grammar of the word 'good' depends not on the object to which it is applied but also on the reasons a person offers for calling something good, for in offering his reasons for using the word 'good', the individual spells out the practice of which its use is a part. Thus 'each different way in which one person, *A*, can convince another, *B*, that so-and-so is "good" fixes the grammar of that discussion' (*AWL*: 35). These points underline how misleading it is to describe goodness as a quality, for this claim suggests that we notice a particular quality in certain objects and then go on to discover it in others. The word 'good', however, does not denote some mysterious quality which occurs in the most varied of forms; rather, in various contexts, we play related games with the same word. The games have certain similarities (e.g. in terms of the connection with action, or through the expressions and gestures which may accompany the use of the word), but there is no one element common to every game. Each can be described as a case of expressing approval, but what this means (the reasons for it, what it entails, etc.) will alter from case to case.

One conclusion that might be drawn from all this is that goodness is a family-resemblance concept. In *Varieties of Goodness*, however, G.H. Von Wright compares the concept 'goodness' with other family-resemblance concepts and reaches the opposite conclusion.[10] To support this claim, he offers two main arguments. First, he argues that it is symptomatic of a family-resemblance concept that cases arise where it is uncertain whether something 'really' falls under the concept; this kind of uncertainty, however, is not one we experience with respect to goodness. Second, he suggests that typically a family-resemblance concept can gain new members (e.g. new games can be invented); again, this seems not to be the case with respect to goodness. These arguments bring out important conceptual differences between a concept such as 'game' and the concept of 'goodness': recognition of these differences, however, does not necessarily lead to Von Wright's conclusion. As Von Wright would accept, concepts such as 'game' are taught via paradigms, e.g. by pointing to a game and saying 'This and other similar things are games.' Here it is the reference to similarity which makes the concept a family-resemblance concept. In contrast, 'good' is not taught by reference to paradigms, but as an expression of approval, and what makes it a family-resemblance concept is the fact that in different contexts approving something will mean different things. Thus from case to case the criteria on the basis of which we call something 'good' vary as do the consequences of calling it 'good'. For example, calling a culinary dish 'good' with a view to eating it is very different from calling a picture 'good' with a view to hanging it on one's wall. Although different, however, these cases are clearly related and it is no coincidence that judgements in the two cases may take the same form. The concept of a game and that of goodness can therefore both be seen as family-resemblance concepts, but family-resemblance concepts for different reasons and in different ways.

On this issue, some of Wittgenstein's comments are in fact

misleading. For example, he claims that the concept good 'is used in different contexts because there is a transition between similar things called "good", a transition which continues, it may be, to things which bear no similarity to earlier members of the series' (*AWL*: 33). Here Wittgenstein's point is that we do not call objects 'good' because they have some one thing in common; what he says, however, is misleading in so far as it suggests that we call different things 'good' because of similarities (or networks of similarity) between them. Shortly afterwards, Wittgenstein ridicules the analogous idea which arises with respect to beauty. Thus he points out that

> we do not as children discover the quality of beauty or ugliness in a face and then find that these are qualities a tree has in common with it. The words 'beautiful' and 'ugly' are bound up with the words they modify, and when applied to a face are not the same as when applied to flowers and trees. We have in the latter a similar 'game'. (*AWL*: 35)

It is this point which is crucial. Goodness and beauty are a different type of family-resemblance concept from concepts such as game, language, etc., because they are a fundamentally different type of concept. One consequence of this is that while a clear-cut definition might roughly correspond to our use of the word 'game', the same is not true with respect to the word 'good' (*PI*: para. 77). This is so for two reasons: first, because to offer a rigid definition of the word would sever the necessary connection with action and so fundamentally change its function (see below); and second, because the range of context, and specificity of meaning within each context, is such that no definition could have even roughly the same application. Not only is a good painting totally different from a good piece of music, but the criteria for a good Michelangelo are quite different from the criteria for a good Velasquez.

Thus, while the word 'good' fulfils a certain general role, its precise meaning changes from context to context: a good car has little in common with a good house, while what an Eskimo may describe as a good house may be very different from the Oxford don's ideal residence. Wittgenstein makes analogous points with reference to beauty, e.g. he notes that the phrase 'beautiful colour' can 'have a hundred meanings, depending on the occasion on which we use it' (*AWL*: 35). Similarly, he points out that 'a difference of meaning is shown by the fact that "you can say more" in discussing whether the arrangement of flowers in a bed is "beautiful" than in discussing whether the smell of lilacs is so' (*M*: 313).[11] This might seem to suggest that words such as 'good', 'beautiful', 'just', etc., have a pernicious ambiguity, and yet to say this would be misguided. The word 'good' fulfils a particular function precisely in virtue of the fact that we can disagree in applying it. Thus the conflicting ways of using the word and the rival reasons for applying it allow the expression of different substantive views. To replace the word 'good' with a rigidly defined term – one which did have agreed criteria for its use – would therefore eliminate the function of the word as a means of expressing disagreement.[12] It would also sever the link with action, for applying the word would no longer necessarily express the speaker's reaction to the object in question: if what it was for something to be a good house was strictly laid down, then there would be no grammatical connection between my noting the fact that a house was good and my wanting to live in it, etc.[13] Here one might also note that the different reasons or criteria we adopt for using words such as 'good', 'just', etc. can provide the basis for moral discussion. However, to treat such a discussion as an attempt to discover what goodness or justice really is would be misleading. The desire, however, to claim that a particular definition of justice is true or correct throws an interesting light on our relation to language, for it illustrates how we sometimes project our moral disagreements onto language itself. Thus we might claim that what someone who disagrees with us calls justice is not 'really' justice at all. Underlining phenomena of this kind, Wittgenstein notes that 'we confer individual words as we confer already existing titles' (*RPP1*: para. 116).[14]

Against what we have said so far, one might object that if 'good' has a different meaning in different contexts, and depending on the reasons supporting it, then two people who say that different things are 'good' are not really contradicting each other. This objection brings us back to the fundamental differences between ethical disagreement and empirical disagreement. In empirical matters, disagreement occurs within the context of a game we all accept (i.e. where there are agreed procedures for resolving disputes); in ethics, however, the disagreement might be said to lie in the fact that we play different games without there being any agreed means of bringing them into harmony. Calling different things 'good', we act in different ways and this may well involve condemning ways of acting other than our own;

to this extent, there is certainly disagreement and contradiction, but there is no framework within which the disagreement can be independently resolved. As Wittgenstein argues, a similar point holds true with respect to religion. Thus a belief in the Last Judgement may form the basis of the life of a religious person, but since the concept plays no part in the life of the non-believer it would only be confusing to say that the latter believes the Last Judgement will *not* occur. Rather than saying this, one might say that the notion of the Last Judgement means nothing to him, for he rejects, as it were, the very concept. Now, of course, 'you can call [that] believing the opposite, but it is entirely different from what we normally call believing the opposite' (*LA*: 55).

In her essay, 'Objectivity and Disagreement', S.L. Hurley considers precisely this issue, for she suggests that one crucial difficulty facing a Wittgensteinian account is that of explaining how individuals in different reason-giving practices (i.e. with concepts which are in a significant sense different) can none the less be in substantive disagreement with each other (Hurley 1985). As we have seen, the solution to this problem lies in a recognition of the grammatical differences between empirical and ethical disagreement, for in the latter case the substantive disagreement may lie precisely in the possession of different concepts.[15] Hurley, however, analyses the problem in very different terms. She claims that the existence of substantive moral disagreement can only be accounted for on the assumption that beneath apparent moral disagreement there lies a necessary commitment to certain specific values. Thus, according to Hurley, the notion that an action ought to be done contains an implicit reference to specific values, and it is these values which provide the common ground which makes substantive disagreement possible. This limitation, she argues, 'is not avoided by insistence on some form of logical link between claims about what ought to be done and action, as the concept of action itself may not be logically independent of specific values . . .' (Hurley 1985: 65). Thus, according to Hurley, describing the behaviour of others as 'action' presupposes that they accept certain specific values. Moral disagreement about what ought to be done is not thereby ruled out; rather, it is explained as reflecting differences in the priorities assigned among those values; hence it is these values that provide the common ground which makes disagreement possible.

The search for a common ground in terms of which substantive disagreement can be explained is, however, misguided, for in ethics, it is our actions themselves that provide the 'locus of disagreement'. If one person rejects all talk of justice as an empty charade, while another strives hard to act justly, then in acting and in judging actions each will invoke different concepts; it would be ridiculous, however, to suggest that therefore they are not actually disagreeing. Their disagreement lies in the fact that they invoke different concepts, and indeed each may condemn the other precisely on this basis. Here Hurley would claim that underlying their disagreement is their mutual recognition as agents – the fact that each can see the other as acting. As we have seen, Hurley is right to point out that much is presupposed in our being able to recognize the behaviour of others as action. It would be misleading, however, to take the mutual intelligibility of our actions as already constituting a kind of moral agreement; rather, it constitutes the basis both for agreement and disagreement, indeed for any relation to the other as a person. Thus we may recognize someone else as an agent and yet find his moral outlook totally abhorrent; here, however, it would be little comfort to reflect that at least his behaviour was intelligible! Similarly, if we are to understand someone else as using our word 'good', we must be able to understand what he is doing as expressing approval; this, however, does not rule out the possibility of his approving something of which we strongly disapprove. The Liberal and the Nazi may share a common humanity, but this does not mean that they are in implicit, if extremely limited, moral agreement.

What re-emerges here is the desire for proof or logically compelling moral argument. Thus it is tempting to try to take the limits of intelligibility as constituting reassuring limitations on the possibility of disagreement. Such a tendency is evident both in the thrust of S.L. Hurley's argument and, more particularly, in her misleading reference to 'specific values'. Thus the claim that we share specific values is inferred from the fact that we recognize each other as conscious agents; *specific* values, however, are precisely what we do not share, and in any normal sense, what substantive moral disagreement indicates is not our common acceptance of specific values but the very opposite. Hurley's aim is to show that there are conceptual limits on the moral values an individual can adopt. The conceptual points she stresses, however, do not exclude any substantive moral positions: what they rule out is not the morally obnoxious but the literally unintelligible.[16] *Pace* Hurley, our recognition of others as conscious agents has nothing to do with whether or not we are in moral agreement with them. To underline this point, it is worth referring back to the distinction between understanding someone's reason and understanding that what the person is saying constitutes a reason. We may, for example, find the actions of a sadist totally abhorrent and hence in a sense incomprehensible; none the less, we still treat him as acting for a reason even if we find this reason repulsive. Similarly, we may find someone's moral views alien and yet still be able to treat what he says as expressing a moral view, albeit one radically at odds with our own.[17]

Thus intelligibility does not place substantive limitations on the moral views an individual can adopt. To make the point in terms of reasons, if we could not recognize something as a reason this would not mean the agent had offered the wrong reason or that the reason was conceptually confused and required rectification by some third party; rather, the agent would not have offered a reason at all. The difficulty would be that we could not understand his action, for *ex hypothesi* we would be unable to make anything of the purported reason he offered for doing it. The parallel here with reasons is not fortuitous, for the agent/speaker has the same priority in stating his values as he does in offering reasons for his action. This can be illustrated with respect to the use of the word 'good'. In judging something to be good the individual expresses his reaction to it, and therefore any supposed implications of that judgement further specify what that reaction is; hence they are only implications of his judgement if he accepts them as such. What follows from a particular judgement cannot be determined independently of the individual that made that judgement, for by stating the implications of his judgement the individual shows which cases he considers to be the same and which different. For this reason, it is misleading to claim that an individual might be implicitly (or necessarily) committed either to a specific value or to a particular judgement. As with reasons in general, only an individual can say what his values are: someone else may, of course, suppose that he holds certain values, but such suppositions are only correct if the individual accepts them. If he does not, then what they define is a moral position other than his own.[18]

Against this, one might argue that certain things follow logically from an individual's judgement; that if he approves of one thing, consistency may require him to approve of another. This line of thought generates two puzzles. First, it suggests that, unbeknownst to the individual, he may believe that a certain act is wrong, and yet this would be highly paradoxical. Second, it seems to transform logic into a coercive force, for it seems that once the individual has made certain judgements, logic imperiously demands that he make others. To clarify this issue let us consider an example. Suppose someone refuses to lie and offers as his reason for so doing the belief that one should always tell the truth. Here it seems clear that the individual is logically committed to condemning lying just as much in other circumstances. What does it mean, however, to say that he is logically committed to so doing? Suppose he doesn't: in that case, either he would be retracting his original reason or his subsequent explanations (and actions) would show that we had misunderstood it, i.e. that he didn't mean always (mean by 'always' what we mean by it). Thus it is not as though an irresistible logical force determines his actions and judgements; on the contrary, the meaning of his original statement is spelt out by what he accepts as following from it. We discover what he means by saying 'one should never lie' by offering other cases and asking for his verdict upon them – he may, for example, explain that embellishing an after-dinner story does not count as lying. Here it would make no sense to claim that as a matter of fact it is lying and that therefore he must condemn it. Rather, it is the agent who decides what for him is a morally relevant difference – a point underlined by his treating the two cases differently, e.g. by avoiding one but not the other. Thus one cannot examine the implications of someone's moral position independently of that individual: what moral judgements he would make in different circumstances form part of his moral position, and in stating what the implications of his views are he simply defines his position more fully.[19]

The grammatical differences which we have highlighted in our comparison of the use of the word 'good' and that of words such as 'yellow' mirror the grammatical differences between believing something to be right and believing something to be true. In both cases, the differences bring out the connection between ethics and action. They also underline the point that in understanding an individual's moral judgements one eventually reaches the bedrock of a reaction – the fact that he acts in a certain way. In this sense, every ethical system implies a distinctive practice, while adopting an ethical system, like embracing religious belief, involves committing oneself to a certain way of living one's life. However, the fact that making a moral judgement ultimately involves a substantive reaction on the individual's part does not entail that there is nothing to choose between the various logically equivalent reactions. Despite the fact that my calling something 'good' expresses a reaction on my part, there is no logical impropriety in my holding that anyone who judges otherwise judges foolishly. Of course, this will be denied by the 'fool', but then that, presumably, is what one would expect. By matching my every reason with its logical antithesis, the fool may demonstrate that the logical status of our arguments is the same; in so doing, he underlines our disagreement but demonstrates neither that it is empty nor that it is merely a question of a difference in reactions. Indeed, when I claim that his judgement is foolish or misguided, this is precisely what I deny.

The grammatical points which have come to the fore in our investigation of the use of the word 'good' can also be used to review (and reinforce) our earlier conclusions about fact and value. Thus one of the ways of drawing this contrast is to note that in stating a fact I make use of a linguistic rule, where the practice of using that rule involves verification or a process of comparison with reality. When I make a value judgement, however, no such process is involved; rather, in making the judgement I express a reaction and this reaction has its point in terms of its connection with a way of acting. A process of reasoning may precede my judgement and this may involve determining the facts (i.e. the nature of the situation in which I act), but what is at issue is a decision about how to act. The importance of this point is that it changes what it would mean to say that a judgement was true or objective.[20] It also underlines the fundamental differences between moral beliefs and empirical beliefs, for these differences do not reflect differences between types of mental state or process but indicate that the word 'belief' is used in a different sense in the two contexts. In view of these points, one way of clarifying the grammatical status of moral beliefs is to use the word 'ethics' to refer to whatever considerations underlie the way an individual acts. Thus an individual's 'ethics' will be manifested in what considerations weigh with him and in the type of reasons he offers for his actions. In this sense, Goering's 'Recht is das was uns gefällt' is 'also a kind of ethics, for it is helpful in silencing objections to a certain attitude' (Rhees 1982: 101). Goering's statement makes clear the basis on which he intends to act and thus fulfils the same logical function as the contrasting claim that there is one universal moral law. In this way, it illustrates the nature of the considerations here at issue, for the rival claims express different ways of understanding and thinking about the world, and in both cases these are grounded neither in proof nor in specific evidence that they are correct or appropriate. Indeed, in this context it is hard to see what 'specific evidence' might mean. If one wishes to say that these viewpoints are grounded in anything, one might say that they are grounded in all the individual has seen, thought, and experienced. Since the question at issue does not involve finding out what is the case, but rather making a judgement about how we and others should act, the notion of evidence ceases to be applicable. Here one may hold that there are independent standards of right action or that there are not; in either case, however, no factual discovery will resolve the matter.[21] For this reason, it would be wrong to treat such views as straightforwardly true or false. One may consider a way of acting and the corresponding way of understanding the world appropriate or inappropriate, sagacious or pernicious, but whatever the case it cannot be said to be true or false in the same sense as an empirical proposition.[22]

As a final way of underlining the grammatical differences between moral and empirical beliefs, it is worth considering the type of basis on which we come to adopt the former. One way of doing this is to consider the related issue of religious conviction. Here we can return to Wittgenstein's lecture on ethics, for having noted the close relation between ethics and religion, Wittgenstein is led to consider the notion of a miracle. The first point he notes is that if a miracle were to occur the attempt to investigate it scientifically would seem to make the miracle disappear. The reason for this is that 'the scientific way of looking at a fact is not the way to look at a miracle. For imagine whatever fact you may, it is not in itself miraculous in the absolute sense of the term' (*LE*: 11). Here the grammatical relations parallel those we discussed earlier; for just as finding a fact significant involves reacting to it in a certain way, so too does describing an occurrence as a miracle. Thus to believe a miracle has occurred is to witness an occurrence which convinces one that God exists, an occurrence to which one reacts with an affirmation of God's existence. In *Culture and Value*, Wittgenstein notes that a miracle would have to be

as it were, a *gesture* which God makes. . . . The only way for me to believe in a miracle in this sense would be to be *impressed* by an occurrence in this particular way. So that I should say, e.g.: 'It was

111

> *impossible* to see these trees and [not believe that their movement was commanded by God]'. . . . Just as I might say 'It is impossible to see the face of this dog and not to see that he is alert and full of attention to what his master is doing'. (*CV*: 45)

The fact that someone else might witness the occurrence and not be affected by it does not necessarily cast doubt on my reaction; where this occurs we are simply faced with two different reactions. One person reacts by saying it was a coincidence or by claiming that one day it will be explained; while the other person reacts by claiming that no scientific explanation will ever be sufficient. Between these two reactions logic can offer no adjudication, for there is no independently given criterion for something's being a 'satisfactory' explanation.[23] Once again, this underlines the importance of philosophy's remaining neutral, for if someone makes an experience of this kind the cornerstone of his life, on what basis can this be questioned by the philosopher? If such experiences play no role in the philosopher's life, then that is his affair. Once again, bedrock is reached and any position adopted reflects the taking up of a stand on the part of the individual.[24]

The conviction that a certain event was a miracle is the kind of unshakable certainty which can underlie religious belief. It shows the sort of thing which might lead one to order one's life in this way. Not all religious belief, however, has to rest on grandiose experiences of the 'miraculous'.

> Life can educate one to a belief in God. And *experiences* too are what bring this about; but I don't mean visions and other forms of sense experience which show us the 'existence of this being', but, eg, suffering of various sorts. These neither show us God in the way a sense impression shows us an object, nor do they give rise to *conjectures* about him. Experiences, thoughts, – life can force this concept on us. (*CV*: 86)

Thus our conviction may have a basis without our being able to put this into words. What leads us to a certain conviction may not be something that can clearly be presented in terms of evidence, for whatever the immediate occasion of our coming to hold a particular belief, its basis could in a sense be said to be the sum total of our previous experience. The basis of our conviction can thus be intangible without our conviction therefore being irrational or arbitrary: it reflects what through experience we have come to hold important.

112

These considerations apply as much to ethical conviction as to religious conviction and further illuminate what it is to believe something to be right or wrong. Here belief is not accepting a proposition on the basis of grounds which everyone might recognize; rather, it reflects acceptance of a way of understanding the world and of the way of acting which this implies. Embracing an ethical system is in this respect very similar to adopting a religious perspective, and here to understand religious belief we have to recognize that 'religious belief could only be something like a passionate commitment to a system of reference. Hence, although it's belief, it's really a way of living, or a way of assessing life. It's passionately seizing hold of this interpretation' (*CV*: 64).[25] Furthermore, while believing in God involves a reaction on the individual's part, one cannot infer from this that it is merely a question of his reacting in a certain way. Rather, part of the content of his reaction is the claim that it is the response to an independently existing reality: hence if one treats it as merely reflecting a human reaction, one thereby expresses one's own rejection of the claim that God exists. The reaction and the negative assessment of it are therefore logically on a par: the choice between them is a substantive one, not one that can be made on logical or conceptual grounds, and hence for Wittgenstein it lies outside the realm of philosophy.

These points illustrate the nature of belief in ethical and religious contexts. The connection between belief and action, whether it concerns believing God to exist or believing a certain action to be wrong, constitutes a crucial grammatical difference between belief in this context and empirical belief. Here a difference in belief is a difference in the way one lives. If, unlike the believer, I do not believe in the Last Judgement, then 'I think differently, in a different way. I say different things to myself. I have different pictures' (*LA*: 55). The differences involved may cover the whole spectrum of what I think, do, and say. Furthermore, I may be unable to specify the basis of my belief, and yet my belief is not without a basis; indeed, in one sense it has the strongest basis possible. Similarly, the individual 'will treat this belief as extremely well-established, and in another way as not established at all' (*LA*: 54). On the one hand, he may cling to it in the face of evidence which would shake any empirical belief, but on the other, he may recognize that his grounds for so doing are nothing like what we ordinarily call 'evidence'. Here we don't talk of probabilities and hypotheses – the game we play is entirely different. The belief forms

the basis of our lives, the way in which we see the world – and here
seeing the world in a certain way means acting in a certain way. Far
from implying that such belief is arbitrary, Wittgenstein's stress on
bedrock allows us to understand the sense in which ethical belief can
have a basis, even if this basis cannot easily be articulated. From this
perspective, someone who finds a certain act just but can 'give no
reasons' for his judgement is not necessarily being stupid or irrational.
He reacts in a certain way, but not necessarily arbitrarily; what lies
behind his reaction may be a lifetime of thought, reflection, and
experience. Indeed, the idea that he should be able to distil this experience into a small number of readily comprehensible reasons is itself
somewhat strange; were this possible, the path to wisdom would
indeed be a short one.

Thus consideration of the 'basis' of moral belief, and of the
question of what evidence such belief might have, throws further light
on the differences between empirical and moral judgements. It also
clarifies the notion of bedrock, for it underlines the fact that the
Wittgensteinian stress on bedrock in no way implies that moral
judgements are arbitrary. On the contrary, a recognition of the specific nature of moral belief enables one to appreciate the confusions
inherent in the claim that moral judgements are groundless unless
provable. As we shall see in Chapter 7, recognition of the specific
nature of moral belief is also important when considering the notions
of objectivity and truth in ethics. Before considering these topics,
however, we must first seek to clarify further the specificity of the
ethical, for in one sense Goering's statement constitutes precisely a
rejection of the ethical, and the sense in which it does this we have yet
to explore.

6

ETHICS: A DISTINCTIVE REACTION

> I can only say: I don't belittle this human tendency; I take my hat
> off to it. And here it is essential that this is not a sociological
> description but that I speak *for myself*.
>
> (Wittgenstein, conversation with F. Waismann, *WWK*: 118)

So far we have tried to clarify ethics by underlining the differences
between ethical questions ('What ought we to do?') and empirical
questions ('What is the case?'). Correspondingly, we have suggested
that an individual's ethical convictions can be seen as those convictions (whatever they may be) which underlie his action. This brings
out the importance of bedrock, the nature of belief in this context and
the type of background and basis such belief can have. However, the
word 'ethics' can clearly be used in a much more specific sense, and in
this respect much remains to be considered. Thus, while we have
stressed the importance of reasons and of the specific type of reasons
we offer, this still leaves obscure our use of the word 'ought', for a
particular feature of this is that we often wish to use the word without
being able to support our doing so with reasons. Similarly, while we
have talked of ethical systems, we have had little to say about spontaneous, less systematic ethical reactions – what are we to make of
these? Here what is needed is to clarify the difference between a moral
reaction or judgement and a non-moral one. What we need to explore
are the differences between moral judgements and straightforward
expressions of preference.

One way of approaching this problem is to ask why we have moral
judgements at all. If, as some philosophers have suggested, moral
judgements are essentially expressions of preference, why is it that we
make such a distinction between the two? That we do so already

suggests that moral judgements express a distinctive reaction; indeed, one of the most obvious ways in which the distinctiveness of the reaction is manifested is precisely the vehemence with which people deny that moral judgements are mere expressions of preference.[1] In what, however, might this distinctiveness lie? In response to this question, Rush Rhees suggests that a value judgement has a significance which 'goes beyond' the circumstances. By this, he means that 'it goes deep with me when I say it; that it is anything but a *trivial* remark' (Rhees 1970: 98). Here he is surely right in emphasizing the importance of the judgement, the sense that it has a wider significance; his statement, however, does little to define its distinctiveness. Thus one might still construe moral judgements as simply a very strong negative reaction: although this goes against the spirit of Rhees's claim it is not clear what response he could make to it, for as yet no qualitative difference has been specified.

What Rhees's claim does hint at, however, is the fact that we attribute to moral judgements a different type of importance. This manifests itself in a variety of ways. Thus in making a moral judgement we hold that there is something at stake other than just our preferences: we claim that one and only one act is the right thing to do and that this is so regardless of whether we or others recognize this. Such claims pose problems, for it is not easy to pin down exactly what they mean. As we saw, to make a moral judgement is to approve or condemn an action, and since such a judgement does not state what is the case, it cannot in that sense be said to be true or false. In view of this, one might have thought all such judgements would be treated as essentially the same, i.e. as simply expressing different preferences. If this were so, the only problem would be that of finding a means of compromise, i.e. of finding a way to live with the fact that our preferences often happen to conflict. This, however, is not how we react. We claim that actions are not just preferable or non-preferable but also right or wrong. Quite apart from the question of whether we would prefer to do an act, we want to know whether we ought to perform it. The concepts introduced in this way are of a fundamentally new type, for they purport to qualify actions and types of action independently of the individual, assigning them an intrinsic value in terms of their moral correctness. Someone who uses these concepts denies that judging actions is a matter of personal choice, and holds instead that there are standards of right and wrong which our judgements (and actions) must strive to embody.

Here it is important not to let the prevalence and hence familiarity of this reaction blind us to its radical and in a sense mysterious claims. Whatever is it, one might ask, that gives us the idea that in judging actions there should be standards independent of human preferences? What is it that on occasion leads us not to do the action we most prefer but instead to determine our action by a standard of right conduct whose force lies precisely in the belief that it is somehow independent of us or objective? Not surprisingly, such questions defy any straightforward response. Philosophically, however, what is important is to recognize the distinctive nature of the reaction to which they are a response and to note the distinctive concepts in which this reaction issues. This may seem a cowardly evasion of the crucial philosophical task; in fact, however, it reflects the need to recognize that explanations and justifications come to an end. The ethical reaction confronts us with the claim that there are certain actions that ought to be done and others that ought not to be done, but if one tries to explain this claim further one either ends up simply re-invoking the very concepts one is seeking to explain or one offers a non-moral explanation of these concepts and one which is therefore necessarily inaccurate. Confronted with this reaction, all the philosopher can do is to underline its distinctive features and help eliminate the unnecessary mystery surrounding it by indicating other human reactions to which it is related, and by pointing to the experiences which lead individuals to take up the notions of right and wrong as the only ones capable of expressing their convictions about the world and Man's role in it.

As we should be clear from the preceding chapter, the attempt to justify the reaction is also misguided, for any attempted justification has the same logical status as the reaction itself and hence cannot eliminate the logical possibility of someone rejecting the reaction as misguided or simply absurd. For this reason, apparent justifications of the reaction are better seen as elucidations of it, for their function is simply to present the wider context in which the reaction has its place. Thus, in the most obvious example, the reaction we have described may go together with religious belief, so that the claim that there is an independent standard of action will be justified in terms of the idea that this standard expresses the will of God. It would be wrong, however, to conclude that the reaction we have described is therefore only intelligible against a religious background. Indeed, as perennial philosophical arguments about the notion of divine law illustrate, the reference to God leaves what is philosophically puzzling in this reaction essentially untouched. Thus, even if we assume the existence of a Creator, why should this assumption bring in its train a new range of concepts? Surely its only implications would be prudential, for in such a situation we would simply be confronted with a new constraint reflecting the existence of a being whose power to enforce preferences was incomparably greater than that of any human? This response, however, clearly misses the point of religious belief, for within the religious perspective the individual's pursuit of his own satisfaction is replaced by the idea of a (God-given) order within which particular courses of action have a unique significance as being the right (and not just preferable) thing to do. Belief in God (as opposed to the belief that some infinitely powerful extraterrestrial exists) involves attributing a special significance to God's Will, i.e. holding that one ought to act according to it not just because this is prudent but because this is right. The circularity here (one ought to do God's Will because doing so is right) is unavoidable, for again we are confronted with the notion of 'ought' and the accompanying claim that there is a uniquely correct way of acting, and it is this claim that must either be accepted or rejected.

To underline further the nature of the ethical reaction, let us consider a non-religious example; and we can in fact use Wittgenstein's own personal views as an illustration. Thus, on one occasion when discussing Kierkegaard with M.O'C. Drury, Wittgenstein said 'I don't believe what Kierkegaard believed, but of this I am certain, that we are not here in order to have a good time' (Drury 1981: 89). Here Wittgenstein as an individual denies that pursuit of pleasure is what is most important in human life, and a corollary of this denial is the claim that some acts are intrinsically worthwhile and others intrinsically wrong. To advance such a claim is to assert that the appropriate standards of human action are independent of the individual – that anyone who fails to recognize these standards goes wrong and by implication that we too would go wrong if we failed to recognize them. The moral use of the word 'ought' thus introduces a new basis for our action (pleasure and related notions are rejected as the decisive consideration) and also claims for our judgements a new status (for it involves denying that they are merely expressions of our own preferences, attitudes, or dispositions). The philosophical difficulty here, however, is accepting that having said this there is no more to say. Instead, we are tempted to demand a further explanation of the idea that the correct standards of conduct are independent of us, but what

118

more could an explanation do here? As should be clear, these standards are not mysterious metaphysical things 'out there'; rather, the idea of these standards simply conveys the notion that the goodness or badness of our actions does not lie in our thinking them so. Specific elucidations of this idea will provide it with a particular background and context (religious, humanist, or whatever) but whether one explains that one ought to act in certain ways because it is God's will or because to act otherwise would be to fail to show proper respect for the human dignity of other individuals, the logical status of one's reaction is the same, and hence it always remains logically possible that others will deny that there is a correct way of acting and maintain instead that any judgement about actions can only be the expression of the individual's own preferences or dispositions.

So far, we have outlined the basic structure of claims which makes the ethical reaction distinctive, and to underline the distinctiveness of this reaction it is worth comparing moral judgements and expressions of preferences in more detail and so bringing out the various ways in which the fundamental grammatical contrasts manifest themselves. Thus it is significant that we respond differently to a clash of preferences and to a clash of moral judgements, for in the former case we don't ask 'Which preference is right?', but simply treat the conflicting preferences as reactions which just happen to be different. With moral judgements, however, a clash creates a problem for reflection: in treating the judgement as a moral judgement, we treat it not as a reaction which might just as easily have been otherwise, but as a valid or invalid judgement concerning the act in question. The significance of this is that it implies that there is a standard for judging action which has validity independently of our recognition of it. Correspondingly, we do not treat those who disagree with us as simply expressing a different reaction; rather, we claim that what they say is wrong or misguided, i.e. we treat their statements as embodying a failure to recognize what ought to be recognized by everyone. Here we may claim that those who disagree with us fail to recognize the moral truth. This claim can, of course, be a source of much confusion, for it may encourage us to confuse the moral claim that on some occasions there is only one right thing to do, with the tautology that empirical judgements either state what is the case or what is not the case.[2] If, however, one recognizes the grammatical differences between empirical and moral statements, one can see that the reference to truth has a different meaning here from that which it has in the context of empirical judgements. Thus here it is simply one way (although perhaps the central way) of expressing the distinctively moral claim that there is a set of uniquely correct standards according to which everyone should act and that these standards are valid quite independently of whether we or others recognize them.

One implication of the above is that if we came to treat two conflicting moral judgements as simply different reactions, then *ipso facto* we would have ceased to treat them as moral judgements at all.[3] This can be seen if we consider the different consequences of a change in one's preferences and of a change in one's moral judgements. In the first case, a change would presumably lead one to act differently, but that would be the end of the matter. In the second case, however, from one's present perspective one would be committed to claiming that one's future perspective was misguided, while from one's future perspective one would make the converse claim. Similarly, if the convictions involved are to be treated as moral, the change could not be seen as arbitrary: from one's previous perspective, the change is a falling-off, a deterioration in one's judgement, while from the new perspective it represents an advance towards a better understanding of what is right or wrong.

Another way of underlining the distinctive nature of moral judgements is to note that one no longer treats one's convictions as moral if one treats them as desires – even odd, overriding desires. If, for instance, my desire for tobacco was leading to my financial ruin, I might take steps to eliminate it (e.g. through a course in hypnotism or by ensuring that tobacco was never available to me). I could not, however, act similarly with respect to my moral conviction that stealing is wrong. Were I to do so, this itself would give good grounds for saying that my aversion to stealing was no longer a moral conviction, i.e. that I didn't really believe stealing to be wrong. The reason for this is that by seeking to eliminate my conviction, I would be demonstrating that as far as I was concerned all that prevented me from stealing was a contingent and inconvenient hang-up. My actions would show that I regarded my aversion to stealing not as the accurate perception of an independent truth (as a correct judgement about how people should act), but rather as a regrettable feature of my own psychological make-up which I would be best advised to eliminate as soon as possible. In this way, the use of moral concepts can be seen to introduce a new dimension into the individual's action: they create a new type of uncertainty prior to action, for it may be clear to the individual what he wants to do, and yet he may still be uncertain how to act. Similarly, with respect to past action, the individual may not merely regret the consequences of what he has done; he may now be full of remorse simply because he acted in a particular way (i.e. because he did something which he considers wrong). Recognition of this new dimension thus creates the possibility of moral struggle (the attempt, as it were, not to do what one wants) and can also lead the individual to act in new kinds of ways; for example, it may lead him to give up something even if doing so is clearly against his own interests.

Against this, one might claim that all that is at stake here is a different type of desire, viz. altruistic as opposed to selfish desire. On this account, moral struggle is of the same kind as the prudential attempt to correlate short-term desires and long-term interests. Once again, however, this misses the point, for it fails to distinguish between doing an altruistic act because one believes that later one will be glad to have done it, and doing it simply because one believes that one ought.[4] Although in the two cases one may perform the same act, the basis of that action differs radically in the two cases. Thus if an individual acts on his wants and his wants change, then obviously so too will his actions. If, however, he rejects this way of deciding how to act, then he is committed to claiming that there is a standard for the individual's action independent of the individual, i.e. that this act (or type of act) ought as such to be done (or not to be done). In this case, the judgement is not conditional on the existence of a special kind of desire either in the agent or in the person who makes the judgement. On the contrary, on this approach the question of the individual's wants and desires is irrelevant to the question of how he should act.[5] To put it another way, if what is at issue is a clash between altruistic and non-altruistic desire, the result may vary from occasion to occasion, i.e. sometimes being altruistic may give the individual more satisfaction, sometimes not. Where the individual's commitment to helping others is moral, however, he is committed to such action independently of whether it will give him more satisfaction than the alternatives. Similarly, where he fails to live up to his convictions he is committed to see his action as wrong and a fitting object for remorse, however much he may have enjoyed it.

The shift away from acting solely on the basis of one's desires, and the related idea that there are considerations other than our preferences which should guide our action, introduces a new way of thinking about human action and brings in its train a whole range of distinctive moral concepts. Thus it becomes possible to distinguish between happiness and 'true' happiness; for the ethical perspective may generate paradoxical claims such as the claim that happiness lies in suffering for others (where, of course, what is at stake is not an enjoyment of suffering). Similarly, from this perspective one may regard a certain way of living as the worst possible, even if it is a way of life totally untroubled by misfortune and unhappiness.[6] Here acting well becomes more important than faring well – or rather the two are identified on the basis of a new conception of what it is to fare well. Wittgenstein makes a point of this kind in the *Tractatus*, for there he notes that ethical action must in some sense be its own reward. Thus one performs the action not in view of some hoped-for advantage but because one ought, and the 'reward' for performing it is that one has done what one ought.[7] Here the notion of reward is altered in order to express the nature of moral action. In the same way, one could modify the notion of the individual's interest and claim that ethical action *is* in his interest, adding, for example, that only by acting in this way can the individual lead a life of true human dignity. From this perspective, one would not claim that acting morally conflicted with acting in one's own interest; none the less, someone who acted on this basis might often act in ways which in non-moral terms precisely were against his interests. Recognizing this, the believer in ethics might respond by claiming that the individual has 'higher' interests and hence, once again, the distinctiveness of ethical claims would become apparent.

The distinctiveness of the ethical reaction also manifests itself in other ways, e.g. in the fact that we make *universal* judgements.[8] Rather than acting on our preferences act by act, we hold that certain types of action are right (or wrong) and argue about the validity of various possible universal judgements. Here, unlike preferences, our moral judgements typically call for some sort of justification or support and hence can lead to wide-ranging debate on which standards of assessment are correct. In contrast, if we held that the only basis for judging actions was our preferences, brute nature would determine whether or not we were in favour of a certain action, and the only scope for discussion would be of purely technical questions such as what consequences a particular act would have (or would probably have). Similarly, with moral judgements, questions arise as to their compatibility, for while I may like oranges without liking mandarins, an explanation will be called for if I accept infanticide but condemn abortion. These differences underline two points: first, that in making a moral judgement one claims a special status for one's judgement, i.e. one denies that it is just one judgement among others all equally valid; and second, that in doing this one attributes to one's reaction a certain type of significance and one which can be elucidated by specifying the moral perspective of which the particular judgement is only a part.[9]

As part of the background to the ethical reaction, one might note the kind of experience which Wittgenstein mentions in his lecture on ethics. There he talks about an experience of his which he can best describe as a feeling of wonder at the world's existence; he also mentions 'what one might call the experience of feeling *absolutely* safe' (*LE*: 8). As Wittgenstein notes, such experiences can have a striking impact upon us and in certain cases may play an important role in determining how we lead our lives. For example, impressed with the wonder of the world, one might come to feel that acting in an upright manner was more important then simply doing what would be most to one's own advantage. Other, perhaps more common, human experiences also constitute part of the background to the ethical reaction we have discussed. The most obvious of these is, of course, the experience of guilt. As we saw in Chapter 3, Smart presented this as an unfortunate reflection of the mistaken metaphysical belief that acting wrongly in some confused sense stains one's soul (Smart and Williams 1973: 52). From this perspective, remorse at one's misdeeds only increases the disutility which those misdeeds involved, and therefore in an optimal situation such feelings would not exist at all. As Norman points out, however, the notion of guilt generally plays a very different role in people's lives; there it is seen as something vitally important, as the recognition of an important truth, the realization that there are standards of behaviour to which we ought to conform even when we would prefer not to. Furthermore, guilt is seen as having a positive function, and one has only to think of the novels of Dostoevsky to see the weight which can be placed on remorse as a sign of spiritual progress and awakening moral responsibility. Similarly, it is significant that having acted wrongly, people sometimes hold that it is not enough simply to repent one's deed, but that one must make amends for it or in some way expiate it. Again one can, like Smart, treat such responses as anomalous or irrational, but in so doing it should be clear

123

that one is expressing one's own substantive position.[10]

The concepts which come to the fore here, however, are not always easy to grasp, for what is one to make of the notion of expiation? More pointedly, isn't Wittgenstein's talk of wonder at the existence of the world nonsensical? Normally one can only express wonder at a state of affairs that could conceivably have been different, but it is by no means clear what it would mean to say that everything might not have existed. In his lecture, Wittgenstein recognizes this point and claims that 'a certain characteristic misuse of our language runs through *all* ethical and religious expressions' (*LE*: 9). For example, with reference to the idea of being absolutely safe, he comments 'to be safe means that it is physically impossible that certain things should happen to me and therefore it is nonsense to say that I am safe whatever happens' (*LE*: 9). The problem with such expressions, he argues, is that they seem to be similes and yet cannot be paraphrased; hence 'what at first appeared to be a simile now seems to be mere nonsense' (*LE*: 10).[11] If these expressions cannot be paraphrased, if we cannot say what we mean by them, should we not conclude that they are meaningless? Such a conclusion seems inescapable, and yet these expressions seem not meaningless, but rather profoundly meaningful. Responding to this difficulty, Wittgenstein seeks to have it both ways. Thus he claims that such expressions thrust against the boundaries of language and are therefore meaningless; he adds, however, that the thrust, the tendency they express, none the less *'points to something'* (*WWK*: 69), so that despite their nonsensicality the expressions retain a certain mysterious significance.

Later in his life, Wittgenstein came to be concerned with similar problems in a rather different context, for he discusses the inclination some people have to use colour words to describe vowels, and emphasizes that, although their use of these words seems metaphorical, in fact it is not. 'If I say "For me the vowel *e* is yellow" I do not mean "yellow" in a metaphorical sense, – for I could not express what I want to say in any other way' (*PI*: 216). Similarly, he argues that in using an expression such as 'In my heart, I understood . . .' we do not just use a figure, for the expression 'is not a figure that we choose, not a simile, yet it is a figurative expression' (*PI*: 178). His concern with such uses of language reflects his recognition of how misleading it is to view language simply and exclusively as a means of communicating information. Thus, towards the end of his life, he came to stress the importance of the fact that we assimilate language with the consequence that language itself can come to be directly expressive.[12] In such cases, words are used to express an experience whose specificity lies in having that particular form of expression, i.e. in the fact that the speaker finds those words and only those words the appropriate expression for it. Thus the statement 'I feel absolutely safe' is based on the assimilation of the use of these words: it does not use them according to the rules in terms of which they were taught, but rather to express a specific experience.[13] Such uses of language may on occasion be relatively trivial ('I had the feeling that the city lay to the north although I knew this could not be the case', 'For me, *e* is yellow'), but on others may give expression to feelings and experiences which the individual holds to be vitally important. The impossibility of paraphrase here reflects the linguistic equivalent of bedrock being reached: like a gesture, the form of words used is directly expressive and another person either responds to it ('knows what it means') or simply finds it opaque. Thus although he cannot explain or paraphrase his expressions, many will understand what Wittgenstein means when he expresses wonder at the existence of the world or describes a feeling of absolute safety. Furthermore, since these experiences often go together with a commitment to acting ethically, understanding them can also offer an insight into why someone might decide to act ethically.

Closely related to such expressions are the pictures which can form a crucial part of an individual's ethical position. Thus someone may supplement his claim that a certain action is wrong by invoking the idea that there is a moral law to which the individual must submit. Here the notion of a moral law may be the only way in which the individual can express his ethical conviction, his understanding of the world. However, to respond (as Williams does) by asking who enforces the law and who enacted it is to miss the point of his statement: the statement expresses a certain outlook in terms of a picture (in terms of a non-paraphrasable simile), and to ask such questions is to draw the picture out in ways that are inappropriate and irrelevant.[14] The notion of guilt and the idea that a misdeed must be expiated have a similar function, for the idea that one is stained by sin gives expression to a distinctive moral position, a distinctive way of viewing one's own acts. The picture it invokes cannot be given a foundation but does not therefore involve an erroneous belief in metaphysical 'yellow stains'; rather, it is the non-paraphraseable expression of a particular moral conviction. To describe it as a picture is not to belittle or call into question the substantive moral position the individual expresses; rather, the intention is to underline the grammatical status of the individual's statement. Thus Wittgenstein stresses that the picture is integral to the moral position expressed. Furthermore, he emphasizes that, since the function of the picture is to express the individual's moral outlook, the significance of the picture can only definitively be elucidated by the individual himself.[15] On the other hand, of course, invocation of a particular picture typically goes together with acting in certain ways. For example, the reference to a moral law generally forms part of a moral position which universally condemns certain types of action and claims that in every situation there is one and only one thing which is the right thing to do. Thus the picture does have an application, but part (or indeed the entire) weight of what is said may lie in the picture itself. The picture is not merely ornamental, for as the individual's insistence upon it shows, it is an integral part of his moral position. Furthermore, it is not a clumsy expression of something which might be better formulated in discursive terms; rather, the picture says what it says and has value as the unique expression of the individual's ethical conviction.

To underline the importance of the role pictures can play in our thinking it is worth considering an example from a very different context, for our relation to others is also expressed in certain fundamental pictures. Thus the notion that others are conscious is in part a picture: for in saying that another person is conscious, a thinking being rather than an automaton, I do not make a particular empirical claim which I can support with clearly specifiable evidence; rather, I express my relation towards the other person – 'my attitude towards him is an attitude towards a soul. I am not of the *opinion* that he has a soul' (*PI*: 178). Here the grammatical status of the picture as an expression of our reaction at bedrock is crucial – hence the sense in which it is misleading to talk of an opinion. What is expressed in the picture could hardly be captured by a list of all that follows from or is related to our treating the other person as having a soul, for this picture permeates our very relation to other people. Thus

> it is true that we can compare a picture that is firmly rooted in us to a superstition, but it is equally true that we *always* eventually have to reach some firm ground, either a picture or something else, so that a picture that is at the root of all our thinking is to be respected and not treated as a superstition. (*CV*: 83)

Experiences such as the one Wittgenstein expresses in the notion 'wonder at the world's existence' point to an important aspect of human life, for it is experiences of this kind that form a crucial background to the distinctive ethical reaction we have described. Other experiences of a more general nature are also important here, for the experience of guilt may lead an individual to see life in a new way – through such experience one may become convinced that acting rightly is more important than simply doing as one pleases. Our discussion of pictures also points to another characteristic feature of human life, for the attempt to understand the world, to form a coherent picture of it, is a characteristic human endeavour. Here what is at stake is not the type of understanding sought by science: in this context, what is important is not finding out more facts, but, as it were, reaching a conclusion as to how one should see the facts as a whole. Here science usually plays only a marginal role, for scientific theories and data typically only form a small part of the material on the basis of which an individual comes to adopt a particular understanding of the world. As we noted in Chapter 4, of its nature science does not (and cannot) determine the significance of its findings. Hence the individual's attempt to draw wider conclusions about how he should understand the world can be said to take place in a different dimension from the scientific, and it is with this dimension that the ethical (and the religious) is intimately linked.

Here we can return to the issues of Chapter 1, for the attempt to achieve an overall understanding of the world brings us back to questions concerning the nature of philosophy. Thus, from what has been said, we can see why ethics should have been such an intimate part of much past philosophy, for in expounding a conception of the universe (a picture of the world) one is also delineating an ethic. In this respect, the shift from metaphysics to linguistic philosophy alters the relation between philosophy and ethics, for in a sense the latter is marginalized. This can be seen in the work of Bertrand Russell; for, as we noted on pp. 15–17, Russell's call for scientific method in philosophy goes together with the explicit desire to eliminate ethical claims from the philosophical domain. Unfortunately, with Russell, the shift to a new conception of philosophy is accompanied by a reductive account of ethics, for he claims that 'ethical metaphysics is fundamentally an attempt, however disguised, to give legislative force to our wishes' (1918: 108). According to him, if this attempt has any value it lies in 'the indication of some new way of feeling towards life and the world, some new way of feeling by which our own existence can acquire more of the characteristics which we most deeply desire' (*ML*: 109).

The reference, however, to ways of feeling is inappropriate, for how can one genuinely come to accept a certain way of seeing the world if one regards it simply as that illusion which happens to be the most comforting? Such a notion fails to capture the distinctive feature of ethical claims which we have been stressing. Thus, although Russell is right to claim that ethical notions have no place in the scientific investigation of reality (this, as it were, partially defines science), he is wrong to infer from this that ethics therefore simply reflects our wishes. Coming to an overall understanding of the world cannot be the direct product of scientific investigation, for it involves attributing a particular significance to the facts, and since doing this involves the taking-up of a substantive position by the individual, it can be no part of a purely factual investigation. Whether the individual is therefore free to understand the world in whatever way he pleases is, however, itself a substantive question, for to assert this is to reject the alternative claim that of the various ways of understanding the world there is one particular conception which is correct and which should be accepted by everyone. Thus, although one may adopt a 'scientific' conception of the world, this does not logically follow from admiration for the achievements of science. Rather, the decision itself expresses a particular attitude and one which involves treating the attempt to understand the world in some further sense as empty or misguided. Only from this particular substantive viewpoint is ethics nothing but the projection of human hopes and desires. Therefore, rather than claiming that science has shown the ethical claims of the metaphysician to be empty, it would be less misleading if Russell had simply noted that the metaphysician, in articulating a particular conception of the world, presents a substantive moral position. Assessment of that position (and of the question as to whether *any* positions of that kind were correct) would then be a separate issue. Making this distinction is vital, for as we have seen no ethic can be supported on logical or conceptual grounds, and hence, as Wittgenstein's lecture on ethics suggests, in assessing (or advancing) an ethical position the individual can only speak for himself. Precisely for this reason, it is crucial to distinguish between the conceptual clarifications of philosophy and the articulation of substantive moral views. To put it aphoristically, the aim of the former is conceptual clarity, while that of the latter is wisdom, and the two are by no means the same.

128

At this stage, it is necessary to re-consider a fundamental objection to our whole account, for it may be claimed that human action is no different from any other kind of action and that it too should be explained in causal terms. In this way, the reactions which underlie our moral judgements can be treated as dispositions whose origin and genesis we can explain. From this perspective, the stress we have placed on bedrock is misguided, for according to this approach rather than our stopping at bedrock it would be (and is) possible to continue our explanations and offer accounts of why we react as we do. On the one hand, science can explain why we make the judgements we do, while, on the other, once we throw off the shackles of a superstitious, religious past, it becomes clear that our moral judgements are simply manifestations of our dispositions and indeed could never have been anything else.

This objection presents itself as a correction of our account; however, what it in fact reflects is a substantive position, one which rules out particular ethical claims and which treats as misguided the distinctively ethical reaction we have discussed. Rather than embodying the truth about human action, it offers a different way of looking at (and treating) such action: again, what it might be said to express is a positivistic 'scientific' conception of the world. One way in which the substantive nature of its claims can be illustrated is by considering the notion of a disposition. Thus the claim that moral judgements manifest a disposition is analytic if the point is simply that all human statements and actions by definition manifest dispositions. The substantive move, however, is to claim that moral judgements *merely* express dispositions. Here the ethical reaction we have described is ruled out, and in so far as this is the case this can only reflect a substantive decision on the part of the assessor, for it represents his (personal) denial of the claim that there are standards of conduct independent of the individual. Another way of making this point is to consider the notion of explanation, for to seek to explain moral judgements already involves a move from considering the object of the judgement ('Is the act right or wrong?') to considering the judgement simply as the manifestation of a certain disposition (a tendency to condemn acts of such-and-such a kind). In this way, the content of the judgement is bracketed off and the claim that actions can be intrinsically right or wrong independently of our dispositions is implicitly denied. The search for explanation treats the judgement as simply the manifestation of a particular disposition and hence implicitly undermines it and rejects the reaction it embodies.

In this way, the objection to our account can be seen to embody a substantive move and one at odds with the distinctively moral aspect of our moral practices. This, of course, does not mean that one cannot embrace it with the intention of reforming our moral practices. What does need to be made clear, however, is that such a reform would be based not on logical or conceptual grounds but on the substantive rejection of a certain type of position. From what we said earlier, it can be seen that this move is not without its dangers, for to incorporate projects for moral reform within philosophy is precisely to encourage the confusion of the conceptual and the substantive. Similarly, it should be noted that such a move involves a change in aim, for we set out to understand our moral practices, to clarify what we mean by 'ethics', and now we are being encouraged instead to reform these practices. This move would indeed be unavoidable if our current practices were self-contradictory; such a claim, however, is suspect on general grounds (see p. 10) and is not sustainable with respect to our moral practices. Hence if we decide to reject these practices it would be because we see them as misguided, not as nonsensical. Here it is also significant that the attempt to reform our practices often seems to replace rather than succeed the understanding of them. Thus our practices are treated as unintelligible either on the basis of misguided philosophical prejudices or through a contingent failure to understand them. Russell, for example, mistakenly takes science and traditional ethics to be in competition. More generally, the stress on the social value of ethical action can also involve a misconstrual of what is at stake in ethics, and as a result may render many ethical claims opaque.[16] Here part of the failure is a failure in imaginative understanding, as we saw, for example, in Smart's discussion of guilt or in Williams's comments on the moral law.

It is also important to recognize the scale of the change implicitly being advocated, for it is not so much a question of the reform of our moral practices as of their abolition and replacement by something quite different. Thus the discussion of whether or not a certain act is wrong is replaced by the consideration of which set of dispositions should be programmed into society's members. To take a concrete example, the argument about abortion ceases to be an argument about the rightness or wrongness of that act and becomes instead a problem of social organization. The notion of rights (the mother's rights versus the foetus's rights) drops out of consideration, and the question becomes 'Do we want a society where people can have abortions and are disposed to accept abortion, or do we not?' This question, however, is itself problematic, for whatever answer one gives to it will, on the account we are considering, simply reflect the dispositions one has happened to acquire. In this way, a reflexive problem is created, for adopting the causal account undermines the possibility of rational discussion: indeed, it evacuates one's own statements of content, in so far as these are no longer taken at face value but instead treated as the manifestation of dispositions. Thus, suppose someone claims that society would be better organized in a certain way, the reply will come back 'Do you really believe that or have you simply been caused to make this claim?' This presents the advocate of the causal account with an inescapable dichotomy, for in discussing a judgement either the reference to causation drops out as irrelevant or the content of the judgement is nullified.[17] Thus if one treats one's belief simply as the product of causation, one must also accept that one might just as easily have been caused to hold the opposite belief. Hence if one sticks with the causal account one must treat one's own belief as arbitrary and so implicitly undermine one's commitment to it. If, however, one does not do this but claims that one's belief is correct or well-grounded, then the reference to causation drops away as irrelevant: in this case, what is relevant is the validity or invalidity of the judgement and the grounds there are for accepting or rejecting it. Adherence to the causal account is therefore incompatible with the affirmation of judgements of the kind we have seen to be distinctively ethical. This applies just as much to claims which are obviously moral as to others which are less clearly so, such as the claim that society would be better (or more just) if organized thus-and-so. These latter claims also imply that there are standards independent of the individual in terms of which such issues can be discussed, and for this reason they too cannot be combined with the claim that such judgements only express our preferences or what we have been caused to believe.[18]

At this stage, it is perhaps also worth noting that our account does not commit us to rejecting all causal explanations of how individuals come to judge as they do. The individual may accept that he was caused to hold a certain belief, but when he advances the belief as correct, questions as to how he came to acquire the belief cease to have any significance. Thus in making moral judgements the individual must distinguish between those of his reactions which he takes at face-value (as it were, identifying with them) and those which he treats as non-significant and simply the product of his upbringing, etc. In this sense, the possibility of causal explanation adds a further dimension to reflection, a further complication to the situation of moral choice. Thus, in deciding how to act, one aspect of the individual's situation may be an awareness of the possibility of treating moral scruples as the product of conditioning. In the face of this possibility, he must decide whether to treat his response as a moral judgement or as a causally explicable hang-up. To say that 'within' the individual's dispositions the two are indistinguishable is beside the point. The sceptical problem this suggestion poses has to be met and has to be met in action. Thus ultimately the individual takes up a position and either treats his reaction as a mere hang-up or holds that the action is in fact wrong, and thereby denies that his making this claim is merely a product of conditioning.[19] If someone asks him how he can be sure that a particular judgement he makes is not simply the product of his upbringing, then he has no answer. In his actions, however, he manifests his conviction that this is not the case. None the less, it always remains logically possible for a third party (or even for the individual himself at a subsequent date) to take up the opposite position, i.e. to treat his scruples as unfortunate hang-ups. Here once again we reach bedrock – one is faced with a substantive choice, and no position can be justified on purely logical or conceptual grounds.

To clarify these issues, let us consider Mackie's forceful exposition of the opposing point of view in his essay 'Morality and the Retributive Emotions'. There he argues that our moral concepts are derived from retributive emotions which can be explained as the product of evolution. He begins his argument by outlining what he calls the paradox of retribution. According to him,

> the paradox is that, on the one hand, a retributive principle of punishment cannot be explained or developed within a reasonable system of moral thought, while, on the other hand, such a principle cannot be eliminated from our moral thinking. (Mackie 1985: 207)

Mackie considers various attempts to resolve this paradox by proving the validity of retributive principles. In each case, however, he concludes that the attempted justification either presupposes its object or is incoherent. For example, he rejects as incoherent the Hegelian claim that an appropriate penalty annuls or cancels the crime, as it were 'trampling on it and wiping it out'. Against this, he argues that the punishment may trample on the criminal, but it does not do away with the crime. It may, perhaps, by way of deterrence, reformation, and the like help to prevent future similar crimes . . . but again all of these are only possible consequentialist justifications, yet it seems that it is merely in confusion with them that it could be thought that the punishment annuls the crime. It should be clear beyond all question that the past wrong act, just because it is past, cannot be annulled. (Mackie 1985: 210)

Thus Mackie claims that the notion of retribution cannot be given a reasonable moral justification. The truly radical nature of his critique becomes apparent shortly afterwards when he points out that his attack on retribution applies *ceteris paribus* to the very notion of a morally wrong action.

The central moral concept of the wrongness of an action includes . . . the synthetic judgement that what is harmful generally and intrinsically forbidden calls for a hostile response: this concept contains a very general form of the positive retributivist principle. In this general form, it applies not just to the special concept of punishment, but pervasively, wherever the central concept of moral wrongness is in force. (Mackie 1985: 214)

According to him, it is impossible to make sense of any such principle; for this reason, he advises us to make the 'Humean' move and so 'ask not, "Why do wrong actions deserve penalties and good actions deserve rewards?" but rather, "Why do we have an ingrained tendency to see wrong actions as calling for penalties and good actions as calling for rewards?" ' (Mackie 1985: 215). He then proceeds to sketch a biological and sociological explanation of how we have come to think as we do. Thus he claims that we can 'describe a possible course of evolution by which retributive behaviour and emotions, co-operative resentment, and the disinterested moral sentiments could have developed in turn' (Mackie 1985: 218). Such an account solves the paradox of retribution by accounting for its genesis. Furthermore, in so doing it offers a general explanation of why we are inclined to make the moral judgements we do.

In response to Mackie, the first issue to consider concerns the so-called paradox of retribution itself. Bearing in mind what we have said in earlier chapters, it should be clear that what Mackie demands is a justification at bedrock, and thus the inability to meet his demand reflects not the incoherence of our practices but the incoherence of this demand itself. The advocacy of principles of retribution manifests a particular ethical reaction. This reaction can be further elucidated in various ways, but as Mackie correctly notes these elucidations pre-suppose the reaction rather than provide independent grounds for accepting it.[20] This, however, is necessarily the case; as we saw, no independent justification is possible, because in this context the notion of an independent justification makes no sense. The same point can be made in terms of reasons for action, for the principle of retribution can be treated as the claim that having done wrong is itself a reason for being punished. Mackie questions this claim and hence effectively asks 'Why is this reason a reason?' To this question there is, of course, no answer, for here we reach bedrock and all we can do is note that for certain people it is a sufficient reason. One might therefore construe his critique slightly differently and take him to be asking 'Is this a *sufficient* reason for action?' Understood thus, however, the substan-tive nature of his critique becomes obvious, for it becomes clear that he wishes to reject a particular kind of reason, i.e. that he is expressing his own belief that such a reason is not sufficient.

Thus Mackie's critique is based on a substantive moral claim rather than conceptual analysis. Furthermore, in so far as he identifies the two his critique is confused, for he believes his objections to be con-ceptual when in fact they are substantive. This suggests that his criti-cisms are at least partly the product of philosophical prejudice and confusion; the failure to understand what he criticizes can in turn be seen as partly a philosophical failure and partly an imaginative failure. This is illustrated by his treatment of the Hegelian justification of retribution, for, although he describes this as 'a more serious attempt to explain the retributive principle' (Mackie 1985: 210), on his interpretation it is not merely misguided, but ludicrously (and implausibly) foolish. Thus Hegel is supposed to have confused the fact that the criminal is 'trampled on' with the notion of the crime being trampled on – some confusion! In fact, however, the fault lies with Mackie, for the notion that the punishment in some sense annuls the crime is one he cannot understand; faced with the moral reaction which Hegel's claim expresses, Mackie can literally make nothing of it. His difficulty, however, is more general, for he has similar prob-lems with the notion that a 'wrong action is not just harmful to this or to that person, [but] is harmful *simpliciter*' (Mackie 1985: 213). For Mackie, the reaction this claim manifests (i.e. the reaction we have described as distinctively ethical) is simply an oddity, a strange phenomenon, and precisely one in desperate need of explanation.

Mackie's paradox is thus not a genuine paradox, or rather it is only a paradox if one both feels that an individual ought to be punished for doing wrong and yet ultimately believes that one's own reaction is unreasonable. Hence an explanation is only needed if one adopts the substantive position of rejecting retributive principles and therefore finds it necessary to explain why one is none the less so inclined towards them.[21] The 'Humean' response to this dilemma is itself a substantive move, for it involves giving up the retributive principles which generate the paradox. Thus Mackie abandons the consideration of retributive principles themselves and instead treats the problem as one of explaining how we have come to have certain dispositions. The explanation he then offers presents itself as a straightforward empirical account. The account he offers, however, does not consist in the presentation of detailed concrete evidence. Rather, he sketches a possible evolutionary schema and underlines certain similarities; in this sense, he presents a picture and encourages us to look at our moral reactions in a certain way, e.g. as similar to an animal's instinctive hostile response to hostile action. Thus Mackie's proposed explanation is not really empirical in nature; it does not simply state how as a matter of fact our moral reactions arose, but rather expresses a commitment to accounting for these reactions in a certain way. What underlies his apparently empirical claims is his substantive belief that it is misguided to distinguish between human moral reactions and the instinctive, conditioned responses of an animal.[22] Since his proffered explanation embodies a substantive move, it is highly misleading for him to claim that his account is simply 'the best explanatory hypothesis to account for the phenomena of moral thinking' (Mackie 1985: 214). The point is that if one thinks it is right to punish those who have done wrong solely because they have done so, then one believes that no further explanation is needed; for the retributivist that is what justice demands and that's all there is to it.

In his essay 'Errors and the Phenomenology of Value', Simon Blackburn, like Mackie, claims that it makes no sense to reject explanation *a priori* and adds that this is especially true when possible explanations actually exist. One counter-example here, however, would be the notion of Providence. Thus, according to some historical sources, the fact that it rained shortly before the battle of Waterloo played an important part in Napoleon's defeat. Most people would not take the fact that it rained at that particular moment as standing in need of explanation; indeed, they would *a priori* reject the attempt to explain this. Others, however, will explain it as providential and offer a possible explanation (e.g. that God wished to punish the hubris of Napoleon and undermine France's domination of the continent). Here, in adopting or rejecting the attempt to explain, one indicates the relation one takes up to the facts, the way one believes they should be looked at. The decision involved is a substantive one, and hence it is wrong to assume that the attempt to explain is always necessarily an appropriate response.[23] To put it another way, explanation comes to an end in action, for in acting one shows what it is that one takes to require explanation and what one does not.

Blackburn's essay raises other problems for our account, for he denies that there is a clash between the claims embodied in traditional moral judgements and the explanation of these judgements in projectivist terms. Thus he treats our moral judgements as manifestations of our dispositions, but also claims that we can assess such judgements, for 'we can turn our judgements on our own appetitive construction, and may find it lacking' (Blackburn 1981: 175). He therefore rejects the idea that a projective theory must involve one in believing claims such as 'If we had different attitudes it would not be wrong to kick dogs.' This counterfactual he takes to express the moral view that what makes it wrong to kick dogs is our reaction, and as a moral view he holds this to be absurd. The projectivist

> like anyone else . . . thinks that what makes it wrong to kick dogs is that it causes them pain. To put it another way: he approves of a moral disposition which, given this belief as an input, yields the reaction of disapproval as an output; he does not approve of one which needs belief about our attitudes as an input in order to yield the same output, and this is all that gets expression in the counterfactual. (Blackburn 1981: 179)

Similarly, he claims that the projectivist can talk of moral improvement and deterioration, for he may judge that someone has acquired dispositions which he considers more worthy or less worthy. In this way, he hopes to have shown that his theory ('quasi-realism') offers an adequate account of what the moral realist wants to say and hence is in harmony with our everyday moral thinking.

Crucial to Blackburn's argument is the claim that we can separate what individuals are doing when they make moral judgements, from claims ('theories') about the nature or status of their activity. On the basis of what we have said already, however, it should be clear that this is not possible. Someone who claims that there are standards independent of the individual is not propounding a theory about the nature of moral judgements; rather, that claim is part of his judgement itself. Hence to claim that moral judgements merely express our dispositions is to reject that type of judgement and so express a rival substantive position. The moral position of the quasi-realist is therefore *not* the same as that of the realist. When the latter claims that kicking dogs is wrong because it causes them pain, his judgement is not concerned with which human dispositions he approves of but rather with the act itself. What is at issue is whether kicking dogs is wrong, not whether we approve of people who are disposed to disapprove of dog-kicking.[24] Thus in the above quotation Blackburn's equation is inaccurate: to say that kicking dogs is wrong because it causes them pain is not simply to say that we approve of a disposition which given a certain input yields disapproval as an output. Rather, it says what it says, viz. that kicking dogs is wrong because it causes them pain. This claim involves no reference to human dispositions however indirect; indeed, *qua* moral judgement what is distinctive about it is the assertion that kicking dogs would be wrong even if we were disposed to approve of such action (and were disposed to approve of those who approve of it, etc. etc.).

Blackburn therefore cannot claim that quasi-realism leaves our moral vocabulary intact, for this theory rejects the central claim made in distinctively ethical judgements. Furthermore, by treating moral statements as simply the product of dispositions the individual has been caused to acquire, it ceases to treat them as judgements at all. Thus the question of whether kicking dogs is wrong (the question of whether this judgement is correct) disappears and is replaced by the question 'What kind of dispositions do we approve of?'. Blackburn makes this shift because he wishes to deny that evaluative judgements reflect something other than our own dispositions, i.e. because he rejects the claim that there are independent standards of human action and correspondingly intrinsic differences between the moral value of different types of action. Because of this denial, the only way he can explain moral judgements is as disguised judgements about dispositions to judge thus or so. As we have argued, however, this account fails to capture the claims embodied in moral judgements. Furthermore, it is also fails to stand up even in its own terms, for even if one accepted that moral judgements were concealed expressions of approval or disapproval of other people's dispositions, a further question would then arise as to what such expressions of approval could mean on the quasi-realist account. The difficulty here is that the assertion that a particular disposition is worthy or deserving of approval involves precisely the kind of claim Blackburn wishes to eliminate, for it claims that some dispositions are intrinsically superior to others. Thus if he is to be consistent the quasi-realist must treat his approval of a particular disposition not as an appropriate response to the merits of that disposition but as the result of his own dispositions which might just as well have been otherwise. If he admits this, however, he effectively undermines his own judgement, for he would be accepting that the various possible dispositions are all on a par and that it is only the contingencies of his causal life-history which lead him to distinguish between them.

Thus a causal account of the kind Blackburn proposes undermines the individual's ethical judgement in so far as it treats the key determinant of the judgement as the disposition of the individual making it rather than the merits of the object supposedly being judged. This clash between the commitment to a causal account and the claims embodied in ethical judgements poses irresolvable problems for Blackburn's entire argument, as can be illustrated by reconsidering his central claim that quasi-realism is quite compatible with holding that, for example, kicking dogs is wrong because it causes them pain. Where the quasi-realist makes this claim, the immediate question that arises is whether the reasons he offers for his judgement are what is crucial or whether what is relevant is the fact that he has been caused to be disposed in a certain way.[25] If the individual affirms the former he abandons quasi-realism, for in doing so he accepts that there can be rational discussion about the merits or demerits of human action and thus that there are correct and incorrect standards in terms of which one should act. If, however, the quasi-realist maintains that moral judgements are simply the expression of particular dispositions then he must accept that a different causal history would have led him to judge otherwise than he does and that is all there is to it.

Thus Blackburn's claims, like Mackie's, are substantive and do challenge established ways of moral thinking. Acceptance of quasi-realism would involve either abandoning our existing moral vocabulary or continuing to use it but in a fundamentally new and confusing way. The approach which leads to the advocacy of such a change is, of course, one possible substantive position, and as such there are no logical or conceptual objections to it. It is confused and inaccurate, however, where it claims either to offer an insight into our moral practices as they actually exist or to be the only approach to ethics that is philosophically adequate.[26] To underline this point let us briefly summarize the argument of this chapter. Thus our starting-point was the recognition that moral judgements do not state what is the case in the way empirical judgements do. One possible response to this grammatical point, we argued, would be to hold that therefore all judgements about human action were on the same level, i.e. that different judgements simply reflected different preferences or different dispositions. Against this, however, we noted the claims of the ethical individual who maintains that there are intrinsic differences between actions (and/or types of action) and that correspondingly some judgements about human action are correct and others incorrect. In making these claims, the ethical individual asserts that there are standards of right action which are independent of the individual and which ought to be recognized by everyone. As we saw, together these claims constitute the distinctive feature of moral judgements; accepting or rejecting them, however, involves the taking-up of a substantive position, and hence the philosopher can say nothing more here *qua* philosopher, for logical and conceptual considerations leave the question entirely open.

7

TRUTH, RELATIVISM, AND OBJECTIVITY

At the end of my lecture on ethics, I spoke in the first person. I believe that is quite essential. Here nothing can be established. I can only appear as a person speaking for myself.

(Wittgenstein, *WWK*: 117)

Although Wittgenstein in his later period wrote little or nothing on the subject of ethics, he did discuss the topic on a number of occasions with Rush Rhees, and some of these discussions are highly interesting. Thus in 1942, Wittgenstein pointed out how strange it was that one could find books on ethics in which there was no mention of a genuine ethical or moral problem. He and Rush Rhees then went on to discuss the case of a man who comes to the conclusion that he must either leave his wife or abandon his work of cancer research:

Such a man's attitude will vary at different times. Suppose I am his friend, and I say to him, 'Look, you've taken this girl out of her home, and now, by God, you've got to stick to her.' This would be called taking up an ethical attitude. He may reply, 'But what of suffering humanity? how can I abandon my research?' In saying this he may be making it easier for himself: he wants to carry on the work anyway. (I may have reminded him that there are others who can carry it on if he gives up.) And he may be inclined to view the effect on his wife relatively easily: 'It probably won't be fatal to her. She'll get over it, probably marry again', and so on. On the other hand it may not be this way. It may be that he has a deep love for her. And yet he may think that if he were to give up his work he would be no husband for her. That is his life, and if he gives that up he will drag her down. Here we may say that we have all the materials of a tragedy; and we could only say 'Well, God help you'.

140

Whatever he finally does, the way things then turn out may affect his attitude. He may say, 'Well, thank God I left her; it was better all around.' Or maybe, 'Thank God I stuck to her.' Or he may not be able to say 'thank God' at all, but just the opposite.

I want to say that this is the solution to an ethical problem. (Rhees 1982: 99–100)

Wittgenstein's conclusion may seem wilfully paradoxical, for far from solving the problem, he gives no indication of what the 'right' answer to it is. This, however, is precisely his point, for the thrust of his discussion is to call into question the notion that there is an independent way of determining the 'right' answer. As Wittgenstein goes on to point out, if the man was a Christian, his problem would be totally different. In that case, the question, 'Should I leave her or not?' would not even arise: his problem would be how to make the best of the situation, what he should do to be a decent husband in these greatly altered circumstances, etc.

The natural response to this is to ask whether the treatment of such a question within Christian ethics is itself right. If there are various possible solutions to the problem, it must surely be possible to decide which of them is right and which is wrong. According to Wittgenstein, however, this demand makes no sense:

we do not know what this decision would be like – how it would be determined, what sort of criteria would be used, and so on. Compare saying that it must be possible to decide which of two standards of accuracy is the right one. We do not even know what a person who asks this question is after. (Rhees 1982: 100)

The difficulty here is conceptual, for it makes no sense to claim that one can stand *outside* the various ways of looking at the problem and adjudicate between them. Within Christian ethics, one conclusion follows, and within another ethic, a different conclusion follows. To decide that the Christian ethic was the right one would itself be a value judgement; as Wittgenstein puts it, 'it would amount to *adopting* Christian ethics' (*RR*: 101). Thus in reaching a conclusion any supposedly independent procedure demonstrates *ipso facto* the bogus nature of its claim to independence: in reaching a conclusion, it shows that it too is one way of looking at the problem and hence logically on a par with that which it is intended to assess.[1] For these reasons, a clash between ethical systems differs fundamentally from a clash between scientific theories; for 'it is not like saying that one of these physical theories must be the right one. The way in which some reality corresponds – or conflicts – with a physical theory has no counterpart here' (Rhees 1982: 101).

The contrast which Wittgenstein draws here is grammatical; his claim is not that nothing as a matter of fact corresponds to ethics, but rather that the notion of correspondence here makes no sense in principle. The fundamental contrast here is that between investigating reality and deciding how to act. The first project necessarily involves some form of comparison with reality, for that is what makes it what it is (viz. an investigation of reality). In the second case, however, although what is the case determines the choice the individual faces, his decision can itself neither correspond nor fail to correspond with reality (with the facts). Where several courses of action are possible, no comparison with reality can decide between them; rather, the individual is confronted with the need to make a decision and the decision he makes will reflect his own substantive moral position, i.e. his convictions as to how people should and should not act.[2] The implications of this point are twofold: first, it means that it makes no sense to talk of empirically investigating the truth or validity of a moral judgement; and second, it implies that any assessment of the judgement is on the same level as the judgement itself, for endorsing or censuring the judgement itself involves expressing a substantive moral position.

These grammatical points might seem to usher in a fearful relativism, for do they not imply that all ethics have the same value and hence that a decision between them is arbitrary? Not surprisingly, Wittgenstein rejects this claim. As we saw earlier, the absence of an independent decision procedure does not eliminate the possibility of considered and meaningful judgement. After much reflection, one may decide that the Christian ethic is right and that other ethics are superficial or misguided. This does, of course, amount to adopting Christian ethics, but the substantive nature of one's decision does not show it to be arbitrary. On the contrary, embracing Christian ethics involves rejecting this claim, for to adopt it is to claim that there are qualitative differences between ethics – indeed, that the Christian way of deciding how to act is the only right one. Here what is claimed for Christian ethics is not a privileged logical status but a privileged moral status, and in this respect the claim that other ethics are wrong or misguided is itself a constitutive feature of the moral outlook one adopts. Thus if you say there are various systems of ethics you are not saying that they are all equally right. That means nothing. Just as it would have no meaning to say that each was right from his own standpoint. That could only mean that each judges as he does. (Rhees 1982: 101)

Although each moral standpoint claims for itself a unique status, Wittgenstein's point is that there is no independent way of adjudicating between them. This, however, does not imply that all moral standpoints are wrong to claim a unique status, for that too would be a particular kind of substantive position, viz. extreme relativism. Rather than making any substantive claims of this sort, Wittgenstein simply underlines two grammatical points: first, that the appeal to 'independent' assessment – be it in terms of logic or of reality – makes no sense; and second, that for this reason assessing a moral standpoint itself always involves advancing substantive (and hence contestable) claims.

Against these points, Wittgenstein notes that 'people have had the notion of an ethical theory – the idea of finding the true nature of goodness or of duty' (ibid.: 100). Mentioning Plato as an example, Wittgenstein points out that the aim of such projects is to eliminate relativity and achieve objectivity, the idea being that 'relativity must be avoided at all costs, since it would destroy the *imperative* in morality' (*RR*: 100). Here, however, the reference to truth and objectivity embodies a grammatical confusion, for the force of an injunction does not lie in its truth. Indeed, it could not do so, for *qua* injunction it would make no sense to say either that it was true or that it was false. Thus to claim that a particular moral judgement is true is simply to reiterate that judgement, reaffirming one's commitment to it.[3] Similarly 'if I say: "Although I believe that so and so is good, I may be wrong"': this says no more than what I asserted may be denied' (ibid.: 100). Thus the reference to truth is misleading in so far as it assimilates moral and empirical judgements; in particular, it is misleading if it suggests that the key to resolving moral disputes lies in investigating reality. The idea that we might discover the true nature of goodness is also misleading, for once again it suggests that moral judgements can be derived from what is the case. Of course, if 'discovering the true nature of goodness' means reflecting upon how we ought to act and coming to certain conclusions, then such a project is far from incoherent. In this case, however, the reference to truth simply drops out of consideration: to conclude that it is true that murder is wrong is simply to conclude that one should not commit murder, and this is not some-thing one discovers from a close inspection of any particular facts.

As we noted, the aim of an ethical theory is to establish the nature of goodness once and for all. The motivation behind such theories is a fear of relativity and the consequent desire for an independent means of justifying morality. However, what needs to be recognized is, first, that no independent justification is possible and, second, that none is needed. The logical impossibility of proving that one ought not to do X does not render incoherent the claim that doing X is wrong: even if the denial of relativity is an important part of one's substantive position, it does not follow that in order to make this claim one has to be able to show that every other moral position is logically incoherent. One reason we may be inclined to overlook this point is the temptation to assimilate moral judgements to unsubstantiated empirical claims. Here the existence of disagreement in both cases encourages us to treat both as 'subjective', i.e. as having no validity in the absence of further evidence or proof. Having made this move, relativity does appear a threat, for now it seems that either evidence must be offered to support the claims of morality or these claims will have been shown to be spurious. The original assimilation, however, is profoundly mis-leading, for with respect to moral judgements there is no such thing as evidence or proof. With empirical claims, one can contrast those that are substantiated with those that are not, and thus both poles of the subjective-objective contrast are given a sense. With moral judge-ments, however, this is not so; what it would be for a moral judgement to be substantiated ('objective') has not been defined, and hence the very possibility of its being objective is excluded. Another way of making this point is to note that the claim that ethics is subjective is incoherently treated as both grammatical and substantive. The incoherence comes to a head in the claim that moral judgements do not just lack evidence, but essentially lack evidence. However, to lack evidence essentially is not to be singularly lacking in evidence; rather, the reference to essence indicates that the concept of evidence here has no application. Thus the initial claim embodies a grammatical con-fusion, for what it reflects is the crossing of different language-games. The claim that moral judgements lack evidence and the attempt to remedy this 'defect' are both the product of confusion; in each case, the source of the confusion is the failure to recognize the particular grammar of moral concepts.

Although one may accept that moral claims such as 'You ought not to do X' do not assert that a certain state of affairs obtains, it may seem more difficult to accept this with respect to other moral statements, for example, the claim that there is a moral law or moral order. Here at first glance the ethical individual's claim may indeed seem to be factual; the nature of the claim, however, needs to be explored carefully. Thus someone who makes this claim is not asserting that some peculiar entity exists; rather, the notion of a moral law expresses the idea that the principles according to which one ought to act are, on the one hand, absolute and, on the other, independent of human attitudes and desires. To point out that this claim could not be true or false in the sense that empirical judgements are true or false is thus not to deny or undermine it, but rather to clarify its nature.[4] Thus the key point to recognize is that the claim to correctness ('truth') does not have the same meaning here as it does with respect to empirical judgements. Furthermore, it is important not to confuse the logical point that moral judgements do not state what is the case, with the claim that moral judgements are (and can only be) expressive of the attitudes or dispositions of the individual concerned. This claim does deny that there are standards independent of the individual, but such a denial does not follow from the logical point we have been stressing; rather, it reflects a substantive position and thus one which conceptual analysis can neither establish nor refute.

One rather different reason why it may be difficult to accept that the claim that there is a moral law is not a factual claim, is the indicative form in which the claim is couched. It may be useful therefore to consider a number of other examples of statements where the indicative form can also be misleading. One example would be statements concerned with the notion of fate or determinism. Here it might be thought that either it is the case that everything is determined or it is not; if, however, one paraphrases this dichotomy as either it is worthwhile to struggle against the tide of events or it is not, then it becomes clearer why the reference to truth is misleading. To embrace or reject determinism is to express one's attitude to life, and hence the use of the notion of fate is bound up with the attitude one takes up towards the future and the past:

in the sense in which asking a question and insisting on an answer is expressive of a different attitude, a different mode of life, from not asking it, the *same* can be said of utterances like 'It is God's will' or 'We are not masters of our fate'. The work done by this sentence, or

145

at any rate something like it, could also be done by a command! Including one which you give yourself. And conversely the utterance of a command, such as 'Don't be resentful' can be expressed as if the affirmation of a truth. (*CV*: 61)

A more complicated but similar example would be the claim that other people are conscious (possess consciousness). Here again one might have thought that this claim is either true or false, but in so far as this statement expresses our relation to others, to say this would be misleading. The claim that other people are conscious characterizes our relation to them; and just as to deny responsibility is not to hold people responsible (*CV*: 63), so too to deny that others are conscious would be to reject the range of concepts this claim implies and hence not to relate to others in certain kinds of ways (for example, one would no longer talk of others as happy, as sad, or as having intentions).[5] Thus the indicative form of a sentence may conceal many different types of claim; hence what needs to be looked at is not the form of the sentence but its use.

Wittgenstein's comments on the notion of truth in ethics highlight the grammatical differences between moral judgements and empirical judgements. These differences are also crucial when considering the question of whether moral judgements are objective, for in view of these differences the claim to objectivity has a different meaning in each case.[6] To put it another way, if objectivity is defined as correspondence with reality, then no meaning is assigned to the notion of objectivity in ethics. Thus if one wishes to claim (or deny) that moral judgements are objective a separate elucidation of this claim is required. However, before we consider this issue in more detail, another general point needs to be made, for as we saw in the previous section, in this context it is particularly important to maintain a clear distinction between statements which are grammatical and those which present a substantive position. Thus, since grammatical points advance no claims, it makes no sense to deny them or reject them as wrong. The only possible grounds for objection to them would be if they failed to offer an accurate account of the concepts they purported to describe. Substantive claims, however, present a particular view, and hence their denial always makes sense, for it is a mark of their having content that they are meaningful both when stated positively and when denied. If, therefore, the issue of objectivity is taken to be substantive in nature, both poles of the subjective-objective dichotomy must be assigned a sense.[7] In that case, however, the claim that ethics is subjective and the claim that it is objective will both be logically possible.

Having made these preliminary remarks, let us consider the question of objectivity itself. The first point to note is that how the objective–subjective contrast should be applied in ethics is far from obvious. What the contrast most immediately suggests is a distinction between appearance and reality, between what seems to be the case and what is the case. One might, for example, say that as an object moves away from one subjectively it gets smaller, whereas objectively it remains the same size. Applied to ethics, however, this contrast makes no sense. As we saw, the grammatical role of moral judgements does not involve stating (or attempting to state) what is the case, hence it would make no sense to ask whether they state what is the case or only what seems to be the case.[8] However, the distinction between appearance and reality does bring to the fore the notion of illusion and hence suggests one way of construing the subjective–objective debate in ethics. Thus we can take this debate to be concerned with whether, and in what sense, moral judgements can be said to be valid. Construed in this way, the claim that ethics is subjective constitutes a rejection of the idea that moral judgements can be correct. Thus the idea that there are certain things one ought to do (or ought not to do) is treated as a superstition or as a social device intended to promote certain kinds of behaviour. A view of this kind is eloquently advanced by Callicles in Plato's *Gorgias*:

> In my view those who lay down the rules [of morality] are the weak men, the many. And so they lay down the rules and assign their praise and blame with their eye on themselves and their own advantage. They terrorize the stronger men capable of having more; and to prevent those men from having more than themselves they say that taking more is shameful and unjust, and that doing injustice is this, seeking to have more than other people; they are satisfied, I take it, if they themselves have an equal share when they're inferior. That's why by rule this is said to be unjust and shameful, to seek to have more than the many, and they call that doing injustice. (*Gorgias* 483b)[9]

On this account, the claim 'You ought to do X' is taken to mean 'I want you to do X', and thus the attempt to distinguish between moral judgements and expressions of preference is treated as a fraud. Correspondingly, it is held that in his actions only the foolish individual will take into account considerations other than his own desires or preferences. By the same token, all talk of justice, nobility, and rights is rejected, for these claims invoke independent standards just as much as the straightforward claim that one ought to act thus-and-so. Construed in this way, to claim that moral judgements are subjective is to claim that they have no validity and that the absolute standards they invoke are fictions of which the individual need take no account.

Having assigned a clear sense to the claim that ethics is subjective, the opposite claim can be explained fairly straightforwardly. Thus, according to this point of view, desires and preferences are *not* the only considerations which should determine our actions; rather, it is held that there are certain types of act that are right and others that are wrong, and that it is in terms of these concepts that one should act. A corollary of this claim is the claim that moral judgements do not simply express one's preferences or dispositions, but express the recognition of standards which everyone ought to recognize on the pain of going morally wrong if they do not do so. Thus, in claiming that a particular moral judgement is valid, the individual claims a unique status for one way of deciding how to act; he claims that it is the only way in which one ought to decide how to act, and that correspondingly it is not just different from others but right where they are wrong. Here it is important to note that the meaning of the claim to uniqueness can only be expressed in moral terms: to say that one way of deciding how to act is the right way is to say not that it corresponds to reality but rather that any other way is wrong. Thus to claim that ethics is objective is not to claim that weird entities exist or that there is something 'out there' which makes moral judgements true; rather, it is to assert that there are standards independent of the individual according to which one should act and against which (and regardless of whether one wishes it) one's actions can and should be judged. To put it another way, the moral 'realist' makes the coherent claim that there are standards independent of the individual according to which one should act, and this claim is quite different from the nonsensical claim that there are entities out there which are those standards.[10]

In Chapter 6, we noted that one way the ethical reaction expresses itself is by reference to the notion of moral truth, and similarly we have just alluded to the notion of ethical realism. It is important to note, therefore, that the grammatical points we have stressed in no way undermine these notions, for the notion of truth (and the vocabulary of cognition in general) provides a direct and natural way of expressing the idea that there are independent standards which everyone should recognize. Thus a statement such as 'I now see [have realized] that to lie to someone is to fail to show that individual the respect which is his due' is perfectly in order. Here, however, one should note that the individual has not as it were discovered a fact of which he was previously unaware; rather, he has changed his convictions about how people ought to act, and come to recognize standards which he previously rejected (indeed, the change may be that before he rejected the very idea that there were independent standards). Similarly, when discussing moral struggle and the attempt to make the right moral decision, it might well be appropriate to talk of the illusions and self-deceptions of egotism. Thus one might condemn the individual's tendency to see himself as all-important, and in contrast advocate humility as a recognition of the way things really are. Recognizing this 'truth' would mean accepting that any one individual has only a small role to play in the scheme of things and that one ought to act accordingly. The sting here is in the tail, for the action-guiding nature of the conclusion indicates that the phrase 'the way things really are' is being used in a special sense – the recognition embodied in the notion of humility is, for example, one that could neither be discovered by science nor authenticated by it. The claim that any individual has only a small role in the scheme of things is not offered as a piece of information, for if it were one might claim that some have less to be humble about than others, or ask from whose point of view the role is small and how this has been established. In this context, however, such questions are irrelevant, for the claim that any one individual has only a small role to play in the scheme of things embodies an injunction to see the world in a certain way and to act correspondingly, and acceptance of this injunction excludes such questions. Here the moral as opposed to factual nature of the claim is further underlined by the fact that part of the claim being made is that to see the world in another way is itself to go morally wrong, for example, by succumbing to pride or the delusions of self.

Thus to claim that ethics is objective is to claim that there are standards independent of the individual in terms of which he should act. As we have seen, this claim must be carefully distinguished from the claim that moral judgements are true in the same sense as empirical statements, i.e. because they state what is the case. The ethical reaction expressed in this claim can, however, be elaborated in many ways and in terms of various pictures, and it is therefore worth concluding our discussion of objectivity by considering some of these pictures. The notion of objectivity most immediately suggests certain kinds of ethic, in particular, theological ethics or ethics involving a reference to there being a moral order or moral law. Here one aspect of the ethic is a stress on the notion that moral standards are independent of mere human concerns and reflect the wider purposiveness or order of the universe. These pictures, however, are not the only ones that are possible, for one may hold that there is right and wrong without wishing to invoke these particular ideas. Thus one may believe that the world is meaningless and has no *telos*, but that for precisely this reason, every human being has an obligation to his fellows and a duty to act justly.[11] Here moral concepts are used against a very different background, but still as part of a rejection of the claim that judgements involving them are subjective (i.e. concealed expressions of preference). In this context, the claim to objectivity may express itself in terms of the idea that certain sorts of action are worthy or noble and others unworthy, or in the claim that only a life of a certain kind is compatible with human dignity. The central claim, however, remains the same, for it is still claimed that there are certain things one ought to do and others one ought not to do, and that not to recognize this (or to refuse to recognize this) is to go wrong, to fail to recognize precisely those standards according to which the individual should act.

Thus, construed as a dispute about the validity of moral judgements, the subjective–objective debate is a substantive issue. To claim that ethics is objective or to claim that it is subjective is to express one's own substantive position, and hence philosophy can endorse neither claim. Both positions are coherent, and hence conceptual grounds can provide no basis for deciding between them. Interestingly, therefore, in ethics, unlike in general philosophy, scepticism is a real possibility: here scepticism may be a matter not just of words but of deeds, for one may decide always to act on one's strongest desire, never to sacrifice one's own interests, and to override one's scruples however strong they may be. Thus the individual's claim that ethics is a fraud may be bodied forth in his life, and while others may judge that in acting thus he acts wrongly, philosophy can neither endorse this claim nor refute it.

In our discussion we have been careful to emphasize that a grammatical investigation cannot yield substantive conclusions. In particular, we have argued that while moral judgements do not state what is the case, this does not imply that they are subjective. Mackie, however, claims that 'one way of stating the thesis that there are no objective values is to say that value statements cannot be true or false' (Mackie 1977: 25). Here the first question to ask is what exactly he means when he claims that there are no objective values. To clarify this point, we must consider the arguments he advances to support his claim, and perhaps the most important of these is the so-called argument from queerness. Here he argues that objective values, if they existed, would have to be 'entities or qualities or relations of a very strange sort, utterly different from anything else in the universe' (Mackie 1977: 38). Roughly speaking, they would have to be something like Plato's Form of the Good. Thus

> an objective good would be sought by anyone who was acquainted with it, not because of any contingent fact that this person, or every person, is so constituted that he desires this end, but just because the end has to-be-pursuedness somehow built into it. (Mackie 1977: 40)

Here Mackie's words echo those of Wittgenstein's lecture on ethics; what they suggest, however, is that the attempt to conceive values as entities is itself misguided. The difficulty of conceiving of an entity with 'to-be-pursuedness somehow built into it' is a conceptual one; indeed, since the notion is incoherent we face not a difficulty but an impossibility. Thus the validity of Mackie's argument lies in the prominence it gives to the logical points we discussed in Chapter 4. In so far as this is the case, however, what Mackie establishes is that it is incoherent to claim that there are values in the world and not false or incorrect to do so;[12] this, however, he explicitly denies (Mackie 1977: 40). Furthermore, while the logical point has no substantive implications, Mackie takes his argument to refute a large number of actual moral viewpoints. How then can this be?

Here we need to look at an earlier part of Mackie's discussion, for doing so reveals a further (and quite different) sense in which he wishes to deny objectivity to ethics. Thus before embarking on the argument from queerness, he considers the notion of the categorical imperative. This he defines as a reason for acting which is held to be 'unconditional in the sense of not being contingent upon any present desire of the agent to whose satisfaction the recommended action would contribute as a means' (Mackie 1977: 29). He then goes on to emphasize that it is precisely this notion which he wishes to reject:

> so far as ethics is concerned, my thesis that there are no objective values is specifically the denial that any such categorically imperative element is objectively valid. The objective values which I am denying would be action-guiding absolutely, not contingently (in the way indicated) upon the agent's desires and inclinations. (Mackie 1977: 29)

Here his reference to desire suggests he is assimilating reasons and causes and hence implicitly treating human action in quasi-causal terms. This has the effect of making the categorical imperative seem unduly mysterious, for reference to it is taken to involve positing a causal mechanism which as it were operates independently of causes (desires). The implicitly causal nature of his account of human action is also one reason why Mackie treats objective values as entities; for looking at human action in this way, he is forced to construe the claim that there is a categorical imperative as the claim that there exist entities which are such that when confronted with them we are forced to act in certain ways regardless of what we desire. However, the claim that these entities operate non-contingently conflicts with the quasi-causal function they are intended to fulfil, and hence the demands placed upon them are mutually contradictory. In this way the conceptual confusions embodied in the notion Mackie sketches lead him to deny as a matter of fact that such entities exist. Another way of making these points would be to note that Mackie equates having a reason with having a desire, and hence has to treat the claim that there are certain actions which everyone always has a reason to do either as the highly implausible (and factually incorrect) assertion that certain desires are possessed by everyone or as the assertion that there are certain peculiar entities capable of somehow overriding the desire mechanism.

The problem here is the failure to distinguish between reasons and causes; if one makes this distinction, it becomes clear that talk of entities is misplaced, for to claim that there is a reason to do X is not to claim that there is something that will cause one to do it. Recognizing this point, we can paraphrase Mackie's definition and treat the claim that there is a categorical imperative as a claim that there are reasons for acting which all agents should accept regardless of their personal wishes or preferences. Thus someone who holds that there is a categorical imperative does not claim that a certain entity (or entities) exist; rather, he holds that in particular situations, there is one and only one thing which the individual ought to do and that this is so independently of the agent. He is not claiming that the individual will always be caused not to act in certain ways, but rather that certain acts are wrong, and that this in itself gives the individual a reason for not doing them. Construed in this way, the claim that there is a categorical imperative cannot simply be dismissed as empirically false. Instead, it becomes clear that the dispute between Mackie and the objectivist is a substantive dispute. For Mackie, ethics is a device for improving the human condition; for him the central question is what principles of action should we as members of society choose, and this question is answered by considering what kind of society we wish to live in.[14] For those Mackie attacks, however, ethics is a question of recognition, not of choice; the question is not 'What principles do we prefer?', but 'What principles are right?' These two approaches provide radically different accounts of how one should decide what to do; one cannot, however, adjudicate between them on logical or on empirical grounds. Mackie's argument from queerness demonstrates the incoherence of the claim that objective values are entities, but the claim that moral judgements are objective involves a quite different notion of objectivity. The claim is not that certain entities have their to-be-pursuedness built into them, but rather that the standards of right action are not a matter of private or social choice. According to this type of view, that certain things are right and others wrong is something the individual has to recognize, since not to do so is to fall into moral error. Thus, while on Mackie's approach there would be no grounds for criticizing a society that adopted different ethical principles from our own, for someone who believes ethics to be objective, social unanimity or the lack of it is morally irrelevant. Similarly, it would be equally irrelevant if some individual protested that he had no desire to fulfil the moral law, or indeed if he said he did not wish others to fulfil it – for the objectivist, all such reference to desires is beside the point.

Thus, in construing the notion of objectivity, Mackie conflates several issues. He uses the phrase 'objectivity of value' in two ways: first, as the description of a conceptual confusion, and second, as a way of referring to a certain type of substantive position. With respect to the first, his argument does have logical force, not because it shows ethics to be subjective, but because it illuminates the grammatical confusions involved in the notion of values as entities. With respect to the second, Mackie's arguments are at best persuasive in nature and simply express one particular substantive view. The ambiguity involved in mixing these types of claims is extremely dangerous, and it is precisely for this reason that Wittgenstein argues that philosophy should restrict itself to description: Mackie's claims are the expression of his own personal substantive beliefs, and hence to weave these together with grammatical or logical points is highly misleading.

This point can be concretely illustrated by considering a passage which comes at the end of Mackie's discussion of the categorical imperative. There he writes:

> What I am saying is that somewhere in the input to [a moral] argument . . . there will be something that cannot be objectively validated – some premiss which is not capable of being simply true, or some form of argument which is not objective, but is constituted by our choosing or deciding to think in a certain way. (Mackie 1977: 30)

The first point to note here is that, although Mackie claims that there will always be some input to a moral argument that cannot be objectively validated, he does not specify what it would be like for this not to be the case. What he seems to mean is that there will always be some input to a moral argument which cannot be verified by empirical investigation (by science). This, however, is a grammatical point; correctly understood, it does not cast doubt on the validity of moral judgements, but rather throws light on their nature. Mackie elaborates on this grammatical point by noting that moral judgements are neither true nor derivable from logic. This, he claims, shows them to be a matter of choice. Here, however, his argument has become substantive, for this conclusion does not follow from the grammatical point which precedes it. Although making a moral judgement involves the taking-up of a position by the individual (a reaction by the individual), it does not follow that this has to be represented in terms of the individual choosing the viewpoint he prefers. The claim that life is sacred and murder always wrong is not an empirical claim and hence cannot be 'objectively validated'. Those who advance such a principle, however, do not do so on the grounds that they prefer it to others. On the contrary, their claim is that murder is wrong whether or not people think it so or choose to call it so. As we argued in Chapter 4, although this claim expresses a reaction on the individual's part, the reaction embodies the claim that it is not merely a reaction (not merely a question of 'our choosing or deciding to think in a certain way'); rather, this reaction's distinctive feature is the claim that it involves a recognition of a standard of action which is valid independently of our thinking it so and which ought therefore to be recognized by everyone.

Mackie has a further argument against the objectivity of value and this is the familiar argument from relativity. The basis of this argument is that 'the actual variations in . . . moral codes are more readily explained by the hypothesis that they reflect ways of life than by the hypothesis that they express perceptions, most of them seriously inadequate and badly distorted, of objective values' (Mackie 1977: 37). Here the reference to explanation and hypotheses points to a failure to recognize the different grammars of moral and empirical claims. Thus people do not hypothesize objective values to explain the beliefs they have; rather, the claim that there are objective values is itself the central feature of their beliefs. The significance of this point can be underlined by considering a passage from Mackie's essay 'Morality and Retributive Emotions'. Discussing the principle of retribution, he writes:

> although many, perhaps most, or even all [!] moral thinkers have an apparent intuition in favour of this principle – a moral intuition not merely a linguistic or conceptual one – it cannot be defended as an immediately valid and authoritative principle with the status of an objective truth. (Mackie 1985: 215)

In view of the nature of moral judgements the contrast here between intuition and objective truth makes no sense. If a large section of the populace had a hunch ('intuition') that there were sentient beings on Mars, this would of course provide no support or evidence for this claim. However, to have an intuition in favour of retributive principles is not to have a hunch about what is or is not the case; rather, it is to believe that those who do wrong ought simply for that reason to be punished. This claim is not a hypothesis nor is it a hunch awaiting 'objective validation'. Rather, it is a substantive moral claim which for that very reason can be neither empirically verified nor refuted. Furthermore, those who accept this claim do not do so on the grounds that its truth is the best explanation of its having been widely held in the past; rather, they embrace it because they believe it encapsulates the correct prescription as to how one should act.[15]

So far we have argued that Mackie's rejection of the notion of objectivity in ethics is a substantive move; in the course of our discussion of Mackie's claims, however, it has become apparent just how radical a move it is. Thus we have argued that in rejecting objectivity Mackie is rejecting the central claim that makes ethical judgements what they are. Against this, one might quote his own claim that his moral scepticism is a second order not a first order view and hence compatible with the holding of strong moral views and views whose content is thoroughly conventional. These two points hang together and we shall question both of them; for the moment, however, it is worth considering the extent to which Mackie himself recognizes the radical nature of his arguments. Thus, in his essay attacking the coherence of retributive principles, he points out that his critique also applies to the conventional concept of a morally wrong action (Mackie 1985: 213) and to moral notions of what is obligatory, of what justice requires, or of rights that must not be infringed (Mackie 1985: 215). By implication, all such concepts are held to be dubious. Thus, as he notes, the apparent impossibility of making moral sense of retributive principles 'casts its shadow over moral thought as a whole' (Mackie 1985: 213). In his *Ethics*, he makes similar claims. For example, he notes that in making a moral judgement

> the ordinary user of moral language means to say something about whatever it is that he characterizes morally, for example, a possible action, as it is in itself, or would be if it were realized, and not about, or even simply expressive of, his, or anyone else's, attitude or relation to it. But the something he wants to say is not purely descriptive, certainly not inert, but something that involves a call for action or for the refraining from action, and one that is absolute, not contingent upon any desire or preference or policy or choice, his own or anyone else's. (Mackie 1977: 33)

Here Mackie provides an accurate statement of the objectivist notion of something being right or wrong in itself, and he makes clear that this is what he wants to reject. Furthermore, he recognizes that the notion of intrinsic prescriptivity characterizes both the particularly moral use of the word 'good' and the distinctive ethical sense of 'ought' (Mackie 1977: 59–62, 76); thus these too are ruled out. He also claims that our sense of justice (and presumably our claim that such-and-such is just) 'has no authority over those who dissent from its recommendations, or even over us if we change our minds' (Mackie

1977: 105–6).[16] Thus he does seem to reject the notion of objectivity in the sense we have outlined; he also seems to recognize just how radical a change this implies.

Having said this, however, Mackie does occasionally adopt a more modest stance; for example, he sometimes argues as if the claim to objectivity were simply a flaw in moral language. Thus he claims that the objectivist 'assumption has been incorporated in the basic, conventional, meanings of moral terms' (Mackie 1977: 35) and seems to suggest that the rectification of this error is simply a matter of discarding an incorrect linguistic assumption. However, the 'error' Mackie rejects characterizes not just moral language but moral thinking itself. The real question therefore is what conception of ethics remains if, like Mackie, we decide to think in terms of inventing right and wrong. As we have seen, on his account 'morality is not to be discovered but to be made: we have to decide what moral views to adopt, what moral standards to take' (Mackie 1977: 106). Thus we must 'decide what to do, what to support and what to condemn, what principles of conduct to accept and foster as guiding or controlling our own choices and perhaps those of other people as well' (Mackie 1977: 106). This proposal may sound quite conventional; on closer analysis, however, this turns out not to be so. Mackie presents morality as a device for counteracting limited sympathies, but it is hard to see what relevance this can have to the question of what principles the individual should adopt. If morality is treated as a device, then one may consider what form of the device would produce the best society to live in, but even if one would prefer a society where everyone believed lying to be terribly wrong, this would provide no grounds for telling the truth where doing so was against one's interests. Similarly, it would provide no reason for adopting truth-telling as a general principle of one's conduct.[17]

On the simplest interpretation, therefore, Mackie would seem to be arguing that morality should be treated as a voluntary (or quasi-voluntary)[18] scheme which a group of individuals adopts to govern their mutual interaction. Here the decisive question would be 'Given our desire to live as part of a group, what principles do we wish to enjoin upon each other in order to promote the best possible communal life?' A large number of Mackie's statements support this interpretation; for example, he notes that the individual is not free to invent a moral system at will, for the proposed morality must be such that it can come to be accepted by a group in their dealings with each other

(Mackie 1977: 147–8). Two points about this conception of ethics are worth making: first, that on this conception what determines the morality an individual proposes is his own self-interest or preferences (what would suit him best); and second, that what determines obedience to the moral code that is agreed upon is again self-interest or inclination.[19] The picture of ethics this presents is radically different from the traditional picture and has a different (more limited) content. For instance, since the old, the infirm, and the sick have 'no benefits . . . to confer . . . and no powers to do harm' (Mackie 1977: 180), they are marginal to the scheme and only qualify for rights through an extension (and sometimes a gratuitous extension) of the moral system. The difference here reflects the fact that concern with what type of acts are right and what type wrong (or with what principles the individual ought to adopt) has been replaced by the pragmatic consideration of what rules for social co-operation one would most like to see enforced.[20] In this way, morality's function and content has been completely altered; indeed, the very notion of morality in the traditional sense has been abandoned.

A further strand of Mackie's argument further supports this conclusion, for he treats morality not just as a voluntary scheme but also as involving the inculcation of particular dispositions into society's members.[21] Here it is significant that the justification of moral principles as such drops out of consideration. Thus Mackie denies that the issue between deontology and consequentialism is best expressed in terms of the question 'Should we always act so as to bring about the best possible results on the whole, or are there some things that must be done, and/or others that must not be done, whatever the consequences?' Instead, he argues that

> our question must rather be, 'Are all the guides to conduct that we want people to adopt, and are the constraints on conduct that we want them to accept, of the form "Act so as to bring about X as far as possible" or are some of them of the form "Do" (or "do not do . . .") "things of the kind Y"?' (Mackie 1977: 154)

The stress here is on what we want people to accept, and in this context this can only mean other people; for if conventional morality does come back into consideration, it only does so as a potentially useful illusion, something one might well want others to believe but not oneself. Although the content of existing morality may be justified as a presupposition for the most preferable form of social organization, this does not provide the clear-sighted individual with any reason to accept moral claims. It may be best if everyone believes that they ought not to commit murder, but the perspicuous reader of Mackie will realize that this does not mean murder is intrinsically prohibited, but only that society (or some group of individuals) chooses to prohibit it. Thus either society will so successfully inculcate moral dispositions that reading Mackie will be unable to dislodge them, or the individual will realize that with respect to this prohibition, as with any other, the only relevant consideration is whether he considers infringing it to be worthwhile given the probable consequences.

These points can be underlined by considering Mackie's account of why one should be moral. Mackie offers two main reasons why we should act thus. First, he claims to have shown that it is in everyone's interests that some system of morality continue; and, second, he argues that since we all actually do have moral feelings, this itself is a sufficient reason for acting morally. The first point, however, does not carry the weight Mackie supposes; for unless one makes the unlikely assumption that the survival of the moral system is causally dependent on my particular actions, hypocrisy (discreet and perhaps selective) is likely to be the best option. The second point has similar weaknesses, for not only does it illustrate the parasitical nature of Mackie's enterprise, but it also draws its force from a misleading ambiguity. Thus if I believe that I ought not to commit murder, and Mackie convinces me that this belief is incoherent (or, as he would say, false), then murder may still fill me with revulsion, and I may anticipate feelings of guilt if I none the less commit it, but this does not amount to my moral conviction remaining much what it was. Now the questions I face are whether I can bring myself to murder and whether the advantages of killing outweigh the 'crisis of conscience' that might follow it. Furthermore, the answer to these questions might be that a processing of hardening oneself through petty wrong-doing would eventually prove successful in eliminating the regrettable constraints on one's action. As Mackie himself puts it, if someone has 'only very weak moral tendencies – or, if that is possible, none at all – then it may be prudent for him to act immorally' (Mackie 1977: 192).[22]

Thus there is no way back to moral belief once one has rejected the notion of objectivity which is constitutive of such belief. If therefore one takes Mackie's claims at face value, one is forced to see him as advocating the total abolition of ethics as traditionally understood. Against this, one might argue that he is only led into this radical position because of his lack of clarity about the nature of the issues at stake; and the fact that he occasionally lapses into judgements of the kind he is committed to treating as incoherent might be seen as supporting this argument.[23] For this reason, one might be tempted to recast Mackie's position and take his real aim as that of advancing a particular kind of ethic rather than rejecting ethics all together. Thus one strand of Mackie's argument which seems particularly important to him is the rejection of theological ethics and ethics invoking a moral order or law. Focusing on this point, one might take Mackie to be arguing that ethics should be *human*-centred and concerned not with determining what God has prohibited, but rather with deciding how individuals living in society ought to treat each other or how that society should justly be organized. Seen in this light, the force of Mackie's claims would be to restrict allowable justifications of moral judgements to those which involve a clear, readily comprehensible reference to human well-being. If we understand Mackie as advancing this particular substantive position, the source of his difficulties can be seen to be his misconstrual of the objectivity question. Believing that values are either part of the furniture of the universe or the creation of human choice, Mackie becomes embroiled in a moral scepticism which runs out of control. Thus he fails to realize that to say we invent right and wrong is effectively to deny that right and wrong exist. Furthermore, in failing to recognize this he is led to reduce distinctively moral thought to the merely pragmatic. If, however, Mackie had recognized the nature of objectivity in ethics, he would also have had to recognize that the disputes he was involved in reflect the conflict of one substantive position with others. He would therefore have had to accept that the positions he opposes are neither false nor incoherent. Furthermore, if Mackie wanted to advocate a human-centred ethic rather than to reject ethics altogether, he would have to accept that he himself wants to make precisely the claim he spends so much time rejecting; for he too would be claiming that the standards in terms of which we should act are independent both of our recognition of them and of our personal desires or preferences.

To underline these points and to show that Mackie's confusions are by no means exclusive to him, it is worth considering another modern discussion of objectivity in ethics; and one account which, like Mackie's, recommends itself by its forcefulness and directness is that of Bernard Williams. Williams begins his discussion by stressing the fundamental differences between science and ethics, and this we can see as corresponding to the grammatical distinction between investigating reality and deciding what to do. As Williams presents it,

> the basic difference lies . . . in our reflective understanding of the best hopes we could coherently entertain for eliminating disagreement in the two areas. It is a matter of what . . . would be the best explanation of the end of disagreement: the explanation of convergence. (Williams 1985*a*: 135)

Williams's point here is that in science convergence can be understood as convergence on what is the case or what is true, whereas this is not so with respect to ethics. While scientific judgements 'track the truth', moral judgements, in particular those involving the terms 'ought', 'right', and 'wrong', do not; for this reason, he 'cannot see any convincing theory of knowledge for the convergence of reflective ethical thought on ethical reality in even a distant analogy to the scientific case' (Williams 1985*a*: 152). According to Williams, the implications of this point are far-reaching, for since moral judgements do not track the truth, we must instead understand them as the expression of dispositions society's members have come to have. This in turn implies that 'ethical thought will never entirely appear as what it is [for it] can never fully manifest the fact that it rests in human dispositions' (Williams 1985*a*: 199–200).

The structure of this argument is similar to Mackie's, for in both cases there is a shift from the grammatical to the substantive. Thus the claim that moral judgements do not state what is the case is a grammatical point and corresponds to a valid and important contrast between moral judgements and empirical judgements. However, Williams then goes on to make a substantive claim, for the claim that moral judgements should be understood as essentially the expression of dispositions rules out a particular type of substantive position and one which (as we have seen) characterizes the ethical. The point here is that Williams moves from the claim that moral judgements are not true to a complete rejection of the claim that judgements about how one should act may be intrinsically right or wrong. For Williams, reflection shows that various ethics are possible, and hence the notion that one ethic may be uniquely correct is treated as misguided. This misses the crucial point, however, for in assuming that the claim to uniqueness must be the (incoherent) claim to truth, Williams fails to recognize the distinctive ethical claim to objectivity. Similarly the move from 'moral judgements are not true' to 'moral judgements are merely the expression of dispositions' embodies an illegitimate shift from a grammatical point to a claim that is rejected by those who advance moral claims.

The type of position Williams rejects is that of someone such as the early twentieth-century philosopher H.A. Prichard; for according to Williams, Prichard 'thinks that objectivism gets its content just from the sense which these experiences embody, of confrontation with something independent. He construes objectivism as a kind of realism' (Williams 1985*b*: 208). Williams claims that this kind of position is 'simply misconceived' and hence that realist objectivism is not an option (Williams 1985*b*: 210). However, the reference to realism is misleading; as we have seen, the claim that moral judgements state what is the case *is* confused, but the claim that valid moral judgements express the recognition of standards independent of the individual is not. Only the latter notion of objectivity makes sense in ethics, and hence it is vital to distinguish it from the former. To make the point in terms of convergence, the ethical objectivist would view the emergence of wider moral agreement not as convergence on what is the case, but as a process of moral improvement, the increasing recognition of those standards that ought to be recognized by everyone.[24] According to Williams, the objectivist seeks 'to conjure objectivity straight out of ethical experience' (Williams 1985*b*: 210); like Mackie's reference to intuition, however, this claim is misleading. The acceptance (or the rejection) of the claim that there are standards independent of the individual expresses a reaction on the individual's part and reflects the way he has come to understand the world; in this sense, it reflects all the individual has seen, thought, and experienced, and hence the claim it embodies is presented misleadingly if treated as a naïve inference from experience.[25] Thus Williams rejects but does not explore the claim to objectivity which is distinctive of ethics. He insists that what seems to come from outside actually comes from deeply inside, but in making this claim he simply expresses his substantive rejection of a certain type of claim.[26]

Thus, by treating ethical objectivity as an incoherent kind of realism, Williams is able to gain an apparent but empty victory over his opponents. His own substantive position, which he takes to be thereby established, then dominates both the direction and the conclusions of his book. However, as we saw with Mackie, the type of substantive claim advanced has radical implications for ethics, for it constitutes a radical break with the past. As in Mackie, moral judgements are treated as the expression of dispositions, and because of this, justification of the judgements themselves disappears and is replaced by consideration of the social utility of certain dispositions. Similarly, the question of whether someone deserves to be blamed is replaced by the notion of blame as a piece of social machinery which can be used in various ways.[27] Thus, in making moral judgements and in talking of blame, people are, on Williams's account, doing something very different from what they have always thought they were doing. This raises the question of whether a Williams-type interpretation of moral practices is compatible with their continuance, and for Williams this is a central problem. According to Williams, while

> ethical practices are felt to be in some sense independent of us . . . in truth they are dependent on us and our motivations . . . they can serve to control and re-direct potentially destructive and uncooperative desires . . . [but] they can do this, or do it most effectively, only if they do not present themselves as one motivation or desire among others, nor as offering one option among others. . . . [Hence] consciousness of what the system is will not happily co-exist with the system's working. (Williams 1985*b*: 211)

In this way, Williams's whole argument, like Mackie's, advocates a radical break with the past; moral judgements as traditionally understood are rejected, for their justification ceases to be their correctness and instead is taken to lie in the role they play in the social system. As we have seen, and as Williams admits, on this account ethics will always be in part illusory; in fact it will always involve an element of self-deception, for coming to have the dispositions we want ourselves to have will also involve coming to see them as not just dispositions. The radical change in the nature of ethics which this involves is manifested in the fact that, for Williams, the ethical question is not 'What ought we to do?' or 'What moral judgements are correct?', but rather 'How would it be best that we were disposed?' or 'The possession of which judgements would be the most effective means of producing the society we want to live in?'[28] Similarly, since the notion of correctness has been rejected, the notion of what Williams calls confidence comes to the fore: what becomes important is social agreement that we are best-off disposed as we are. This, however, brings with it a form of relativism, for ethics is reduced to the same level as the ways and customs of a particular society: on this account, confidence in the ethics that prevail in our society would essentially be satisfaction with how our society was arranged, with how we do things.[29]

The new approach to ethics which Williams advocates also manifests itself in his suggestion that our moral practices might be given an objective foundation by science, in particular, by psychology. Having presented ethics as a question of what dispositions we want to come to have (or to feel justified in having), the natural step is to seek independent discursive grounds for favouring one set over another. Thus Williams holds that it might be the case[30] that psychology would support some ethical conception as a necessary part of human happiness. Here two points are important: first, that such a notion of objectivity has little or nothing to do with the traditional ethical claim to objectivity in the sense of independence; and, second, that on traditional accounts the fact that only by acting in a certain way will the individual be happy is actually morally irrelevant – on these accounts, it may be the case that we all ought to do certain things even if this will necessarily make us miserable. According to Williams, if the ethical life was objectively grounded 'one could come to know that it was so grounded, by developing or learning philosophical arguments which showed that ethical life satisfied the appropriate condition of being related in the right way to practical reason or to well-being' (Willams 1985b: 207). Such a claim contrasts markedly with the traditional claim to objectivity, for, on this account, to recognize the ethical life as objectively grounded is not just to recognize that there are good reasons in favour of it, but rather to recognize that it is correct, that that is how an individual *ought* to live. In contrast with Williams's account, the central claim here is that certain acts are right and others wrong and that all individuals should, whether they wish it or not, recognize this and act accordingly.

To sum up, in this chapter we have been concerned to emphasize a number of points. First, we have stressed the distinction between empirical judgements which state what is the case and moral judgements which concern how we should act. Second, we have argued that moral judgements are not true or false in the sense that empirical judgements are, but rather that if they are to be assessed they can only be assessed in terms of being either morally right or wrong. Thus we have claimed that objectivity in ethics has to have a special sense; for since moral judgements do not state what is the case, to claim that they are objective cannot be to claim that they depict the way things really are. Rather, the claim must be understood as asserting that one ethic is uniquely morally correct and that in this sense there are independent moral standards which ought to be recognized by everyone.

As a final illustration of this point, let us briefly reconsider Blackburn's quasi-realism. Like Mackie and Williams, Blackburn does not recognize the distinctive ethical claim to objectivity and takes the central issue to be whether or not moral judgements describe a feature of reality. Thus Blackburn mistakenly takes the (correct) claim that moral judgements do not describe reality to justify the claim that we project value and that our value commitments are therefore the product of our choices and sentiments. To illustrate his position, Blackburn mentions another 'projected' quality, viz. funniness (1985: 9). Here the treatment of these two cases as parallel is itself indicative of confusion, for in the case of funniness there is no correlate of the ethical claim to objectivity. Thus the very fact that the two are treated as if they could be analysed in the same terms suggests that an important feature of ethical claims is being neglected and hence implicitly denied.

The significance of this point can be brought out by considering Blackburn's discussion of a particular moral dilemma. Precisely in response to the claim that his account leaves something out, Blackburn considers a case of obligation:

> Mabel and Fred want to marry each other. The opportunity is there, the desires are aflame, the consequences are predictably acceptable or even desirable. There is only one thought to oppose it: they have a duty to do otherwise, so it would be wrong. And this feeling that it would be wrong can wrestle with and sometimes overcome all the rest. (Blackburn 1985: 7)[31]

He now asks whether a projective plus quasi-realist account of Fred's scruples will undermine them and concludes that it would not. Invoking the notion of 'funniness', Blackburn points out that a projective account of what it is for something to be funny need not prevent us from laughing as before:

> So Mabel is not irrational if she accepts Fred's theory of laughter and continues to laugh at his moustache, and by analogy he may be perfectly rational to accept the projectivist account of morality, and to maintain his resolve as forcefully as before. (Blackburn 1985: 9)

The two cases, however, are *not* parallel: if Fred comes to see his scruples as essentially the expression of a disposition he has contingently come to acquire, he may continue to take them into account, but in a significantly different way from when he took them to embody standards which everyone ought to recognize. This can be illustrated in two ways. On the one hand, one could note that Fred's dilemma ceases to be a moral one, for it ceases to be concerned with the question 'What ought I to do?' where that means 'What would it be right to do?' Instead, he faces a practical problem, one factor in which is the fact that he is disposed to feel he ought not to marry and hence presumably will feel guilty, etc. if he does so. Here the question 'What ought I to do?' means simply 'What action should I take?', and this might involve considering whether his feelings of guilt would ruin his marriage or whether, all in all, it is worth getting married none the less. Another way of looking at the issue would be to say that in an important sense Fred, when he adopts the projective account, ceases to believe that he ought not to marry. Thus, according to Blackburn, Fred comes to believe that were he otherwise disposed, no obstacle to the marriage would exist; hence he comes to see his scruples not as a moral obstacle but as a practical obstacle. On the other hand, if Fred continues to advance the *moral* claim that anyone in his position ought not to marry, then he would also be committed to claiming that if someone were disposed to marry none the less, the situation would be worse not better. Hence if he does think marrying would be wrong, he cannot wish he were otherwise disposed. More generally, if he does believe marrying would be wrong, he must treat the claim that one ought not to marry not just as the expression of a disposition he happens to have, but as the recognition of a moral standard which holds independently of the dispositions of any individual. Thus Fred must either stand by his moral conviction and reject quasi-realism or accept quasi-realism and understand himself as simply disposed in an unfortunate way.

Against this, Blackburn argues that, on his account, Fred does not have to regard himself as the victim of his upbringing; for 'Fred need not regard himself as a victim, so long as he can endorse the general policy of producing human beings whose motivational states are like his' (Blackburn 1985: 20). This, however, does not restore to Fred his original moral views; rather, it offers him an incidental consolation; one supposes, for example, that he would still regard himself as in some sense a victim – not a victim of chance, but a victim of a policy which may justify itself overall, but which in his own case is simply a nuisance. Here Fred would accept society's policy of causing people to be disposed in this way, not because he believed having these scruples to be *correct*, but because he has been convinced of their social utility. Once again, however, this demonstrates that Fred is not left with the moral convictions with which he started, for he no longer believes that in these circumstances getting married is *wrong*; rather, he believes that it is for the best that people believe this, even though the belief in its own terms has no justification. Hence, although he is in favour of the widespread acceptance of moral beliefs, his philosophical account commits him to treating as misguided the idea that one should believe them because they are right or correct. Since this latter claim is an integral part of moral beliefs, he is implicitly committed to rejecting these beliefs in their traditional sense; hence in favouring their widespread acceptance he is, like Williams, committed to favouring the perpetuation of what he believes to be an illusion.

Thus Blackburn's argument is misleading, for he fails to recognize the radical change in our moral thinking which would result from stripping moral judgements of their claim to objectivity. His argument also provides a further illustration of the misleading confusion of the grammatical and the substantive, for once again there is a shift from a grammatical point (the point that moral judgements do not describe reality) to a substantive claim which rules out a certain type of ethical position. In conclusion, therefore, the final point that needs to be emphasized is that in ethics the objectivity question presents us with a *substantive* choice and not one which can be resolved by philosophical or conceptual analysis: whether he believes that there are absolute standards independent of the individual is something each person must decide for himself.

8

REASONS AND THE WILL

How is 'will' actually used? In philosophy one is unaware of having
invented a quite new use of the word by assimilating its use to that,
e.g. of the word 'wish'. It is interesting that one constructs certain
uses of words specially for philosophy wanting to claim a more
elaborated use than they have, for words that seem important to us.
(Wittgenstein, *RPP1*: para. 51)

The notion of bedrock has figured prominently in our investigation of
ethical concepts, for we have stressed that in considering human
action (and judgements about human action) a point is reached where
the offering of reasons comes to an end and where we are confronted
with a substantive reaction on the part of the agent/speaker. Non-
Wittgensteinians, however, may find this invocation of bedrock hard
to accept; indeed, the invocation of bedrock may easily seem a glib
expedient whereby a host of thorny issues are avoided through the
blank assertion that explanation comes to an end. It might also be
objected that we have shirked the task of offering a concrete account of
human action, failing in fact to explain what is actually involved in
someone's *doing* something. Another way of making this objection
would be to complain that we have offered no account of the will, and
this complaint might be continued by arguing that it is precisely with
regard to the will that the inappropriateness of our attempt to distinguish between reasons and causes becomes apparent. Against this, we
shall argue that a satisfactory account of the will is only possible if one
embraces the Wittgensteinian perspective we have been advocating.
Consideration of this issue will also enable us to place the claim that
reasons come to an end against a wider background and so underline
the importance and the necessity of the notion of bedrock.

Just as we earlier approached the question of the grammatical differences between moral and empirical statements via consideration
of the fact/value distinction embodied in the *Tractatus*, so too here
we can approach the issue of the will by tracing Wittgenstein's comments on this topic from his earliest writings to those of his later
period. Although he says little about the will in the *Tractatus* itself,
Wittgenstein's notebooks of the period indicate that the problem of the
will exercised him considerably at this time, confronting him in two
related ways. First, it arises in the context of his attempt to give an
account of the subject of experience and of the notion that this subject
can intervene in the world as agent. Second, it arises in the context of
Wittgenstein's attempt to understand ethics, for Wittgenstein also
seeks to make sense of the idea that the subject's intervention in the
world, and hence the subject itself, can be good or bad, worthy or
unworthy, etc. However, these two sets of demands seem to generate
insuperable difficulties. Thus, while there is clearly something more to
the subject than just the succession of experiences, it seems impossible
to specify what this is. The notion that the subject acts is similarly hard
to capture; for once talk of processes or causes is introduced, one is
forced to extend the chain of causes backwards as well as forwards,
with the result that every sequence of events is endowed with an
impersonal necessity that excludes reference to a subject and *a fortiori*
to the notion that this subject acts. These difficulties are then further
accentuated when one seeks to give an account of ethics, for if it seems
impossible to give an account of what it is to do something, how much
more so to explain what it is to do wrong!

In an attempt to avoid both sets of problems, Wittgenstein transposes the subject to a position beyond the world, dogmatically
asserting that:

> the philosophical I is not the human being, not the human body or
> the human soul with its psychological properties, but the meta-
> physical subject, the boundary (not a part) of the world. The
> human body, however, my body in particular, is a part of the world
> among others, among animals, plants, stones etc, etc. (*N*: 82)

That ethical considerations play an important part in prompting this
radical separation of world and subject becomes clear in other comments Wittgenstein makes about the human body. For example, he
claims that 'a stone, the body of a beast, the body of a man, my body,
all stand on the same level. That is why what happens, whether it

comes from a stone or from my body, is neither good nor bad' (*N*: 84). According to the early Wittgenstein, the only thing to which the predicates 'good' and 'bad' can be applied is the subject itself, for 'what is good and evil is essentially the I, not the world'; unfortunately however, 'the I, the I is what is deeply mysterious!' (*N*: 80). The mystery here arises in part from the need to account for ethical concepts, for Wittgenstein's two sets of problems interact, so adding to his difficulties. One problem, for example, is the clash between the contingency of the will's effects and the fact that the ethical value of an act of will is not contingent. Another problem is that, while willing the Good must in some sense be attractive, in order to give us a reason for willing it, what makes it attractive cannot be its consequences, for as we have noted these are contingent. Recognizing these points, Wittgenstein concludes that willing the Good is its own reward. He explains this claim by arguing that how the subject wills determines its relation to the world as a whole:

> if good or evil willing affects the world it can only affect the boundaries of the world, not the facts . . . In short, it must make the world a wholly different one. The world must so to speak, wax or wane as a whole. As if by accession or loss of meaning. (*N*: 73)

Thus the will is good (and consequently happy) when it achieves the right relation to the world and bad when it does not do so. What this right relation is, however, remains unspecifiable: the mark of the good life cannot be described, for 'this mark cannot be a physical mark but only a metaphysical one, a transcendental one' (*N*: 78).

The mystical conception of the will which Wittgenstein puts forward runs into several important difficulties; ironically, the most obvious of these is ethical in nature. Thus, as a consequence of his emphasis on the contingent nature of the will's effects and because of his identification of the good life and the happy life, Wittgenstein is forced towards a form of Stoicism:

> How can man be happy at all, since he cannot ward off the misery of this world?
> Through the life of knowledge.
> The good conscience is the happiness that the life of knowledge preserves.
> The life of knowledge is the life that is happy in spite of the misery of the world.

The only life that is happy is the life that can renounce the amenities of the world.

To it the amenities of the world are so many graces of fate. (*N*: 81)

This Stoicism, however, and the conclusion that goodness and happiness lie in renouncing the world and consequently willing nothing, is in radical conflict with traditional views of an individual's ethical duties; as Wittgenstein notes, ' "to love one's neighbour" means to will!' (*N*: 77). To accept the traditional view, however, would seem to render the value of ethical action contingent, and it certainly fractures the straightforward identification of the good life and the happy life, for 'can one want and yet not be unhappy if the want does not attain fulfilment? (And this possibility always exists)' (*N*: 77). Here Wittgenstein's reflections seem to reach a dead-end: 'Is it, according to common conceptions, good to want *nothing* for one's neighbour, neither good nor evil? And yet in a certain sense it seems that not wanting is the only good' (*N*: 77). Caught between a conception of the world as a contingency from which the subject must seek to escape and the conception of it as a task the subject is set and must strive to fulfil, Wittgenstein can find no way out. Ironically, and much to his own bewilderment, his attempt to give an account of ethical action ends in an advocacy of inaction.

Wittgenstein's account also runs into other, more fundamental difficulties. Thus, having outlined an ethical doctrine of the will, Wittgenstein faces the difficult task of making clear the connection of ethics with the world (*N*: 84). Faced with the problem of what it actually means to will something, Wittgenstein's first suggestion is that a willed movement of the body happens just like any other unwilled movement in the world, except that it is accompanied by an act of will on the part of the subject. However, this suggestion fails to capture the notion of agency; for, on the one hand, the connection between the act of will and the action is too weak (mere accompaniment), and, on the other, the relation of the subject and his acts of will is inappropriately passive (the act of will appears as something that happens to the subject). As Wittgenstein points out, when someone says 'In five minutes, I shall raise my arm', it would be nonsense to suggest that he was simply predicting that he would will this movement (*N*: 87). The nature of the connection between the will and the body also poses problems. Thus whatever connection between the body and the will we postulate it will always be conceivable that this connection should fail; this point, however, seems to clash irremediably with the fact that it makes no sense to talk of someone trying to will something and failing. From this, Wittgenstein draws the mysterious conclusion that 'the act of the will does not relate to the body at all . . . in the ordinary sense of the word there is no such thing as the act of will' (N: 86). Pursuing this line of thought, he reaches a further unexplained conclusion: 'This is clear: it is impossible to will without already performing the act of will. The act of will is not the cause of the action but the action itself. One cannot will without acting' (N: 87).

Wittgenstein also runs into other difficulties in his attempt to clarify the nature of the will. For example, there are problems about how the individual knows that he willed a certain action.

> Have the feelings by which I ascertain that an act of will takes place any particular characteristics which distinguish them from other ideas? It seems not! In that case, however, I might conceivably get the idea that, e.g., this chair was directly obeying my will. (N: 87)

If this is nonsense, however, the opposite thought (that the will has limits) seems equally perplexing, for as we noted earlier the idea of trying to will something and yet failing also makes no sense. Talk of the will's limits also has unacceptable ethical consequences, for it locates the subject in the world, so threatening to turn it into a mere cog in the world machine:

> consideration of willing makes it look as if one part of the world were closer to me than another (which would be intolerable) . . . in this way then the will would not confront the world as its equivalent, which must be impossible. (N: 88)

The tensions and obscurities of Wittgenstein's account manifest themselves most dramatically in a puzzling separation of the will into an ethical part and a part concerned with physical action. This split becomes apparent when Wittgenstein seeks to bring the threads of his discussion together:

> What really is the situation of the human will? I will call 'will' first and foremost the bearer of good and evil.
> Let us imagine a man who could use none of his limbs and hence could, in the ordinary sense, not exercise his *will*. He could, however, think and *want* and communicate his thoughts to someone else. Could therefore do good or evil through the other man. Then

it is clear that ethics would have validity for him too, and that he in the *ethical sense* is the bearer of a *will*.

Now is there any difference in principle between this will and that which sets the human body in motion? (*N*: 76–7).

In the *Notebooks*, Wittgenstein can find no answer for this question; however, that the question itself should arise indicates just how unclear Wittgenstein was on this subject – as he himself admits, 'here I am still making crude mistakes! No doubt of that!' (*N*: 78). The solution to his difficulties, however, lay in the radical shift from the philosophy of the *Tractatus* to that of the *Philosophical Investigations*; only after making that shift was Wittgenstein in a position to approach the problem of the will more fruitfully.

When Wittgenstein later returned to consider the will, he took as his starting-point the very difficulties that had preoccupied him at the time of the *Tractatus*. Thus, in line with his earlier comments, he points out that volition cannot be conceived of in terms of an act of will, for then willing comes to seem a mere experience or idea, something which 'comes when it comes, and [which] I cannot bring . . . about, (*PI*: para. 611). On this occasion, however, Wittgenstein seeks to explore this idea further: 'Not bring it about? – Like *what*? What can I bring about, then?' (*PI*: para. 611). These questions lead Wittgenstein back to the ordinary contrast between what the individual can bring about and what he cannot, 'between the movement of my arm and, say, the fact that the violent thudding of my heart will subside' (*PI*: para. 612). Thus the contrast invoked is that between voluntary and involuntary action. What then did Wittgenstein mean when he tried to apply this contrast to willing itself? 'Doubtless I was trying to say: I can't will willing; that is, it makes no sense to speak of willing willing' (*PI*: para. 613). The reason for this, however, is not that willing is an involuntary action, but rather that ' "willing" is not the name of an action; and so not the name of any voluntary action either' (*PI*: para. 613).

The source of confusion here is the temptation to think of willing as a type of 'bringing about'. Willing is treated as a peculiar type of causal mechanism, a super-mechanism which cannot fail to operate: 'one imagines the willing subject . . . as something without mass (without any inertia); as a motor which has no inertia in itself to

overcome. And so it is only mover, not moved' (*PI*: para. 618).[1]
Thought of in this way the real act, the essence of doing, seems to lie in
a mental act; and hence there arises the notion of the act of will, for
'the phenomenal happenings [seem] only to be consequences of this
acting. "I do" seems to have a definite sense, separate from all experience' (*PI*: para. 620). To combat this picture, Wittgenstein quotes an
old thought, viz. that 'willing, if it is not to be a sort of wishing, must
be the action itself. It cannot be allowed to stop anywhere short of the
action.' In the *Philosophical Investigations*, he continues this line of
thought by pointing out that

> if it is the action, then it is so in the ordinary sense of the word; so it
> is speaking, writing, walking, lifting a thing, imagining something.
> But it is also trying, attempting, making an effort, – to speak, to
> write, to lift a thing, to imagine something etc. (*PI*: para. 615)

This underlines the point that willing is not a process and *a fortiori* not a
mysterious process which cannot fail. Thus the fact that one cannot
fail to will is simply the converse of the fact that one cannot try to will,
and hence 'one might say "I can always will only inasmuch as I can
never try to will" ' (*PI*: para. 619).

A further source of confusion here is our tendency to treat certain
types of voluntary action as paradigmatic. As Wittgenstein points out
in the *Brown Book*, we think of cases such as that of someone lifting a
heavyish weight as 'fully-fledged' examples of willing. 'One takes
one's ideas, and one's language, about volition from this kind of
example and thinks that they must apply – if not in such an obvious
way – to all cases which can properly be called cases of willing' (*BB*:
150). Thus it is through concentrating on the deliberation preceding
the action and on the effort involved in the actual lifting that we are led
to conceive of willing in terms of an act of will. Similarly, we are
encouraged to think of willing as wanting something and then trying
to obtain it. The temptation to think about willing in these terms,
however, is greatly reduced if one considers other examples of voluntary action, e.g. reaching someone a lighted match after having lit
one's own cigarette and seeing that he wishes to light his, or moving
one's hand while writing a letter, or moving one's mouth, larynx, etc.
while speaking (*BB*: 150). As such examples indicate, if we are to give
a convincing account of willing, a quite different approach is going to
be necessary.

Associated with the idea of willing as a process is the idea of the will as 'an influence, a force, or again: a primary action, which then is the cause of the outward perceptible action' (*RPP1*: para. 900). Wittgenstein, however, rejects all such conceptions, stressing that there is no gap between willing and action. 'When I raise my arm "voluntarily" I do not use any instrument to bring the movement about. My wish is not such an instrument either' (*PI*: para. 614). In line with this claim, Wittgenstein also denies the will requires a point of application or foothold in the world. To underline his point, he considers an apparent counter-example, viz. the fact that when our fingers are crossed in a certain way we are unable to move a particular finger until someone touches the finger to be moved. Here one feels inclined to describe this situation in terms of the idea that one cannot find a point of application for the will. Wittgenstein argues, however, that this is misleading:

> one would like to say: 'How am I to know where I am to catch hold with the will, if feeling does not shew me the place?' But then how is it known to what point I am to direct the will when the feeling is there? (*PI*: para. 617)

Even if we suppose a feeling which shows us where to apply our will, what does 'applying our will' involve? What are we supposed to do with the information the putative feeling conveys to us? Medical specialists apart, most people are unaware which muscles are involved in any particular movement, and when an individual seeks to move part of his body but is unable to do so, it is certainly not because he is unsure which particular muscle to move! Rather, the fact is that with our hands held in a certain way we are unable to move a particular finger until that finger is touched, and *that is all there is to it*. This phenomenon appears strange because normally we can move our fingers as we wish; but the problem is not that we cannot do as we normally do when we will, for normally when we will we don't do anything other than just move the part of the body in question!

Having rejected the above ideas as confused, Wittgenstein restates his central problem: 'let us not forget this: when "I raise my arm", my arm goes up. And the problem arises: what is left over if I subtract the fact that my arm goes up from the fact that I raise my arm?' (*PI*: para. 621). The fact that it is me that raises my arm cannot lie in the wish that my arm should rise; indeed, as Wittgenstein points out, voluntarily doing something excludes the possibility of wishing that it should happen (*PI*: para. 615). My willing the action also cannot be said to lie in the kinaesthetic sensations which accompany the action, for like any other sensation, these sensations, as it were, happen to me (*RPP1*: para. 753). Recourse to introspection also proves fruitless. We may, for example, try to explain willing by invoking a 'feeling of innervation', for this 'expresses what one would like to say: that it [willing] is like an *impulse*. But a feeling like an impulse? What is an impulse then? A physical picture. The picture of a push' (*RPP1*: para. 754). Here, as in the case of other philosophical problems, we seek to solve our difficulties by invoking sensation as an irrefutable given; on closer examination, however, such an invocation turns out to be an empty charade. In this case, in an attempt to bring our search for the essence of doing to an end, we invoke a feeling of innervation and yet this supposed feeling is no more than a picture, and thus the essence of doing is held to lie in 'a feeling of doing'.[2]

The problem of what it is to will (and the related issue of what makes an action voluntary) thus seems irresolvable. The key to clarifying this topic, however, lies in the shift from attempted explanation to description, for only by returning to the everyday use of these concepts can we clarify their significance. Thus Wittgenstein focuses on an everyday example of voluntary action and notes that calling such action voluntary does not involve hypothesizing a special process or special feelings on the part of the subject:

A child stamps its feet with rage: isn't that voluntary? And do I know anything about its sensations of movement, when it is doing this? *Stamping with rage is voluntary*. Coming when one is called, in the normal surroundings, is voluntary. Involuntary walking, going for a walk, eating, speaking, singing, would be walking, eating, speaking etc in abnormal surroundings. E.g. when one is *unconscious*: if for the rest one is behaving like someone in narcosis; or when the movement goes on and one doesn't know anything about it as soon as one shuts one's eyes; or if one can't adjust the movement however much one wants to; etc. (*RPP1*: para. 902)

Here Wittgenstein rejects the idea that the voluntariness of an action is conferred on it by some external fact or by its having come about in some special way. Instead, he stresses that we distinguish between types of action in terms of their context: 'what is voluntary is certain movements with their normal *surroundings* of intention, learning, trying, acting. Movements of which it makes sense to say that they are sometimes voluntary and sometimes involuntary are movements in special surroundings' (*Z*: para. 577). Thus what distinguishes voluntary actions from involuntary ones is their relation to a wider pattern, the way they connect up to other elements in our lives. 'An involuntary movement is, for example, one that one can't prevent; or one that one doesn't know of; or one that happens when one purposely relaxes one's muscles in order not to influence the movement' (*RPP1*: para. 761). Another way of putting this is to note that the mark of involuntary movement is (e.g.) that it does not obey orders as voluntary movement does – that 'we have "Come here", "Go over there", "make this arm-movement"; but not "make your heart beat" ' (*Z*: para. 593).

Thus Wittgenstein rejects the attempt to give our concept of voluntary action a foundation in truth and instead stresses that the bedrock of the language-game is the fact that we distinguish between different types of pattern in human behaviour and have a different relation to each. Thus against the background of normal human behaviour, we pick out a pattern to which we attribute a particular significance:

> There is a particular interplay of movements, words, expressions of face, as of manifestations of reluctance or readiness, which are characteristic of the voluntary movements of a normal human being. If one calls a child, he does not come automatically: there is e.g. the gesture 'I don't want to!' Or coming cheerfully, the decision to come, running away with signs of fear, the effects of being addressed, all the reactions of the game, the signs and effects of consideration. (*Z*: para. 594)

The bedrock of the language-game is our making a distinction (both in words and in deeds) between action that is voluntary and action that is involuntary. It makes no sense, however, to try to offer this distinction some further basis. The attempt, for example, to prove either to oneself or to others that human behaviour is voluntary gets nowhere.

> How could I prove to myself that I can move my arm voluntarily? Say by telling myself: 'Now I will move it'? But how do I know that I did it, and that it did not just move by accident? Do I in the end feel it after all? And suppose my memory of previous feelings were to deceive me and those were not the right feelings to go by! (And which are the right ones?) (*Z*: para. 595)

Here to ask how we know that our actions are voluntary or what grounds we have for believing this would be misguided, for knowledge and belief are only possibilities within our language-games and precisely for this reason cannot lie at their base. That in general my movements (and those of others) are voluntary is not something about which I can assemble evidence or which I have grounds for believing; rather, this conviction is one of those which characterizes my relation to myself and to others, for I manifest my conviction that certain types of action are voluntary by treating them as voluntary, e.g. by offering an explanation of the act when I am the agent and by seeking one when somebody else is.

The fundamental role which the notion of volition plays in our lives can be illustrated by considering what would be involved in denying that human actions are in fact voluntary. The first problem that emerges here lies in the reference to the factual, for the denial that our actions are voluntary incoherently seeks to measure our concepts against reality and conclude that they are inadequate. However, since there is no independently given concept of voluntary action, it makes no sense to claim what we call voluntary actions are not in fact voluntary: in such a sentence the second reference to voluntary action just as much as the first invokes our concept of voluntariness. Such a claim suggests that we do not really have control over our own actions, but in the ordinary sense we do; how then should we understand the reference to 'real control'? What the phrase does is conjure up a picture, e.g. that of our movements miraculously but contingently coinciding with our wishes; the application of this picture, however, is far from clear. What would taking it seriously involve? Would it mean that we would stop making decisions or giving orders on the grounds that we supposedly had no 'real control' of our actions? As we have noted, the treatment of the actions of others as voluntary characterizes our relation to them; when someone stands up to leave the room, we unquestioningly take the action to be voluntary and do not think that maybe his body has just got out of control. Suppose, however, that we did entertain such thoughts, what consequences would this have? Would we also worry about whether what an individual said in the ordinary course of conversation might not be involuntary? And when the individual assured us that his utterances were voluntary, would we have doubts about this utterance too? Here the intrusion of doubt where it has no rounds threatens to overturn the whole language-game. Furthermore, it introduces a relation and attitude to the behaviour of others which is quite different from our own. Thus if someone really did doubt that the actions of others were voluntary, a certain wariness would presumably characterize his approach to others, for he could never be certain what movements their bodies might make next. Similarly, if he doubted that his own movements were voluntary, he might be expected to observe these movements carefully, perhaps occasionally exclaiming 'Why, look – my hand went up just when I was hoping it would!' Thus the claim that our own behaviour and that of others is voluntary is presented misleadingly if presented as an unsupported assumption;[3] rather, this notion governs our relation to others and to ourselves, and to question it is not to exhibit laudable caution but to express an attitude (and adopt a way of acting) which differs totally from our own. Indeed, such an attitude would diverge so radically from our own that we might well treat someone who expressed it as suffering from a strange form of mental disorder.

Here, however, one should also note that our ability to play this language-game presupposes certain regularities: if others suddenly started to behave without rhyme or reason and could offer no account of their action, or if we suddenly found ourselves inexplicably performing strange actions, we would no longer be able to apply our concepts as before, and our relation to ourselves and to others (and, indeed, our conception of ourselves and others) would undergo a radical change. As Wittgenstein notes when discussing the idea of feeling dependent, preoccupation with logical possibilities of this kind is one source of the idea that we do not 'really' control our actions.

> The feeling of dependence. How can one *feel* dependent? How can one feel 'It doesn't depend on me?' But what a queer expression of feeling this is anyway!
>
> But if, e.g, every morning one had difficulty in making certain movements at first, in raising one's arm and the like, and had to wait till the paralysis passed off, and that that sometimes took a long time, and sometimes happened quickly, and one could not foresee it or adopt any means of speeding it up – wouldn't that be the very thing to give us a consciousness of dependence? Isn't it the failure of the regular, or the vivid imagination of its failing, that lies at the bottom of this consciousness?
>
> It is the consciousness: 'It didn't have to go like that!' When I get up from a chair, I don't ordinarily tell myself 'So I can get up'. I say it after an illness, perhaps. But someone who did habitually say that

to himself, or who said afterwards: 'So it worked this time' – of him one might say he had a peculiar attitude to life. (*RPP1*: para. 221)

Recognizing therefore that our language-game cannot be given (and does not require) a foundation, Wittgenstein does not seek to prove that our actions are voluntary; instead, he emphasizes the characteristic differences between our relation to our own action and to that of others, and in this way underlines the role which the notion of agency plays in our lives. Thus he notes that 'in a large class of cases it is the peculiar impossibility of taking an observant attitude towards a certain action which characterizes it as a voluntary one' (*BB*: 153). This feature of our relation to our own action connects up with other asymmetries between our relation to our own acts and to that of others. Thus, while we often observe the behaviour of others in order to predict how they will act, only very rarely and in special circumstances do we observe our own (*Z*: para. 591). Similarly, we do not assess the chances of our acting in a certain way, but rather reflect and *decide* how we shall act; for 'asked: "Are you going to do such-and-such?" I consider *grounds* for and *against*' (*RPP1*: para. 815). Here the close connection between voluntariness and intentionality becomes apparent: as Wittgenstein puts it, 'voluntariness hangs together with intentionality. And therefore with decision as well. One does not decide on an attack of angina and then have it' (*RPP1*: para. 805). Because of the connection with intention, one characteristic of voluntary movements is that they do not come as a surprise to the agent. Such points may seem obvious; the aim in making them, however, is to underline the nature of the differences between voluntary and involuntary action and so bring out the role which the notion of agency plays in our lives.

> Active and passive. Can one give an order to do it or not? This perhaps seems, but is not, a far-fetched distinction. It is like: 'Can one (*logical* possibility) decide to do it or not?' – And that means: How is it surrounded by thoughts, feelings, etc.? (*Z*: para. 588)

The claim that voluntariness and intentionality are connected may seem a step backwards; for having denied that voluntary action is characterized by a special process, aren't we now invoking another process, viz. intentionality? This, of course, is not our aim. Indeed, Wittgenstein would argue that the attempt to treat intentionality as a process is just as misguided as the attempt to construe willing in this way. Rather than involving a reference to a mental process, the attribution to others of intentionality (and the corresponding ability to offer reasons for their actions) hangs together with our treatment of their behaviour as voluntary, for these ideas provide the framework which govern our relationship to another person as a conscious, thinking being. Thus in our daily intercourse with others, questions as to what mental processes may or may not be taking place inside them are irrelevant:

> If someone tells me of some incident, or asks me an everyday question (e.g. what time is it), I'm not going to ask him whether he was thinking while he was telling me or asking me. Or again; it would not be immediately clear in what circumstances one might have said that he did this without thinking – even though one can imagine such circumstances. (Here there is a relationship with the question: What is to be called a 'voluntary' act.) (*RPP2*: para. 222)

Actions such as these *are* 'thinking' actions: to behave in this way is to behave as a normal human being does, and such behaviour is characterized by intentionality and purposiveness. Correspondingly, after he has acted, a normal human being can explain why he acted as he did or what his intention was. However, the individual does not read off his intention from some form of mental record, nor does his statement of intention correspond to the occurrence of a particular mental process. Someone, for example, who is interrupted in conversation and later asked whether he knew what he intended to say will in most cases answer 'yes', but not because he had previously silently completed the sentence to himself or because his intention to complete the sentence in a certain way was somehow recorded so that he could later read it back. Rather, he simply says 'I was going to say . . .' and states what his intention was. This, of course, provokes the question 'What difference is there between this and the individual just saying anything?'; such a question, however, approaches the issue from the wrong angle. In reply to it, the first point to stress is the importance of sincerity, for there is such a thing as saying 'I was going to say . . .' and being conscious that in so doing one is lying. It should also be noted that there are cases where the individual says that he has forgotten what he was going to say or that he was going to say one thing but would now prefer to say something else. The second case indicates that we do make a distinction between what the individual intended to say and what he may now wish to say. Furthermore, the rarity of the first case is important, for it is crucial to our language-game that in the vast majority of cases the individual can tell us what he intended to say. Here the possibility of the individual's having forgotten occurs only as the exception to the rule. To clarify the importance of this point it is worth considering the parallel case of explaining what one meant, for there too we are dependent on the individual's present utterance as a guide to his past intention. In this example, however, the function of the assumption that the individual can state what his intention was is clearer, for it can be seen to be the converse of the assumption that his action was intentional, i.e. that he was not just speaking aimlessly but saying something.

Despite these points, one may still be tempted to claim that 'reliance on the individual's say-so' is pitifully inadequate; surely the individual may have meant something else, one might argue, for in the end all we have is his word *now* that he meant such-and-such (intended to say such-and-such) *then*. Here the temptation is to seek a stronger basis for the claim that someone had a certain intention, and the obvious candidate to appeal to is memory. Such an appeal, however, gets nowhere.

> 'My intention was no less certain as it was than it would have been if I had said "Now I'll deceive him." ' But if you had said the words, would you necessarily have meant them quite seriously? (Thus the most explicit expression of intention is by itself insufficient evidence of intention.) (*PI*: para. 641)

Unable to find an alternative explanation of intention, one may try to appeal to a 'feeling of tending towards', arguing, for example, in the case of the interrupted sentence that one feels as if only certain words could possibly complete it. This move parallels that of invoking a feeling of innervation in connection with voluntary action, and as an explanation it is similarly empty. Thus the supposed feeling is simply a restatement of the fact that the individual knows what he intended – the reason the words 'feel' as if they were the only possible continuation of the sentence is that those words and only those words were the ones the individual intended to say! Thus one is forced back onto the language-game itself and recognition that within the language-game the individual is simply taken to be able to state what his intentions were and are. The statement 'I intend to X' is an expression of intention not a report on a state or process, while the statement 'I intended to X' is as it were an expression of past intention – through such an utterance the subject fills out the picture of his past actions and, although this must of course connect up with what he did and said, his facial expressions, gestures, etc. at the time, etc., there is no independent means of confirming it nor does the truth of the statement reporting the intention lie in its being an accurate representation of something that occurred at the time. Rather, part of what is involved in relating to someone else as conscious is the attribution to him of the possibility of saying what he does intend and what he did intend, and within that framework truthfulness (with respect to both past and present intention) is identified not with accuracy but with sincerity.

These remarks about intention reinforce our earlier comments about the will; for they bring out the importance of recognizing the ungrounded nature of our language-games and hence underline the importance of the notion of bedrock. As we have seen in the case of the will, the conceptual difficulties which we encounter are to be resolved not through explanation or by postulating special processes, but by gaining a better understanding of the language-games in relation to which the difficulties occur. Thus, rather than seeking to give an account of how the will operates (as he did at the time of the *Tractatus*), the later Wittgenstein simply seeks to clarify the grammar of concepts such as voluntary and involuntary. Instead of answering the question as to how we move our bodies, he points out that there is no 'how', no method; rather, that an individual can raise his hand when he wishes to is part of the background of our language-games, and it is against the background of the general possession of such abilities that we talk of acting and of voluntary and involuntary action.

Acceptance of the Wittgensteinian account of the will makes it possible to understand why the agent necessarily knows the actions he intends; for the necessity here is grammatical and reflects the agent's privileged position in the language-game. Thus it is the agent who says what he wills, while his being aware of an action is a precondition for it making sense to describe that action as voluntary. The Wittgensteinian account also illuminates other aspects of the will which cannot be accounted for by any account which treats willing as a process or mechanism. Thus the absence of duration (the inadmissibility of 'I was in the middle of willing that . . .') and the impossibility of the will's misfiring (the inadmissibility of 'I tried to will, but . . .') are rendered transparent on the Wittgensteinian account. A better understanding of the will also enables us to see better why the early Wittgenstein was led to make the claims he did. For example, at the time of the *Tractatus* the impossibility of the will's misfiring led Wittgenstein to conclude that the act of will must some-how be the deed itself, not something that brings the deed about. When Wittgenstein first made this claim, it was thoroughly opaque, almost mystical; placed within the context of his later account, how-ever, it comes to seem self-evident, for just as to speak thoughtfully is not to do two things simultaneously, so too raising one's hand volun-tarily does not involve an act of will which has as a consequence the raising of one's hand. The shift away from willing conceived of as a mental act or process also has the virtue of allowing one to recognize the full range of voluntary action from very deliberate action to semi-automatic gestures or actions such as writing where one acts voluntarily without paying attention to (or even necessarily knowing of) each and every movement this involves. Thus, although the Wittgensteinian account involves a radical shift in one's approach to understanding mental concepts, it is only by making this shift that one can achieve a clear and comprehensive account, an account which accurately repre-sents our concepts and the conceptual structures that pervade our lives.

Within modern moral philosophy there is little direct discussion of the will outside the more specialized debates concerning free will and weakness of the will. One important way, however, in which the problem of the will does arise is with regard to questions concerning how reasons motivate; for in this context it is often asked how moral considerations are supposed to 'engage with the will'. This question arises because of the so-called categorical element in morality, viz. the claim that moral injunctions apply to everyone and hence to each agent regardless of what his desires and dispositions may happen to be. Approached in this way, the moral claim seems difficult to under-stand, and this is one reason why such claims are often rejected as incoherent. We shall try to show, however, that the basis of the diffi-culties here is not the incoherence of traditional moral claims, but a misguided conception of the will and a correspondingly mechanistic account of human action.

The underlying source of objections to the claim that everyone ought to act in a certain way is, of course, its universality – the claim seems to ignore the fact that individuals have very different interests and concerns, and offers no explanation of how the abstract consider-ation that a certain action is right can none the less be expected to provide everyone with a motive for action. The universal validity attributed to the moral reason also seems to undermine its explanatory power, for if moral reasons are always valid, it would seem that they cannot explain why some people act in one way and others in another. If we are to explain the actual behaviour of individuals, it seems we must look to differences in their subjective motivations and treat these as the real explanation of their actions. Furthermore, it might be argued that the claim that certain reasons for action are universal is simply empirically false, for it is plainly not true that certain considerations (viz. moral considerations) motivate everyone. Consideration of this point generates a further objection, for if one supposes that moral considerations did motivate everyone and necessarily motivated them, then such reasons would be nothing like what we normally call reasons – rather than guiding our action, such reasons, if they existed, would constitute strange compelling forces, for *ex hypothesi* it would be impossible to act otherwise than they dictated.

Here the mixture of conceptual and empirical objections, however, is itself an indication of confusion. The source of confusion becomes apparent if one probes the account of human action which lies behind these objections, for if motivational states (or desires, wants, etc.) are seen as causing an individual's behaviour, all human action, and not just moral action, comes to seem strangely compelled. Thus within an account of this kind there is no scope for notions such as decision, choice, or voluntariness; hence the moral claim that one *should* act in a certain way disappears in the face of the apparently factual question of what the agent's motivational states will actually lead him to do. The reference to motivational states assimilates the individual to a machine whose present state explains his future actions. The attraction of such an assimilation is that it seems to render the nature of human action as unproblematic as that of any other type of action. The invocation of motivational states seems to provide the link between reasons and action and hence explain how reasons motivate. However, as we saw in Chapter 4, the attempt to forge such a link is misguided, for the gap between reasons and action is categorial and is bridged not by a further link in the chain of reasons, but by the individual showing he accepts the reason by acting on it. Furthermore, the putative explanation in terms of motivational states does not actually explain anything, for the individual's motivational states are not independently identifiable but are simply attributed to him on the basis of his having acted in a certain way. Hence the claim that he acted because he was in such-and-such a motivational state becomes a mere paraphrase of the statement that he acted for such-and-such a reason: the sentence offering the reason for his action is simply cast in a pseudo-causal form.[4] To attribute a motive to someone, however, is not to posit the existence of a state which produced that action, but rather to characterize the action and offer a way to understand it – the motive presents the particular action in terms of a more general pattern of human behaviour, connecting it up with past and possible future action of the agent on the basis of his past actions, what he may have said before or during the action and also perhaps the 'manner' (facial expressions, etc.) in which it was done. The attribution of a motive allows us to understand the action not because it specifies the action's cause but because it intelligibly presents the action as the voluntary action of a conscious agent.

The attack on the coherence of moral injunctions is thus misguided, for it arises from a mechanistic conception of human action and the related failure to recognize the nature of a reason. A moral injunction (like any other reason) urges on the individual a particular consideration, calling for a decision on his part as to whether to act in accordance with it or not. Given a particular consideration, there is no need to show how it motivates, how it is possible for the reason to 'engage with his will'; indeed, one could say that the fact that it would make sense to say that someone acted in such-and-such a way because he believed such-and-such is all that is required for that consideration to be able to engage his will! For example, the belief that lying is wrong is a perfectly intelligible reason for not lying; when someone offers such a reason, we do not respond by asking 'But how did this abstract consideration *motivate* you?' – rather, it is precisely such principles that can motivate us. Someone who says that is not the sort of thing that motivates *him* and hopes thereby to shipwreck the moralist's universal claims by reference to purported facts about his motivational state only indicates his own confusion. In making such a claim the individual treats his own action as something that happens to him, and the moralist might reply that to make these considerations motivate you, all you have to do is act on them. Thus the case of someone not acting on a moral injunction does not undermine the injunction's claim to universality, for the moralist can simply reply that the agent *ought* to have acted on it, that he ought to have made this consideration the decisive one, and that in not doing so he did wrong.

The above points highlight the fact that putting forward a moral reason is always a substantive move, the claim of a certain individual (or group of individuals) that one ought to act in a particular way. With non-moral reasons, the substantive element is cancelled out by a reference to the agent's desires or interests ('Don't smoke, *if* you want to minimize your chances of getting cancer'), and the reason is withdrawn if the agent rejects it as irrelevant ('For me, the pleasure of smoking outweighs the risk of cancer'). With moral reasons, however, this is not so, for the reason is not advanced as a consideration which might be of interest to the individual but as a consideration which *should* be of interest to him, as the consideration which ought to govern his action regardless of how he feels about this. In this way, therefore, the moral claim is substantive, for it urges a particular course of action as such rather than noting a factual connection (e.g. between smoking and the risk of cancer) which will be relevant if the agent has a particular aim or desire. In view of these points, phrases such as 'It is true that the agent has a reason to . . .' or 'There is a reason to . . .' may be misleading, for such phrases obscure the substantive nature of moral reasons and hence invite confusion with factual claims. Presented in this way, non-moral reasons appear straightforward and demonstrable (one can put forward evidence of the link between smoking and cancer), whereas moral reasons seem to lack necessary proof and hence may be ruled out as adequate.

A line of thought similar to this can be detected in Philippa Foot's essay 'Morality as a System of Hypothetical Imperatives', in *Virtues and Vices* (Foot 1978). Using the Kantian terminology of hypothetical and categorical imperatives, Foot distinguishes between hypothetical imperatives which tell an individual what he ought to do if or because he wants something and categorical imperatives which are held to be valid irrespective of the individual's interests or desires. Identifying moral injunctions with the latter type of imperative, she notes that their claim to inescapability distinguishes them from hypothetical imperatives; she adds, however, that 'the problem is to find a proof of this further feature of moral judgements' (Foot 1978: 160). She argues that no such proof is available and that therefore it is wrong to claim that certain reasons (i.e. moral reasons) necessarily give all individuals reason to act. Instead, she suggests that morality only gives reasons to an individual if he is disposed in a certain way, i.e. if he happens to want to further the ends morality promotes. Thus Foot claims that morality is best understood as a system of hypothetical imperatives. Acceptance of this claim would radically change

187

morality's status, for on this account morality is literally irrelevant to anyone who does not have certain desires. The argument which leads to this claim, however, is misguided, for that a moral injunction should be taken into account by everyone is not something that requires proof; rather, it is precisely the substantive claim which gives the injunction its specific character. Foot treats the 'automatic reason-giving force' of morality as if it were an unsupported empirical claim; in fact, however, it is a substantive claim which of its very nature admits of no independent support. In a footnote, she claims that if one were to accept morality's claim to categorial status without proof, then it would be possible 'to create a reason for acting simply by putting together any silly rules and introducing a non-hypothetical "should" ' (Foot 1978: 168). The reference to creation here illustrates the tendency to think of reasons almost as if they were things, and the effect of this is to draw attention away from the fact that reasons are simply considerations which some particular person puts forward as a relevant (or in the case of morality, the overriding and necessarily relevant) guide to action. Since this is so, however, it is of course possible for someone to advance silly rules and say everyone ought always and necessarily to follow them regardless of their desires or interests. This, however, is no threat to the moralist for, as in his clash with rival moral positions, he will simply reject these rules and deny that one ought to follow them, and presumably in so far as the rules are silly everyone else will agree with him.

Similar confusions about the nature of moral reasons can be seen in Bernard Williams's well-known essay 'Internal and External Reasons' (Williams 1981: 101–13). The internal/external reason distinction which Williams makes is broadly the same as Foot's distinction between hypothetical and categorical imperatives, and, like Foot, Williams concludes by rejecting the possibility of the latter kind of reason (i.e. a categorical or external reason). His path to this conclusion, however, is somewhat different from Foot's and worth considering in detail. Williams begins by discussing internal reasons and argues that what gives rise to an internal reason for action is some element in the individual's subjective motivational set. Taking a simple example, Williams claims that if the desire to drink gin is part of the agent's motivational set and if he is correct in believing that the bottle in front of him contains gin, then he has a reason to drink from it. Conversely, if he has no such desire, he has no such reason, while if he falsely believes the bottle to contain gin, then he will also falsely believe that he has a reason to drink from it.

This sketch of the notion of an internal reason for action may seem innocuous, but a close examination of Williams's account reveals first, that the explanatory role of the motivational set is empty, and second, that his account implicitly undermines the element of volition central to our notion of human action. The easiest way of making these points is by considering Williams's account of reflection. Williams presents reflection as the matching-up of elements of our motivational set with possible courses of action. The desire to drink gin, for example, is matched up with the apparent perception of a gin bottle to yield the action of drinking from this bottle. One striking yet disconcerting aspect of this account is the way consciousness appears as little more than a bothersome veil between our desires and their satisfaction. Its principal role seems to be perception, and correspondingly its main function seems to be to introduce the possibility of misperception and false belief. What this strange picture of consciousness reflects, however, is the disappearance of choice and reflection in a real sense. On Williams's model it would seem that, if there is any room for choice and creative reflection, this is only so when we are more or less indifferent (i.e. when the various elements of our motivational states are in equilibrium); however, as we shall shortly see, even here Williams's model is problematic.

In an attempt to pre-empt such criticisms, Williams seeks to emphasize the scope his model allows for the creative functions of the mind:

> A clear example of practical reasoning is that leading to the conclusion that one has reason to X when X-ing would be the most convenient, economical, pleasant etc way of satisfying some element in S, and this of course is controlled by other elements in S, if not necessarily in a very clear or determinate way. But there are very much wider possibilities for deliberation, such as: thinking how the satisfaction of elements in S can be combined, eg by time-ordering; where there is some irresolvable conflict among the elements of S, considering which one attaches most weight to (which, importantly, does not imply that there is some one commodity of which they provide varying amounts); or, again, finding constitutive solutions, such as deciding what would make for an entertaining evening, granted that one wants entertainment. (Williams 1981: 104)

Here Williams stresses the possibilities for deliberation which his account leaves open; in themselves, however, these possibilities are highly limited. Furthermore, in so far as they do widen the scope for deliberation they clash with the spirit of the rest of Williams's account. The reference to attaching weights to one's desires and finding constitutive solutions to the problem of fulfilling one's desires allows some notion of choice to be re-introduced but at the price of calling the rest of the model into question. Thus, in both cases, after the individual has acted we face a dilemma. Either there is no explanation in terms of his motivational set for why the individual acted as he did; in which case the demand for explanation has been abandoned and one might as well accept straight off that people act on reasons. Or, in line with the original model, we must attribute a more specific desire to the agent to explain why he chose as he did, for example, treating his decision to go to the cinema rather than to a party as a demonstration that his original desire for entertainment was in fact a desire to go to the cinema. In this second case, however, the reference to desire explains nothing, for it simply reiterates the fact that the agent chose as he did. This underlines the point that the reference to motivational states offers no real explanation of the individual's action. It also indicates why the notion of choice disappears, for the effect of this model is simply to cast human action in a terminology which presents it as the necessary result of a preceding state. Such a model can of its nature allow no scope for rationality or responsiveness to reasons; for either reflection is held to be unable to bring about an essential change in the individual's motivation (and hence can only be concerned with the clear and accurate perception of the possibilities of action) or reflection becomes responsible for the creation of a new motivational element, in which case the original reference to the agent's having such-and-such a motivational set drops away as unnecessary. Thus if reflection can change the individual's motivation taking him from motivational set *A* to a different motivational set *B* which contains the new element responsible for his action, then it can surely lead straight to action itself. If reflection is assigned this creative role, however, the positing of two distinct motivational sets *A* and *B* fulfils no function, for the motivational set simply changes automatically to conform with whatever voluntary action the individual finally decides to perform.

Bearing these points in mind, let us consider Williams's account of an external reason. Here Williams presents his case by considering the situation of Owen Wingrave, a character from a Henry James story. The problem which forms the basis of this story is that Owen, who comes from a long line of soldiers, has no desire to conform to the family tradition and adamantly refuses to become a soldier. His father, however, urges on him the necessity and importance of his doing so, thus claiming that there is a reason for Owen to join the army irrespective of his personal inclinations. The first claim Williams makes in considering this case is that the external reason could never by itself constitute an explanation of any action Owen might take:

> if it were true (whatever that might turn out to mean) that there was a reason for Owen to join the army, that fact by itself would never explain anything that Owen did, not even his joining the army. For if it was true at all, it was true when Owen was not motivated to join the army. (Williams 1981: 107)

Here the straightforward reference to truth (and Williams's self-confessed uncertainty over its meaning) points to a failure to recognize the substantive nature of a reason. Furthermore, it is this failure which blinds Williams to understanding how reasons 'explain'. If Owen joins the army and offers family piety as his reason for doing so, reference to the external reason *would* allow us to understand why he acted (what 'motivated' him to act) – quite simply, it would indicate that, like his father, Owen had come to accept the substantive claim that out of respect for his ancestors he should join the army, even if this is totally at odds with his own personal feelings.

For Williams, however, a change in Owen's behaviour can only be understood if it is seen as the result of a change in his motivational set; according to Williams, any alteration in his behaviour must be attributed to his having come to have an internal reason for acting as he does. However, the claim that this must be so simply reflects the misguided insistence that human action be explained in terms of a subjective motivation conceived of as its cause. Furthermore, this assumption prevents Williams from recognizing the nature of external reasons. Thus he is led to claim that 'the external reasons statement . . . [has] to be taken as roughly equivalent to, or at least as entailing, the claim that if the agent rationally deliberated, then, whatever motivations he originally had, he would come to be motivated to X' (Williams 1981: 109). However, this stress on rationality is misguided; for the person who holds that the agent has an external reason to X does not claim that acting otherwise would be irrational but rather that it would be wrong. Recognition of the reason is not a measure of rationality but a sign of having adopted the morally correct viewpoint. *Pace* Williams, Owen's father is not offering his son a disguised and misguided lesson in logic; rather, he puts forward a reason, which it would be possible to reject and not act on, but which he holds ought to be treated as decisive by his son, even if it clashes with his son's personal inclinations. Thus for the believer in moral reasons the question of motivation and motivational sets falls away. What he demands is that the individual act on a reason which is held to be valid independent of anyone's inclinations, and here the implicit assumption that the individual could act on this reason simply reflects his treatment of the other person as an agent, i.e as a thinking being whose actions are voluntary.

Thus lack of clarity about the will can have the same radically opposed effects as confusions about fact and value. While the early Wittgenstein sought to avoid difficulties about the will and preserve the ethical domain by transposing the subject to a position outside the world, contemporary philosophers respond to the same difficulties by adopting an implicitly causal approach and hence eliminating the scope for moral concepts. Ironically just as Wittgenstein sought to shroud the workings of the will in a transcendental aura of mystery, so too modern accounts seek to mask their weaknesses through certain ambiguities. Williams, for example, sees the indeterminacy and vagueness of his model as a virtue, a reflection of the fact 'that there are a wider range of states, and a less determinate one, than one might have supposed, which can be counted as A's having a reason to X' (Williams 1981: 110). However, mere reference to indeterminacy and complexity cannot mask the categorial differences between the implicitly causal concepts in terms of which Williams presents human action and the non-causal concepts which we in fact use in this context. As Wittgenstein's later reflections on voluntary and involuntary action indicate, what is necessary here in order to attain clarity is a radical re-thinking of our approach. Only in this way can we understand our mental and psychological concepts and through doing so recognize what is at stake in moral claims.

Our criticism of Williams raises the thorny issue of free will, for having argued that an account in terms of motivational states involves an implicit (and misplaced) determinism, we ourselves need to give some account of the free will question. This question presents itself as empirical in nature, for whether or not human action is the product of free will would seem to be a factual matter. However, attempts to resolve the issue empirically quickly run into difficulties, for what would an empirical proof that we are in fact free involve? Further-more, although from one perspective the question seems empirical, from another it seems conceptual – indeed, there seem to be good conceptual reasons for answering it in the negative. Such a conclu-sion, however, would constitute an implicit challenge to much ethical thinking, for within our culture individuals are traditionally held to be liable to blame only where it is also held that they could have acted otherwise. How then is this conflict to be resolved? In what way can free will be either proved or disproved?

Wittgenstein addressed this question in a lecture at Cambridge in 1936. According to notes made by Yorick Smythies, Wittgenstein began his lecture by summarizing the question at issue:

> There seems to be a point in saying if it [a person's decision] is determined by natural laws, if the history of people can be deter-mined if we know their anatomy etc, then a decision can't be said to be free. (*NFW*: 1)

However, Wittgenstein points out that there is something curious in this, for if natural laws are simply general descriptions of what has happened in the past, why should they be thought of as determining the future? Why should a description of what has happened and a prediction about what might happen be seen as compelling things to happen as they do? Here the idea of compulsion arises from our way of thinking about these descriptions, for we see them as revealing natural laws and view these natural laws as rails along which things have to move. Thus if a natural law does not hold we 'compare it with a rail that has changed its shape, or say we had not known the exact shape of the rail'. In this way, the inescapability of the law is built into it, for the law is re-written to cover anything that escapes it. Thus 'to say that the natural law in some way compels the things to go as they do is in some way an absurdity' (*NFW*: 1).

The approach that is evident here generates problems when applied to human action, for in this context we do not actually possess the 'laws' of such action, and yet we are none the less inclined to claim that such laws *must* exist. What, however, is this opposed to? To no law at all? But, Wittgenstein notes, it is with respect to such action that we *say* there are no laws at all! (*NFW*: 2). To bring out the nature of the claim that there are natural laws here too, Wittgenstein stresses the claim's radical nature and its lack of an empirical basis. Furthermore, he argues that it does not rule out the possibility of free will:

> Suppose I said 'our decisions are determined by the circumstances of our education and our whole anatomy. We don't know in what way they are determined. We can't predict except in very rare circumstances and then very roughly. All the same it is reasonable to think they follow natural laws and are determined.' 'They follow natural laws' would only mean that one day we may, through it is most misleading and out of the question in fact, forecast a man's actions. But thinking this is no reason for our saying that if the decisions follow natural laws – that if we know the laws which they follow – they are therefore in some way *compelled*. (*NFW*: 3)

Here Wittgenstein distinguishes between the possibility of discovering a regularity in human behaviour (on the basis of which we could make predictions) and the claim that such behaviour is compelled. The move from regularity to compulsion is a further step, for it connects up with a kind of fatalism – the belief that what did happen had to happen, that the prediction could not possibly have been wrong. What this belief reflects is the idea we have already mentioned, the idea that 'somewhere the rules are laid down . . . [that a book listing them] would really contain an authoritative description of those rails on which all these events run' (*NFW*: 3). Thus the commitment to determination expresses a particular way of looking at events; and what lies behind this way of looking at things is the success of science. 'Had the case always been that of the apple tree with its leaves dancing about, don't you think we would have thought about natural events in a different way?', Wittgenstein asks.

> As things are now, you might say: 'if only we knew the velocity of the wind, the elasticity of the leaves etc, then we could forecast the movement of the leaves.' But we would never dream of saying this if we hadn't already been successful and colossally so. (*NFW*: 3)

Thus the claim that some natural law must determine human action reflects our commitment to finding regularities to explain what happens and our inclination to view such regularities as manifesting universally valid rules. The point about human action, however, is that it is not characterized by regularity of this kind. Furthermore,

> there is no reason why, even if there was a regularity in human decisions, I should not be free. There is nothing about regularity which makes anything free or not free. The notion of compulsion is [only] there, if you think of the regularity as compelled, as produced by rails. (*NFW*: 4)

To illustrate these points, Wittgenstein considers a concrete example, viz. the claim that the action of a thief is as inevitable as that of a falling stone. Here the first point to note concerns the notion of inevitability, for, as Wittgenstein puts it, 'the whole point of inevitability, I thought, lay in the regularity of the observations. And the point with the thief is that there is no such regularity' (*NFW*: 4). Against this, one might argue that we will eventually discover regularities here just as we have done elsewhere. To this, Wittgenstein replies 'Who will? In 1,000 years or in 10,000 years? Is there really any reason to say we will find this out?' These questions highlight the way in which one approach has come to dominate our thoughts, blinding us to the alternatives to it. Impressed by the success of science and a particular way of understanding that success, we feel forced to conclude that all action must be determined. In fact, however, this claim's pretension to necessity is misleading, for nothing forces us to adopt it. Furthermore, our attitude to human action in everyday life (our talk of decisions and choices, etc.) involves a rejection of this claim, and hence Wittgenstein suggests that, once we have freed ourselves from the grip of a certain picture, the claim loses its attraction.

Another way of bringing out these points is to ask when we would say of something that it moved freely. If, for example, we imagine a car the steering wheel of which appeared to move of its own accord, what would convince us that it was in fact moving freely? Presumably the impossibility of finding the cause of its movement or some law governing it. But, Wittgenstein notes, 'you might go on looking . . . [And] even if you discover a regularity, you might say "it is free, but now it chooses to go regularly" ' (*NFW*: 7). Thus, confronted with a particular phenomenon, the positive or negative results of empirical research still leave us facing a decision as to whether to treat the action as determined or free. The same point holds with respect to human behaviour and to illustrate this Wittgenstein asks his audience to imagine a case where we might indeed be inclined to say of someone that he thought he was deciding freely but was not in fact doing so. Wittgenstein suggests we imagine the case of someone moving about in an upstairs room while someone downstairs claims to be able to control this person's movements. The person upstairs would, of course, claim to move freely. However, if his movements conformed to the unheard 'commands' of the person below, we might conclude that his action was in fact determined. However, this is not the only possibility open to us. Indeed, one might argue that it is the person downstairs who is deluded, for maybe he only predicts where he thinks he commands. On the other hand, if the person upstairs were to act very oddly (e.g. in ways alien to his character) then we might well feel inclined to say his actions were controlled by the other. Here it becomes clear what sort of considerations might lead us to judge the issue one way or the other. As Wittgenstein notes, 'the law court gives us some idea of what we call "free", "responsible" . . .' (*NFW*: 11), for one way the relation we take up to a piece of behaviour manifests itself is in who (if anyone) we hold responsible for it. Thus, in our example, should the person in the room upstairs commit a crime, we would have to decide who to punish – the person upstairs, the person downstairs, or perhaps both.

This example indicates how responding to the question as to whether or not a certain action was free involves taking up a certain attitude and relation to the piece of behaviour in question. Furthermore, how one responds has important ethical consequences, for within our moral tradition, the assertion that the individual could have acted otherwise is generally treated as crucial in assessing the individual's guilt. However, if one asks, as Wittgenstein does, what criteria there are for determining whether a person could have acted otherwise, the answer is that in general there are no criteria. Rather, this assertion constitutes a substantive postulate, the claim that the individual's action should be thought of in a certain way, viz. as the result of a free choice for which the individual is responsible. The substantive nature of this claim can be illustrated by considering the cases where we do make a distinction between the individual's having been able to act otherwise and his not having been able to. Thus

> certain circumstances will make it easy for me to be patient, other circumstances will make it difficult. If I have a bad headache and there is a very tiresome person, it may be very difficult. But one person may say, nonetheless you *chose*. Or someone may say: 'If you are drugged, well that is too much'. (*NFW*: 14)[5]

At this point, it is instructive to consider what is involved in rejecting free will and taking up a fatalistic position. Here we can revert to an earlier example, for rather than embodying a rejection of our everyday notion of volition, the comparison of the thief to a falling stone may be the expression of a particular substantive view. In such a case 'the form "inevitable as a stone" is nothing else but a comparing his action with a stone. The readiness is also a sign that you don't want to make him responsible or be too hard in your judgement' (*NFW*: 6). Thus, in comparing the thief to a falling stone, one views his action fatalistically and suggests that the notion of blame is no more relevant here than it is with respect to natural events. This illustrates a wider point, for it shows how fatalism involves taking up a certain attitude to human action rather than embracing a particular empirical proposition. As Wittgenstein puts it in *Culture and Value*, '*denying* responsibility is not *holding* people responsible' (*CV*: 63). The remarks leading up to this comment illustrate the sort of considerations which may lead someone to a position of this kind:

> Life is like a path along a mountain range; to left and right are slippery slopes down which you slide without being able to stop yourself, in one direction or the other. I keep seeing people slip like this and I say 'How could a man help himself in such a situation!'. And *that* is what 'denying free will' comes to. That is the attitude expressed in this 'belief'. But it is not a *scientific* belief and has nothing to do with scientific convictions. (*CV*: 63)

Thus, despite their empirical form, statements expressing fatalism do not play the same role as empirical propositions, for their basis and implications are of a quite different nature. The denial of free will is not an assertion that a particular state of affairs is the case; rather, it is a rejection of the concepts of freedom and responsibility, an expression, for example, of the conviction that the attempt to apportion guilt and innocence makes no sense, that we are, as it were, all caught up in a tragedy over which none of us has any control.

The attempt to reject such claims and to justify free will through an appeal to introspection is just as misguided as the attempt to refute free will on the basis of scientific research. To justify the conviction that we act freely we may remind ourselves of ordinary cases of choosing, i.e. cases where we faced no obvious external compulsion. Similarly, we may call to mind occasions where one of our decisions was of great consequence, for this too may give us a strong sense of our freedom. However, as Wittgenstein points out, there are also experiences of the opposite kind, for when placed in a difficult situation we may feel we have no choice, that we did not choose the circumstances and that we do not have the strength to overcome them. Thus the appeal to introspection decides nothing, for it still leaves us facing the decision as to whether or not we believe human action to be free. As Wittgenstein (somewhat polemically) puts it, 'there are no grounds [for the conviction of being free]. And as for feelings you can chose whatever you consider most interesting' (*NFW*: 15).

Thus the question of free will is not empirical; rather, whether we see human action as free or determined involves taking up a substantive position and one which no amount of factual evidence could justify. The assertion that one day we will be able to predict (and explain) human action in the same way that we can explain other phenomena is itself a substantive postulate reflecting commitment to a particular way of understanding the world. Furthermore, even if one supposes that we might discover regularities in human behaviour and so come to be able to predict it, such a discovery would not show that our actions were not the product of free will.[6] Here, if prediction and regularity do seem to rule out free will, this is because we tend to think of these notions in terms of the idea of a natural law, i.e. in terms of determination. Thus we assume that the ability to predict must reflect the fact that what is about to occur is already determined, that it is the inevitable product of the present situation. However, we do not have to see what happens as inevitable, and we certainly do not have to treat every sequence of events in terms of causal determination. Furthermore, as far as human action is concerned we do not in general see this in causal terms (rather, we employ the network of concepts linked up with the notions of volition and agency). Finally, where we do see human action as inevitable, this does not typically involve treating it as caused; rather, it expresses the rejection of concepts such as responsibility and guilt, etc.

To sum up, we have argued that the notion of volition is central to our idea of human action and that attempts to explain this notion in terms of a causal conception of the will necessarily fail since causal concepts are incompatible with the notion of agency and reflective choice. Our criticism of the attempt to construe human action in causal terms has been based on the rejection of the claim that this is the only way (or the objectively correct way) to understand human action. Instead, we have argued that the attempt to apply causal concepts to human action often arises from a failure to understand the nature of the concepts we actually use in this context. Rather than excluding the possibility of a causal approach to human action, however, our aim has been, first, to show that this is not the approach we adopt in our everyday lives, and second, to emphasize that adopting it would involve a radical change in our very concepts of ourselves and of others.[7] As far as free will is concerned, we have not sought to decide the question one way or the other. Indeed, we have argued that the question cannot be decided on purely conceptual grounds. Even if one recognizes that the concepts we use in the context of human action (the notions of volition, agency, reflection, etc.) are not causal in nature (indeed, embody a rejection of causal concepts), one is still left facing a substantive choice between fatalism and free will, between the belief that individuals are responsible for their action and the view that whatever happens is tragically inevitable.

CONCLUSION

> Here we come up against a remarkable and characteristic phenomenon in philosophical investigation: the difficulty – I might say – is not that of finding the solution but rather that of recognizing as the solution something that looks as if it were only a preliminary to it. 'We have already said everything. – Not anything that follows from this, no, *this* itself is the solution!'
>
> This is connected, I believe, with our wrongly expecting an explanation, whereas the solution of the difficulty is a description, if we give it the right place in our considerations. If we dwell upon it, and do not try to get beyond it.
>
> The difficulty here is: to stop.
>
> (Wittgenstein, *Z*: para. 314)

As we noted at the outset, our investigation of ethics has had a dual aim. Its primary aim has been to use Wittgenstein's approach to philosophical problems to dissolve some of the difficulties which arise in the attempt to understand the nature and significance of ethical concepts. At the same time, a further aim has been to clarify the nature and force of this approach by showing it in operation. Thus we have tried to show how certain central questions of moral philosophy can be eliminated simply by clarifying the conceptual structures in relation to which they arise. Rather than seeking to offer these structures a foundation, however, we have sought to resolve difficulties about them through description, i.e. through the perspicuous representation of the conceptual relations they embody. Our stress on description rather than explanation reflects the central Wittgensteinian claim that grammar is autonomous. Our investigation, however, also throws light on the notion of grammar, for it shows the importance of distinguishing grammatical claims not only from empirical claims but also from substantive claims. Thus we have argued that no substantive claim can be demonstrated (or supported) by purely conceptual argument, and that correspondingly making a substantive claim involves taking up one particular position in the face of other equally coherent possibilities. The wish to deny this point and to seek illegitimately to use grammatical points to establish substantive views is thus one of the dangers against which Wittgenstein's stress on the descriptive nature of philosophy constitutes a warning.

As we saw, a failure to recognize the nature of moral claims, and a corresponding lack of clarity about the status of one's comments on those claims, is apparent in much contemporary moral philosophy. One sign of confusion here is that grammatical points which underline the nature of moral claims are taken to demonstrate their inadequacy. However, the features which define moral concepts can only seem to indicate their inadequacy if these features are inappropriately contrasted with the features of some quite different type of concept. Ironically, the distinctiveness of moral claims is here both recognized (in so far as the defining features are underlined) and yet denied (in so far as moral claims are implicitly assimilated to other types of claims). For example, it is misleading to note that moral judgements are not supported by evidence and then to treat this as a weakness. Such a claim assimilates moral judgements to unsubstantiated empirical claims; this, however, is confused, for that moral judgements *as such* cannot be supported by evidence (that it makes no sense to talk of evidence in this context) underlines the fact that they belong to a different category from empirical judgements and hence have a completely different grammar. The notion of supporting a moral judgement with evidence of its truth makes no sense because, unlike an empirical judgement, a moral judgement does not assert that a particular state of affairs holds; rather, it asserts that a certain act should be done (or should not be done), hence the notion of evidence for the truth of the judgement gets no grip.

The purported criticisms of moral judgements thus turn out to be a distorted representation of the defining features of such judgements. Such criticisms, however, can also be seen in a different light. As we noted, they confusedly seek to use grammatical statements to advance the substantive views. Thus, if one concentrates on the grammatical element, which lends these criticisms their apparently irresistible force, one can see them as distorted representation of correct and logically undeniable points. Alternatively, one can focus on the substantive element, in which case they can be seen as attempts to cricitize moral claims. In particular, what may lie behind them is a rejection of the distinctive ethical claim that certain judgements about human conduct are uniquely correct and should be recognized by everyone.

In an attempt to avoid the confusions apparent in such criticisms, we began our attempt to clarify ethics by stressing the distinction between moral and empirical judgements. Here we underlined the truism that moral judgements are concerned with how to act rather than with stating how things are; and we noted that, in view of this, the nature and basis of belief are fundamentally different in the two contexts. With empirical judgements, the fact that we all use use the same concepts to represent the world means that our judging takes place within the context of an agreed framework such that disagreement is in principle resolvable. Thus the rules of language embodied in our concepts lay down what it would mean for such-and-such to be the case and hence provide criteria which (if accessible to us) enable us to determine whether the assertion is or is not correct. Moral judgements, however, do not make assertions about the world but propose rules of conduct, and hence disagreements about them cannot be resolved by reference to the facts. In making a moral judgement the individual adopts a substantive position, and hence the bedrock of the judgement is a reaction on the part of the individual. However, this does not imply that moral judgements are arbitrary or that they all have the same status. On the contrary, what differentiates a moral judgement from an expression of preference is the claim to general validity, the claim that it is not just one way of judging human action but the correct way of judging it.

Perhaps the central difficulty in understanding ethics is accurately construing this claim to correctness, for one is tempted either to treat it as a claim to truth in the same sense as empirical judgements or else to dismiss it as incoherent or illusory. However, in view of the grammatical differences between empirical and moral judgements, it should be clear that truth and objectivity cannot mean the same thing in the two cases. With respect to moral judgements, there is no such thing as correspondence with the facts or with reality. Rather, in this context the claim to truth or objectivity expresses the claim that one set of judgements about how people should act is uniquely correct and that the standards embodied in these judgements ought to be recognized by everyone just because this is so. To ask for a further explanation of what correctness means here would be misguided, for further explanation is neither needed or possible. The moralist denies that there are several equally acceptable sets of standards of conduct or that one is free to judge as one pleases; instead, he asserts that one set of standards is correct and ought to be followed by everyone. Once this has been clearly stated, what more is there to explain? The moralist may seek to persuade us to recognize the validity of his claims, but the considerations he advances fill out the background to his position rather than provide it with an independent foundation. His claims present us with the need to make a substantive decision and hence one which cannot be made on the basis of empirical evidence or conceptual analysis. The moralist claims that not all judgements about actions have the same validity, and it is up to the individual to decide whether he considers this claim a ridiculous (perhaps dangerous) superstition or a profound insight into the correct way to live one's life.

Here it is worth underlining that any claim that a certain action or type of action is better than another embodies the claim to objectivity which we have seen to be distinctive of the ethical. The only type of value statements which avoids this claim are relative statements, e.g. the claim that X is better than Y with respect to achieving goal Z or from the perspective of individual A. Here the reference to a given goal or a particular individual transforms the value judgement into a factual claim. Any judgement which is not relative, however, embodies the claim that there are intrinsic differences between actions or types of action, and the corollary of this claim is the idea that such differences obtain independently of our judgements.[1] This underlines a further point, for it shows that the claim to objectivity cannot be treated as a non-essential aspect of moral claims. If one rejects the idea that moral judgements reflect independent standards and hence denies that there are intrinsic differences between actions, then one is committed to claiming that in judging actions all we can possibly be doing is expressing our own preferences or dispositions. To make such a claim is to rule out the possibility of moral judgements, for it abolishes the notion of objective right and wrong.

At this stage, it is appropriate to note a certain ambiguity in our use of the word 'ethics', for we have used this word both to refer to whatever conviction may underlie an individual's actions and also to designate a certain type of conviction with highly distinctive substantive claims. This reflects the fact that our attempt to clarify ethics has been in two stages. We began by seeking to clarify the fact/value distinction and this involved stressing the differences between empirical and moral judgments. Thus we underlined the different natures of the two types of language-games, and hence the different meaning and basis belief has in the two contexts. To emphasize these points we used the word 'ethics' to refer to whatever convictions form the basis of an individual's action. Later, however, we saw that moral judgements involve a much more specific type of claim, viz. the claim to reflect independent standards or intrinsic differences between actions. Faced with this claim, the individual has to make a substantive decision about the type and nature of the considerations on the basis of which he intends to act. In terms of our more specific use of the word 'ethics' only one of these positions is ethical, for only one of them issues in the distinctively moral claim that certain acts are right and others wrong. Whatever decision the individual makes, however, will be substantive, and the claims it involves and their basis will be totally different from in the case of empirical claims.

In both stages of our argument the notion of bedrock has been fundamental. Thus we have emphasized that making judgements about action and how one should act necessarily involves a substantive reaction on the part of the individual. In the face of a number of logical possibilities, the individual must take a stand and decide which he considers to be correct or indeed whether he believes all possibilities to be equal (and hence rejects the notion of correctness). Here one's reasons for judging have the same logical status as one's judgement itself. Rather than giving the judgement an independent or unquestionable foundation, they elucidate the reaction which it manifests and hence leave someone assessing the judgement facing the same substantive decision as that made by the person who first advanced it. Just as the offering of reasons for action eventually gives way to acting, so too the offering of reasons for one's moral judgements eventually gives way to one's judging thus-and-so and acting accordingly – ultimately, one reaches bedrock and is confronted by a reaction, a substantive commitment to the idea that acting and judging in one particular way is correct.

Our emphasis on bedrock, and hence our account of ethics in general, may seem to undermine the scope for discussion in ethics; to illustrate that this is not so, it is worth considering the implications our conclusions have for moral argument. As we have seen, because of the nature of moral judgements there is no such thing as bringing evidence to demonstrate their correctness nor is it possible to prove their validity. Evidence may play a role in establishing the nature of the case at issue, but how one should judge the case cannot itself be deduced from any particular evidence. Similarly, while there may be 'proof' within a particular moral framework, that framework will itself always be potentially controversial – from a logical point of view, it is simply one possibility among others. However, if moral judgements can be established neither empirically nor conceptually, what possibilities for argument and rational discussion are there?

In the previous chapter, we noted that Wittgenstein in his discussion of free will suggested that 'an argument is all right, if it convinces you'. Here it seems that the floodgates of irrationality have indeed been thrown wide open; however, Wittgenstein's remark needs to be seen in a wider context if it is to be properly understood. Thus it is important to recognize that, in contrast to empirical belief, the basis of moral belief is not specific evidence but, as it were, the entirety of the individual's experience. On the basis of what he has seen, thought, and experienced, the individual comes to see the world in a certain way and develops convictions about what is right or wrong (or, indeed, about whether he wants to use such concepts at all). One implication of this is that the field of moral argument has a similar breadth: anything that one person can tell another which will lead him to change his way of seeing the world or alter his sense of right and wrong constitutes a possible form of a moral argument. Thus, as Cora Diamond points out in her essay 'Anything but Argument?' (Diamond 1982: 23–41), *Oliver Twist* or *David Copperfield* can be seen as an attempt at moral persuasion just as valid as any other. Dickens indirectly appeals for a more humane treatment of children and seeks to bring the reader to see certain ways of treating children as unjust or unworthy. His aim is to convince the reader to take precisely that substantive step embodied in the judgement that such things should not occur and should not be allowed to occur: since this substantive step is one which cannot be made on purely conceptual grounds, the appeal to the imagination and sympathies of the reader is by no means inappropriate. It would be wrong, however, to see this as an appeal to the heart rather than the head, for such a dichotomy prejudges the issue. Indeed, to claim that the appeal is merely to the emotions would be one way of rejecting the case Dickens advances. The possibility of rejection, however, is inherent in *any* attempt at moral persuasion and hence demonstrates nothing against the particular form Dickens's 'moral argument' takes. Here, as when assessing any moral position, we are confronted with the need to make a substantive choice. On the one hand, we may read Dickens and feel sympathy for the children he depicts but none the less judge that no injustice is involved ('Life is harsh and the earlier a child realizes that the better'). On the other hand, our sympathy may combine with indignation, and we may conclude that in our actions and institutions we too should take more account of the needs and desires of children.

The starting point of the Cora Diamond paper mentioned above is her dissatisfaction with a review of Stephen Clark's book, *The Moral Status of Animals* (in the *Journal of Philosophy* 77, no. 7, July 1980: 445). In particular, Diamond objects to the reviewer's claim that 'if the appeal on behalf of animals is to convince those whose hearts it does not already so incline then it must, like appeals on behalf of dependent human beings, reach beyond assertion to argument' (Diamond 1982: 23). Diamond argues that this conclusion embodies an excessively limited conception of moral reflection and one which ignores the important role imagination plays in moral argument. The occasion for her making these points is instructive, for the question of the moral status of animals is precisely the type of question where it becomes clear that deductive arguments have little role to play. Although the claim that animals should be treated with respect *can* be expressed in deductive terms, little is achieved by so doing. Consider, for example, the following, simplified arguments. Animals are akin to humans; we treat humans with respect; therefore we ought to treat animals with respect. Causing humans to suffer is wrong; there is no essential (or morally relevant) difference between humans and other animals; therefore causing animals to suffer is also wrong. Both these arguments are clearly valid; what make them contentious, however, are their premises. The notion that animals are akin to humans expresses a vision of the unity of the living world and may form the basis of the individual's judgements about how animals should be treated. The task, however, of persuading others to adopt such a vision is not one which could proceed by deductive argument – the considerations at issue are simply not of that kind. This may seem to suggest that the position of the advocate of animal rights is less rational than that of his opponent. In fact, however, both parties to the dispute are in the same position, for the assertion that there is a morally relevant difference between humans and animals (the idea that Man has a special dignity) presents a moral vision just as much as the claim that humans and animals are akin. Both points of view present substantive claims which cannot be justified in terms of purely empirical or logical considerations.

The example of the treatment of animals brings out two points: first, it illustrates the sense in which a moral argument presents a particular vision and appeals to us to take up a substantive position; second, it indicates one central form this appeal may take, viz. the comparison of cases. Clark's aim is to make us see animal suffering and human suffering as similar – indeed, in moral terms as the same. The implicit accusation he makes is that those who do not assign rights to animals are inconsistent or judge and act differently in cases which are relevantly the same. Such a claim is of course substantive, but may none the less form the basis of argument in so far as each party can express its substantive view by seeking to articulate its reasons for thinking the cases either essentially the same or fundamentally different. Here the fact that discussion is possible does not diminish the importance of the notion of bedrock. The believer in animal rights may accept that there are differences between humans and animals, but not accept that these are sufficient to justify a difference in our treatment of them. Thus it may be only at this stage that the two parties are confronted with the fact that they fundamentally disagree. On the other hand, the disagreement at bedrock may become apparent much more quickly, for the advocate of the special dignity of the human may refuse to specify any one characteristic which distinguishes human beings from animals and instead take this difference as axiomatic, as something denied only by the perverse or the sentimental. The question of how quickly bedrock comes to the fore is secondary (in part perhaps a question of character). The real point is that, however many reasons are offered, at some stage we are confronted with the need to make a substantive move and hence cannot avoid the possibility that our discussions with others may end in irresolvable disagreement.

The notion of comparing cases and of finding morally relevant differences to justify differences in one's judgements reflects the importance of consistency in ethics; and this in turn is a reflection of the substantive claim embodied in the idea that moral judgements are *judgements* and not simply expressions of the individual's preferences or dispositions. The distinctive feature of moral judgements is the claim that they do not simply reflect how an individual is disposed at a particular moment in time but express the recognition of standards of human conduct which ought to be recognized by all. As such they need to exhibit a certain coherence, and hence to understand an individual's rejection of a particular action as wrong it must be possible to see that rejection as part of a more general way of acting and understanding the world.[2] In fact, the criterion of consistency may play a dual role here; for, in addition to being crucial to our recognition of a moral judgement as a moral judgement, it may also determine our attitude to the judgement expressed. Thus, although someone may satisfy us that his position is not logically inconsistent, we may none the less be unable to see his judgements as a coherent and compelling whole. The differences he invokes may strike us as too trivial to be morally relevant, and we may be unable to see any coherent principle as lying behind them. In such a case, the individual's moral position may strike us as self-indulgent or self-deceiving, and we may be reluctant to show such a view the same tolerance or consideration as that we show towards a view with which we disagree but which we none the less find internally compelling.

Of their nature therefore moral judgements demand to be put in a wider context, and correspondingly the probing of a moral position often takes the form of extending it by considering its implications in other areas and with respect to other cases. On the one hand, the presentation of a wider system underlines the claim that what is at issue is not just the expression of what the individual happens to prefer. On the other, it demonstrates the consistency of the position in question and underlines its claim to offer the correct way of understanding the world. It is important, however, to note that the implications of a particular moral position cannot be determined independently of the person whose position it is. Specifying what is and is not an analogous case is a substantive move – indeed, each particular moral position is constituted by the distinctions it makes and the grounds it offers for those distinctions. To take an apparent counter-example, it might be thought that anyone who opposes abortion must by the same token reject infanticide. From a logical point of view, however, this is not so. One could, for instance, imagine a group of people who held that it was impious and a sign of monstrous hubris to interfere with pregnancy once destiny had ordained that a child should be born. However, they might also hold that it would be impious to bring up a child that was weak or sickly ('Destiny determined that it should be born, but the same destiny marked it out for an early death'). Thus rather than appearing as opposites these people's rejection of abortion and their commitment to infanticide may be seen as the product of precisely the same moral impulse. Of course, such reasoning may seem alien to us, a moral position both dangerous and repugnant, but this does not mean that the substantive position it embodies is incoherent or logically untenable.

The importance of analogy in moral argument and the way in which argument may determine our attitude to another person's moral position can be illustrated by considering another example. Thus suppose someone condemned stealing but claimed that shop-lifting was acceptable (i.e. that shop-lifting was not stealing in a morally relevant sense). Such a person might defend his position by arguing that in stealing from a shop, in particular one belonging to a large chain, no particular individual suffered from one's action and that, furthermore, the very system of which such shops were a part was unjust, so that if one's shop-lifting diminished the profits of such stores so much the better. Someone who rejected such an argument might criticize it in various ways. For example, he might begin by focusing on small stores where shop-lifting could have serious implications for the store-owner. On the other hand, he might criticize his opponent's notion of honesty and sarcastically point out that on his argument stealing is acceptable as long as it never rises above petty thievery. However, someone's rejection of this position could also manifest itself in a refusal to take it seriously. Thus someone might treat the above position as purely self-serving, a rationalization put forward to mask immoral action with specious argument intended to delude others and perhaps also the individual himself. 'If you think the system is so unjust what are you doing about changing it apart from lining your pockets?', the critic might ask. As this example shows, what may be at issue in moral argument is not just the attempt to convince the other, but also the attempt to gain his respect even in disagreement. What all of our examples have sought to underline, however, is that in ethics there can be arguments which have weight but which it is none the less logically possible to reject. Furthermore, we have also tried to show that the most important of these arguments cannot be expressed formally or at least gain little or nothing from being expressed in this way.

As this discussion has shown, our account of ethics by no means eliminates the possibility of moral argument. Our discussion also illustrates the scope for moral philosophy. Thus, in addition to the grammatical investigation of ethics which is non-substantive in nature, there is also scope for personal reflection on moral issues and the attempt to outline a particular substantive view in a convincing way. Furthermore, in so far as the search for greater comprehensiveness and system is an inherent feature of ethics, there is scope for the attempt to think through a particular moral position and elaborate the particular view of the world it embodies. In part, of course, this is the role metaphysics played in the past. Our investigation of ethics has shown, however, that any such accounts would be neither empirical nor conceptual but substantive. The error of both contemporary moral philosophy and traditional metaphysics is the failure to distinguish between conceptual and substantive issues; our aim has been to show that recognition of this distinction is the *sine qua non* of any clear thinking about ethical matters.

APPENDIX: ETHICS AND SOCIETY

One feature of our investigation of ethics which may seem surprising is the fact that we have said little or nothing about the connection between ethics and society. This may seem all the more puzzling in view of our Wittgensteinian starting-point, for the few writers who have tried to apply Wittgenstein's method to the problems of moral philosophy have all ended by stressing the social nature of ethics. For example, Richard Norman, whom we quoted with approval in Chapter 3, concludes his book *Reasons for Action* by claiming that ethics is inherently social. As we shall try to show, however, this claim is unduly dogmatic and misleading. Norman's criticisms of contemporary moral philosophy are forceful and perspicacious; and he is right to stress the importance of recognizing the nature of reasons for action and the differences between reasons and causes. In the course of making these points, however, he is led to claim that reasons for action are only validated in or through society. Ironically, he thus mirrors the approaches he criticizes, for he too reduces ethics to an aspect of social existence. Thus he argues that 'moral standards are rooted in paradigmatic human behaviour' (Norman 1971: 130) and claims that these paradigms can only exist (and come into existence) in a social context.

To understand what leads Norman to these conclusions, and to appreciate the differences between his account and our own, it is necessary to consider his argument in more detail. His explicit aim is to explore 'the social nature of ethics' (Norman 1971: 165). Using some of the conclusions from G.E.M. Anscombe's book *Intention*, he argues that there are special concepts (ethical, or more generally evaluative, characterizations) which within a particular society provide reasons for action. These concepts constitute socially endorsed norms and offer members of society a variety of possible meanings for their actions. According to Norman, it is only in terms of these concepts that members of a particular society can make intelligible moral claims. Against the objection that this reduces moral concepts to social conventions, he argues that the systematic and interconnected nature of moral concepts gives them a distinctive status. Thus he claims that the notion of gratitude, for example,

> is so embedded in our conceptual scheme, so closely tied up with so many other ethical notions, that a society which did not possess the notion of gratitude would have a completely different way of seeing human actions and human relationships. (Norman 1971: 131)

This stress on the social has two contrasting implications. On the one hand, it limits the claims of morality, implying a certain relativism; for the applicability and meaningfulness of particular moral concepts is restricted to the society in which they have their origin. On the other, it implies that within that society certain moral claims can be argued for conclusively. Thus Norman seems to agree with Miss Anscombe that the desire for pleasure cannot by itself constitute an adequate reason for cruel action. Similarly he claims that, *pace* Hare, racialism *can* be said to irrational 'if it consists in saying that the colour of a man's skin is in itself a relevant and rational ground for determining how one is to treat him' (Norman 1971: 68).

The explicit basis for Norman's claims is his interpretation of Wittgenstein's arguments on rule-following and the possibility of a private language; for Norman takes Wittgenstein to have showed that rule-following and language are necessarily social. However, as Baker and Hacker have persuasively argued, this is inaccurate, for the point of Wittgenstein's arguments is not that rule-following and language are necessarily social but that they are necessarily *public*.[1] Like Peter Winch (1958) and others, Norman misguidedly takes the correctness of an application of a rule (and the meaningfulness of language) to be determined by communal agreement; and hence he claims that practices with only one participant are logically impossible. Wittgenstein's point, however, is that the connection between a rule and its application is set up in the practice of following that rule. Thus the meaning of a rule is given by the practice which determines what counts as its correct application. Since there is no such thing as an internal or private practice, the conclusion follows that all rule-following is public. As Baker and Hacker point out, 'it is a misinterpretation to take

"Praxis" here to signify a social practice . . . All the emphasis is on the regularity, the multiple occasions of action . . . Whether others are involved is a further question' (Baker and Hacker 1984: 20–1). The error here is to move from the insight that rules do not determine their own application to the claim that correctness in rule-following is therefore determined by the community. Norman's argument follows a similar path, for he moves from the idea that not anything can be a reason for action to the claim that society determines what can (and cannot) count as a reason. The grammatical point here is that for something to be a reason for action it must fulfil the role of a reason, i.e. intelligibly place a particular action within a wider context. Tautologically, the limits to what we can find intelligible are the limits of our understanding; such limits, however, are not social in nature. Indeed, the grammatical point involves no reference to society, nor does it imply that society places conceptual limits on how its members can act.

To illustrate these points it is worth considering a concrete example. Suppose that some individual claimed that, when walking along the pavement, it was morally wrong to tread on the cracks in the paving stones. This claim seems unintelligible because of the difficulty of conceiving how moral considerations could get a grip here; unless the individual can offer some account of why doing this is morally wrong, we should probably treat his avowed moral scruples as a strange but harmless eccentricity. To imagine a whole society making this claim (and acting on it) would not render it any the more intelligible. On the other hand, if the purported moral judgement was connected to a network of other beliefs and practices, then perhaps we would come to understand it as moral. However, in so far as this is true, it applies just as much in the case of the individual as in that of the society. Here too the offering of a fuller account might enable us to come to see the significance of the individual's claim and hence to see that it *was* significant.

This may seem to avoid the crucial issue, for the point of Norman's claims is that there may be reasons for action which we cannot find (or hope to find) intelligible, but which are perfectly intelligible for members of another society. This suggestion is somewhat paradoxical, for the natural thought is that either something is intelligible or it is not. If something seems unintelligible to us, what could be meant by suggesting that it might none the less be perfectly intelligible? Here it is worth reconsidering the case of rule-following. Suppose we came across a group of people (or an individual) who engaged in practices which appeared to be rule-governed, but whose rules we were quite incapable of either learning or understanding. Faced with such a case, we might conclude that in fact the practices were not rule-governed. On the other hand, we might persevere in our attempts to understand the practices and see our failure to date as merely contingent. The claim that, despite their apparent unintelligibility, the practices *were* intelligible would reflect our determination to continue the task of seeking to understand; it would imply a rejection of the conclusion that this task was futile because there was nothing there to be understood. Similarly, to treat a particular claim about how one should act as a moral claim but one we cannot understand would be to treat our failure to understand it as a reflection of our own imaginative limitations rather than the limitations of intelligibility.[2] However, this does not imply that there is one standard of intelligibility for us and another standard for others. The suggestion that an apparently unintelligible claim may none the less be intelligible is simply a plea against overhasty judgement. Furthermore, if we might make this plea with respect to an alien society, there is no reason why we could not also show the same modesty in relation to a particular individual. The question of whether one person, a small group, or a vast multitude have advanced a particular claim (or set of claims) is irrelevant to the logical status of those claims; the attitudes we might take up to an alien society are exactly the same as those we could adopt with respect to a member of our own society.

Norman's claim that the limits of intelligibility are social ignores these points, and in doing so threatens to elide the difference between social acceptability and intelligibility. This is evident in certain key ambiguities which pervade his argument and infect his very use of the phrase 'reason for action'. Thus Norman establishes his claim that not anything can be a reason for action, by arguing that reasons for action must be in some way related to notions such as generosity, justice, self-interest, honesty, etc. This grammatical point – that if something is to be called a reason for action we must be able to recognize it as a reason for action – is then taken to demonstrate that reasons for action are culturally specific. This is misleading, however, for the phrase 'culturally specific' suggests that a particular conception of generosity, justice, etc. is what is at issue, whereas the grammatical point concerns generosity, justice, etc. as a *type* of consideration and hence includes the way these notions have been conceived of in various times and places. Furthermore, even in this broader sense generosity and justice are only *examples* of what we call a reason for action. To be intelligible, conceptions of how one should act neither have to correspond to the specific norms of our society nor do they have to match our broadest evaluative terms. The reason for action must provide an intelligible background for acting in a certain way, and in so far as it fulfils this function it will of course be related to other reasons for action. However, this does not mean that there are *social* limits on the reasons we can advance. Thus it entails neither the ethical relativism nor the cultural determinism which Norman proclaims.

The relativism embraced by Norman is itself of a peculiar kind, for it seems to suggest that we are imprisoned within the concepts of our own society. He claims, for example, 'that in our society it is rational to perform an action solely on the grounds that it is just, because there does exist a norm of justice within our society' (Norman 1971: 65). The shift here from concept to norm mirrors the shift from the grammatical to the cultural and highlights the tendency to replace intelligibility by social acceptability. What is even more striking, however, is that, on this account, acting in a similar fashion in a society where such a norm did not exist would not even be logically possible – a somewhat strange conclusion, for how could logic prevent an individual from deciding that certain types of action were wrong? The notion of relativism here implied is made more explicit in the work of Peter Winch, to whom Norman acknowledges a debt. Thus Winch claims that there are 'intimate conceptual connections between the possible ways in which individuals may live their lives and the institutions of society' (Winch 1972: 5). Similarly, he argues that 'the ability to see (a particular) sort of sense in life depends not merely on the individual concerned . . . [but also] on the possibilities of making such sense which the culture in which he lives does or does not provide' (Winch 1972: 41). Here society is seen as providing the conceptual oxygen without which no individual can breathe. The constraint this implies seems ghostly and yet awesome, for it seems no matter how much he may reject society the individual can never break out from the concepts it offers him.

The misleading nature of this claim becomes apparent when one notices that a constraint which rules nothing out can hardly be called a constraint. In this version of cultural relativism, anything one may do will be treated as culturally determined; since this is the case, it is little wonder that cultural determinism seems mysteriously inescapable. The confusion here is similar to that embodied in the claim that, despite appearances, all sequences are law-like, only some are more complex than others. Extended in this way, the term 'law-like' can no longer be used to describe some specific feature of a sequence, for on this definition no meaning is assigned to the notion of a sequence not being law-like. Thus the definition embodies in a grammatical rule the determination to find laws, i.e. it advocates the adoption of a terminology which presents all facts in a certain light. Similarly, the claim concerning cultural determinism stresses the importance of social context and recommends a certain way of understanding members of a society. Building on certain empirical generalizations concerning the way social forces *do* influence the individual, it seeks to represent this influence as a necessary truth, as if necessary truths constituted a kind of super-generalization. Any individual brought up in a particular society will, of course, be exposed to a greater or lesser extent to the prevailing norms of that society. The individual's awareness of these norms thus creates a relation between these norms and whatever moral position he himself comes to adopt; however, this relation is no constraint on his action, for he may accept these norms, vigorously reject them, or simply ignore them. Here if we claim that the individual's actions and convictions *must* be explained in terms of social background, then it is we ourselves who are the source of this necessity. If the action is necessarily related to social background, then this is because *we* relate it to that background, i.e. assume that in understanding the individual this relation must be crucial. However plausible and attractive this postulate may be, it remains a substantive postulate: while an individual's cultural background *may* provide a key to understanding him, if it does so, this is a contingent not a logical truth.

A slightly different perspective on Norman's claims and the motivation lying behind them can be gained by considering R.W. Beardsmore's book *Moral Reasoning*. Beardsmore's account parallels Norman's and contains similar ambiguities. For example, Beardsmore talks of morality as a 'tradition' and sometimes using this phrase as if it referred to a specific moral code, at others using it to refer to justice, honesty, etc. in a general sense. For our purposes, however, what is particularly interesting about Beardsmore's book is the light it throws on the motivation for the claim that society is the source of ethics, for his arguments show that this claim arises from difficulty in making sense of the notion that moral judgements are independent of the individual. Thus Beardsmore argues that moral judgements are independent of the individual in so far as they reflect established norms within his society. He claims, for example, that 'our moral decisions and judgements are based on considerations we did not decide to accept, but which stem from the way of life in which we were brought up' (Beardsmore 1969: 134). Similarly he argues that

> certain things count as reasons for me not, as [Hare] thinks because they are the sort of things to which I consistently appeal, but because they are the sort of things to which I and others have been brought up to appeal to and accept within some social context. (Beardsmore 1969: 34)

However, these claims misconstrue the notion of objectivity at stake in ethics. The ethical claim is that the moral judgement is *correct*, and this is quite different from the claim that it functions as a social norm. In fact, Beardsmore's implicit relativism is precisely what the ethical individual rejects, for he denies that the standards of moral correctness are determined by individuals either alone or in groups. For the ethical individual, the question of whether a particular judgement is accepted by a particular society is a contingent matter and one irrelevant to the question of whether that judgement is correct.

The confusions inherent in Beardsmore's claims manifest themselves in his implausible suggestion that an individual cannot coherently question the viewpoint which he has been brought up to accept (Beardsmore 1969: 79). On Beardsmore's account, this is impossible because without the fundamental values provided by society, the individual has no basis for judgement. Beardsmore thinks that denying this implies either the incoherent idea that an individual can deduce his moral judgements from a 'neutral' assessment of the facts or the reductive suggestion that moral views merely reflect the psychological state of the individual. As we saw in Chapter 4, however, this is misguided, and hence if we recognize the mistaken nature of Beardsmore's dichotomy there is no reason to embrace his reductive claim that society is the fountain of ethical value. *Pace* Beardsmore, an individual can reject the fundamental values of his society. Against this, it will be objected that the individual cannot just invent concepts and reasons for action; but why not? If Robinson Crusoe wishes to alter his colour concepts and set up a practice where the rainbow is divided into twelve colour segments, then he is quite free to do so. Similarly, he may develop a particular moral position within which certain types of action are assigned a special dignity or worthy. In so far as this moral position is new, he may invoke a new concept of moral worth or he may advance a new conception of one of our broader evaluative term (e.g. justice).[3]

Against this, one might object that the ethical values of other societies are surely in some sense inaccessible to us, for what sense would it make for a twentieth-century Westerner to seek to live the life of an early Christian ascetic or a classical Stoic? Well, what is there to stop someone trying to do this? The first obvious point is that our situation is different from that of an individual of that society and time. Thus we possess a variety of pieces of knowledge they did not (scientific, historical, etc.). Furthermore, since our society differs from theirs in its organization, values, and technology, we face problems they did not, while problems they faced may barely arise for us. However this does not mean their ethical values are inaccessible to us for we may seek to act according to the spirit of these values, adapting them to the admittedly new circumstances. Of course, it is a measure of our distance from these cultures that doing so would strike the average contemporary individual as misguided; however, holding that a moral viewpoint is obsolete is not the same as holding that it is unintelligible. To attempt to lead the life of the perfect Stoic in modern-day London may seem an artificial and perverse enterprise, but it is not therefore logically impossible. Here the reference to artificiality brings out another important point, for it is certainly true that our attitude to a classical Stoic may be very different from our attitude to someone who makes exactly the same moral claims today. Thus the attempt to ignore all that has happened since Stoicism flourished may undermine our respect for the contemporary advocate of this position: what was then a noble doctrine may seem a self-indulgent evasion as a moral code for the contemporary individual.[4] Again, however, what is at issue here is our attitude to the possibility of someone adopting these values today, and this does not entail that the views themselves are unintelligible.

Thus a conceptual relativism which suggests that social determinism is inescapable is confused. In pointing this out, however, our aim has not been to deny the important ways in which social forces influence the individual's perspectives and moral judgements. Our aim is not to question obvious truths about the role of society in the individual's moral and spiritual development, but to undermine the confused tendency to transform such truisms into a mysterious form of social determinism. Similarly, if in the course of our investigation we have had little to say about the connection between society and ethics, the reason for this is that, while this connection may be crucial from a sociological and historical perspective, it has no special significance in logical terms. Our aim has been to clarify the conceptual structure of moral claims, and with respect to this task, questions concerning whether one or many people make these claims (or how individuals came to make such claims) are irrelevant.

NOTES

PREFACE

1 A list of all abbreviations used in the text is given with the bibliography on p. 240.
2 Since these points concern the basic nature of moral concepts, it is not surprising that many of them will already have been the subject of much philosophical discussion. In the 1950s, for example, the notion that moral judgements are action-guiding was widely discussed. Much of this discussion is illuminating, but it is unfortunately flawed by a failure to recognize certain key Wittgensteinian notions. Thus some of the same points will appear here but in a slightly different context and hence with a different significance.

1 WITTGENSTEIN, PHILOSOPHY, AND ETHIC

1 For further discussion of the profundity of philosophy see pp. 21–5.
2 Problems in philosophy are the best example of intellectual difficulties of this kind; Wittgenstein believed, however, that the notion of an *Übersicht* could also be fruitfully applied in a wide variety of contexts from aesthetics to psychoanalysis. We may, for example, improve our understanding of a piece of music not by trying to 'explain' its impact upon us, but by connecting it up with other pieces of music and with things outside the musical sphere, e.g. other works of art or thoughts and feelings we consider important.
3 This brings out an interesting feature of Wittgenstein's writings, for his analysis of the nature of philosophical problems and his stress on the notion of an *Übersicht* leads him to reject all attempts at philosophical proof or demonstration. Thus, like the Indian mathematicians he mentions, Wittgenstein's 'arguments' often have the form 'Look at this' (*PI*: para. 144).
4 For a fuller discussion of Wittgenstein's concept of grammar see G.P. Baker and P.M.S. Hacker *Wittgenstein: Rules, Grammar and Necessity*, Oxford: Blackwell (1985: 263–347).
5 Such statements are what Baker and Hacker call 'synoptic descriptions' (1985: 23).
6 One might accept this point and none the less argue that, although the language-game is not responsible to reality, it must still measure up to certain canons of consistency or coherence. Thus the rules of an ordinary game are 'arbitrary', but none the less must be mutually

consistent. The point here, however, is that if the 'rules' are not consistent, then *no* game is defined. Conversely, if a game exists, it makes no sense to suggest that it might embody hidden contradictions. Hence any attempt to use a stronger notion of consistency or coherence only leads back to the illusory notion of validating or invalidating the language-game by reference to reality.

7 Furthermore, from a Wittgensteinian point of view it is hard to see what justification there could be for calling such an investigation philosophical, for if it was indeed concerned with beliefs and assumptions then presumably it would be empirical (indeed, scientific) in nature.

8 *King Lear*, Act 1 scene iv.

9 As we shall see later (pp. 21–5), like analytic philosophy Wittgensteinian philosophy eschews the ethical content (and the profundity) of previous metaphysics; however it does so in a different way and for different reasons.

10 Thus, where for example the dominance of science leads to inappropriate applications of scientific method, the struggle against this influence will not be a struggle against science, but against confusion and the failure to recognize the specific nature of the subject matter at issue.

11 This does not invalidate the claim that a Wittgensteinian investigation is non-substantive in the sense of advancing no theses, for this 'ethical demand' arises from the commitment to clarity and is 'substantive' only in its drive to eliminate nonsense and confusion.

2 MISUNDERSTANDING HUMAN ACTION (I)

1 One might add that generally speaking we are not interested in probabilistic laws either.

2 It is, of course, no coincidence that Frazer's work should later have been a source of poetic inspiration, as it was to T.S. Eliot.

3 Methodologically, it is important to note that Wittgenstein's aim is not to defend ritual practice, but to clarify its nature. On the other hand, it is of course true that the stimulus which led to Wittgenstein's investigation was irritation at the crassness of Frazer's confusions. Hence in *this* sense, that Wittgenstein should be concerned to attain clarity in this area is an indirect reflection of his own personal respect for ritual and his corresponding impatience with the inadequacies of Frazer's account.

4 In his essay 'Wittgenstein and the Fire Festivals', in I. Block (ed.) *Perspectives on the Philosophy of Wittgenstein*, Cambridge, Mass.: MIT Press (1981), Frank Cioffi accuses Wittgenstein of failing to make a clear distinction between issues concerning the inner nature of the practice and those concerning its relation to ourselves. The two themes, however, are necessarily closely linked, for the inner nature of the practice is only accessible to us in so far as the practice relates (directly or indirectly) to our own experience.

5 Here it should be noted that one can understand what gets expression in the idea of appeasing the gods without having to believe that such gods actually exist. As Wittgenstein notes, 'if I, a person who does not believe that there are human-superhuman beings somewhere which one can call gods – if I say "I fear the wrath of the gods", that shows that I can mean something by this, or can give expression to a feeling which is not necessarily connected with that belief' (*RFGB*: 68).

6 The case of ritual action offers a particularly clear example of the difference between understanding human action in terms of its reasons and understanding a sequence of events in terms of its causes. We shall argue, however, that the differences between the two are just as important in human action which can be seen in means–end terms as in that which cannot.

7 The problem here is not one of sceptical doubt, for the difficulty is not that we could never know whether or not the report was true, but that what this would *mean* has not been specified.

8 This feature of psychological concepts involves a related modification in the concept of lying. Thus the knowledge that one is lying does not reflect possession of evidence that the opposite of what one says is true; rather, it reflects the privileged position assigned to the agent in the language-game, for it is part of our concept of truthfulness (sincerity) that the individual is aware of when he is being untruthful.

9 On the other hand, even if inner processes were taking place inside the agent, these really would be irrelevant; for whether an individual's soul turns red, blue, or green is not what interests us, nor do we typically want to know what neurological processes are taking place in his brain.

10 Probabilistic causal explanations where the resultant state is not pre-determined are no closer to these concepts than classical deterministic explanations, for the idea of randomness is as alien to choice and decision as that of pre-determination.

11 To reply that this is just the peculiar way in which belief-states *cause* action would be to hide behind words, for used thus the notion of causation loses its content. For example, reflection would have to be treated as the spontaneous self-generation of causes!

12 Here if a conflict arises the choice one faces is a real and practical one, for a conflict raises the question of what value one places on the reasons other people offer, and the way one answers this question will determine the nature of one's relationship to them.

13 Thus the experiment described above has no implications over and above its direct conclusion. It shows that the larger the groups people are in, the less responsive they tend to be to appeals for help. As a point of grammar, the results of the experiment show nothing about the *reasons* of those involved. The experiment might change the way we see such situations, perhaps persuading us that on such occasions what people say is of little interest. On the other hand, it might not, for we could continue to place more importance on the individual's

account of why he did not act than on the statistical correlation the experiment points to. A third possibility would be to attach a certain importance to both.

14 Here there is a further connection between Wittgenstein and Freud, for when Wittgenstein describes someone's practice, like Freud, he is articulating that individual's reasons for action. Thus in both cases only if the 'explanation' is accepted is it correct.

3 MISUNDERSTANDING HUMAN ACTION (II)

1 As should be clear from ch. 1, our aim in discussing Smart's utilitarianism is not to reject or endorse the particular moral claims it makes, but rather to show that the arguments Smart advances in its favour (and hence perhaps the reasons he adopted it) are run through with conceptual confusion.

2 If we are interested in understanding our moral practices the only considerations which can be relevant are the reasons people actually give. A consideration which plays no role in a practice may persuade an outsider that it is a good thing the practice continues, but *ex hypothesi* since it plays no role in the practice, it cannot be the participants' justification for acting as they do.

3 As far as act-utilitarianism is concerned, one might also note that not to know that the fact of making a promise is *by itself* sufficient to create an obligation is not to know the meaning of the words 'I promise'. What weight the individual assigns to this obligation – as against, for instance, the consequences of fulfilling it – is of course a different matter.

4 As Norman rightly argues (Norman 1971: 53–83) it is based on similar misconceptions to those lying behind the notion of a private language; to explore this point, however, would require a discussion of Wittgenstein's treatment of the Inner–Outer distinction – a topic too broad to be broached here.

5 Oddly enough(!), many of the members of these categories are precisely those to whom we are normally thought to have a special moral obligation.

6 Even this might be questioned, for like Smart, Mackie seems to offer the account he does largely because he cannot see what the alternatives to it might be. One might therefore do well to pay him the compliment of suspecting that his practice contained many of the elements of morality which his account excludes.

7 Cf. 'Moral Beliefs', in P. Foot *Virtues and Vices*, Oxford Blackwell (1978).

8 For a discussion of this issue cf. D.Z. Phillips and H.O. Mounce 'On Morality's having a Point', *Philosophy* 40.

9 Here too it is symptomatic that in his search for proof, Williams looks to science, in particular to psychology and sociology; and yet such considerations typically play an ancillary role, if any, in convincing

the individual to adopt the moral beliefs according to which he leads his life.

10 Like Frazer, Williams tends to view earlier societies as slightly dull-witted or at least not much given to thought; by contrast, today's society is, he believes, 'pervasively reflective' (Williams 1985 a: 2). One suspects, however, that since well before Plato, people have been aware of the notion that morality might simply be a matter of dispositions, and yet many (including some of those who have reflected the most) have concluded otherwise.

11 Whatever one may think of Kierkegaard, for example, his outlook could hardly be described as crude or insufficiently reflected upon.

12 Here, however, the dichotomies embedded in Williams's account create problems; for while on the reflective level Williams holds that we should recognize the illusory nature of traditional moral claims, on the practical level, he believes that we should continue to hold beliefs which are clearly intended to be similar in kind to traditional moral beliefs. The tensions such a position generates we shall discuss later.

4 THE INEFFABILITY OF VALUE

1 For Wittgenstein, understanding ethics involves understanding why we attach the importance to it that we do, why we hold that ethical questions are in some sense profound. The philosophical task is to elucidate the nature and meaning of this profundity. In this respect, however, contemporary accounts are singularly weak, for they succeed neither in bringing out the significance of ethics nor in clarifying the nature of the role ethical considerations play in our lives. According to these accounts, the only profundity of ethics is the profundity of its illusions.

2 Not long after giving the lecture, Wittgenstein made the obvious point that language is *not* a cage, and when such metaphors recur in his later work, their point is quite different. As Wittgenstein himself might later have remarked, if one is imprisoned it is not by language, but by one's own philosophical confusions.

3 On this issue, modern moral philosophy has produced a variety of related views. G.E.M. Anscombe, for example, argues that such a use of the word 'ought' only makes sense against the background of a belief in God and a divinely sanctioned moral law. By contrast, A. MacIntyre suggests that the attempt to use such terms absolutely arises from a historical misunderstanding concerning their actual relative character.

4 Understanding a ritual manifests a similar kinship: the meaning of the ritual is not separable from the specific acts which make up the ritual, and hence the gesture constituted by the ritual is either accessible to one or it is not.

5 To look for a further explanation would be to undermine (and reject) the very reaction we have expressed; for to do so would be to understand the reaction not in its own terms as something correct or

incorrect, appropriate or inappropriate, but as something *pathological*, something precisely in need of external explanation.

6 The point here is that moving from the fact that such-and-such is the case to acting in a particular way always involves a reaction on the part of the individual. The claim that facts themselves are value-loaded raises very different issues, reflecting, for example, the idea that the forms of description and classification we use reflect our own concerns and interests.

7 Here one might also note the fundamental categorial difference between science and ethics, for where the one is concerned with investigating what is the case, the other is concerned with what we should do. Hence the fact that ethical notions play no role in science is simply a reflection of the nature of each. Thus whatever objectivity in ethics might mean it cannot mean the same as objectivity in science.

8 Whether they should do so is a different question. Here one must disentangle substantive value claims from questions of grammar. The claim that we *should* all act in one way is substantive and unrelated to the grammatical point that every way of acting has the same logical status.

9 We shall discuss the nature of this claim further in Ch. 6.

10 For a discussion of the basis on which moral beliefs may come to be adopted cf. pp. 136-40.

11 Here it is also significant that scientific evidence typically plays no part in the adoption of moral convictions or of a particular moral position. Thus to look to science to *found* one's moral convictions is confused; while to look to science at all retards rather than promotes the attempt to understand those moral practices we actually engage in.

12 A Wittgensteinian account of ethics bears the same relation to Wittgenstein's lecture on ethics as the *Philosophical Investigations* does to the *Tractatus*. In both cases, a change in overall approach has the effect of making apparently similar points take on a completely new significance: on the one hand, everything changes, and yet, on the other, much remains the same.

13 A comment made by Wittgenstein in the period of the *Tractatus* illustrates a similar reaction. Thus writing to Engelmann in praise of a poem by Uhland, Wittgenstein claims that 'if only you do not try to utter what is unutterable then *nothing* gets lost. On the contrary, the unutterable will be – unutterably – contained in what has been uttered!' (*LLW*: 7). Interestingly, like so many of Wittgenstein's earlier ideas, this one too re-emerged as the raw material for later reflection. Thus, at the end of his life, Wittgenstein was keenly interested in the relation between language and music and in the notion that a particular linguistic utterance may have a unique expressive value.

5 ETHICS AND HUMAN ACTION

1 'Right is whatever we want it to be'.
2 Our reference here to the judgement's expressing a reaction is intended to underline the grammatical status of the judgement and in particular its substantive nature. It does not imply that the judgement *merely* expresses a reaction or that it is arbitrary.
3 The notion of bedrock is therefore important in ethics for two related reasons: first, because the language-games involved in ethics are based on the development and extension of a natural reaction rather than on the learning of a set of rules; and second, because in addition the function of the language-game may be that of giving expression to differences of reaction. This second point underlines one distinctive aspect of ethical language-games, for here disagreement at bedrock is not just something we can imagine, it is something we actually encounter.
4 The word 'good' is used in a parallel fashion with respect to objects and with respect to actions; in order therefore to avoid unnecessary duplication we shall henceforth refer simply to objects.
5 Our discussion of the word 'good' draws both on Wittgenstein's lectures on aesthetics and on the Ambrose lectures. At this fundamental level, the similarities between the use of words in aesthetics and in ethics are more important than the differences. As Wittgenstein notes in the Ambrose lectures, 'what has been said of "beautiful" will apply to the word "good" in only a slightly different way' (*AWL*: 36).
6 As Wittgenstein notes in *RPP2*, with colour predicates 'our agreement is essential to the language-game. But with "pleasant", "unpleasant", "beautiful", "ugly" it is otherwise' (*RPP2*: para. 896). Likewise with respect to words such as 'good', 'noble', etc.
7 While this distinction is not important in the original teaching of the language-game, later on it can become very important. As we shall see in ch. 6, this is particularly true with respect to moral judgements.
8 Wittgenstein's discussion (*AWL*: 34–6) is concerned explicitly with beauty, but, as we noted in note 5, Wittgenstein indicates that the points he makes hold equally with respect to goodness.
9 We shall see later on that this does not entail that evaluative judgements must necessarily be relative, i.e. just a question of perspective. For the moment, however, what is important is to recognize the fundamental grammatical differences between evaluative and empirical judgements.
10 G.H. Von Wright *Varieties of Goodness* London: Routledge & Kegan Paul (1963: 16–17).
11 The question 'Has "good" (or "beautiful") one meaning or an indefinite number?' is otiose. We use the same word to play a variety of games; the variety and the relatedness are both equally important. One way of putting it would be to say that the word has many meanings but one role.

12 The notion of essential contestability reflects this logical point, but
    confuses it with the substantive claim that the actual existence of
    disagreement is a good thing. Similarly, the idea that certain concepts
    are essentially contestable can be misleading if it suggests that this is a
    deep metaphysical truth about the terms themselves rather than
    simply a reflection of the way we use these terms. It is not that justice
    is a concept which is extraordinarily difficult to pin down; rather, in
    using the word 'just' in different ways (in putting forward different
    criteria for its application), we articulate different visions of society
    and different substantive moral positions.

13 This is, in fact, what happens when an evaluative term is used in
    (what is sometimes called) an inverted commas sense, i.e. in a
    situation where it has taken on a purely descriptive meaning.

14 Our reaction here parallels that we noted earlier on p. 92-3.

15 Against this, it might be argued that it is too weak just to say that we
    act differently, for this does not explain the sense in which what is at
    issue is *disagreement*. What this points to, however, is an important
    feature of ethics, but one which is quite in harmony with our account.
    Thus the point is that in this context we are not content to treat other
    ways of acting as simply different; rather, we claim that one
    particular way of acting is uniquely correct, and consequently
    condemn other ways of acting as wrong. The claim to unique
    correctness already relates each particular way of acting to the other
    possibilities so that for this reason the various ways of acting are not
    simply related to each other as different. The issues here are complex,
    and we shall explore them more fully in chs. 6 and 7.

16 The sterility of the attempt to use these points to eliminate actual
    disagreement is illustrated by the fact that the terminus of the
    argument would not be 'your position is ruled out on conceptual
    grounds', but rather 'I don't understand what you are saying', and
    that could hardly be said to constitute a conceptual refutation!

17 Of course, at the limit the two considerations are not totally
    independent, for a stage may be reached where we simply cannot
    make sense of what the other person says. However, this would not
    be because what the other person says is too different from our moral
    view in the sense that he approves of that of which we disapprove;
    rather, we cease to see the point of what he says and so can only treat
    his statements as meaningless or pathological.

18 This has crucial implications for philosophy, for, on the one hand, it
    emphasizes the importance of philosophy's restricting itself to
    description, and, on the other, it underlines the dangers of the search
    for conceptual arguments.

19 These points may seem to offer the individual excessive freedom to
    combine various moral judgements as he sees fit and hence virtually
    to abolish moral argument. However, in the Conclusion when we
    discuss moral argument and the role of consistency in ethics, we shall
    see that this is not the case.

20 Cf. ch. 7.

21 Suppose we discovered a being with fantastic powers, who proved that he had created us, etc. Would we therefore have to treat his commands as universally binding? Even if non-compliance inevitably led to punishment, it would still be logically possible to hold that compliance was only a matter of prudence or indeed that one had a moral duty to rebel despite the necessary futility of so doing (cf. *RW*: 108). The logical point is that whatever may turn out to be the case, how one decides to order one's life is a logically distinct issue.

22 Thus even if one wishes to continue using the words 'true' and 'false', the fundamental logical differences between the propositions to which they are applied mean that in the two contexts the words have a fundamentally different meaning. Cf. ch. 7.

23 Here it would be wrong to claim that the non-religious response is, if not absolutely, at least relatively more justified by the facts. To make this claim is simply to express one's own acceptance of the non-religious perspective. If from this perspective the invocation of God seems unnecessary, from the religious perspective the belief that science will always get to the bottom of the matter seems equally unfounded.

24 The fact that a scientific investigation excludes the miraculous is a reflection of the nature of science (of what counts as a scientific explanation, etc.). Furthermore, what is important in a miracle *qua* miracle is that it convinces the individual that God exists, and this aspect of the event can hardly be discovered in the event itself. Of course, the discovery of a scientific explanation may convince one that the event was not miraculous, but even this is not necessarily the case. The tile that falls on the head of the dictator undoubtedly obeys the law of gravity, but its doing so may not be sufficient to convince someone that Providence was not at work.

25 For this reason, one might well say that in an important sense religious belief is not belief at all, i.e. that its grammatical status is not the same as that of what we ordinarily call beliefs, viz. empirical beliefs. Examples of other beliefs whose grammatical status is fundamentally different from that of empirical belief would be the beliefs involved in ritual, belief in fate, and the belief that others are thinking beings and not cunningly programmed automata.

6 ETHICS: A DISTINCTIVE REACTION

1 From what has already been said, it should be clear that it would not make sense to seek to explain this on the basis of an 'error theory'. If an individual denies that his moral judgements are expressions of preference, his statement is not a claim about the status of his reaction: rather, it is part of this reaction itself. Consequently, since he is not making a claim, the individual cannot be in error; rather, his statement characterizes what he is doing as 'making-a-judgement-which-is-not-an-expression-of-preference'. What needs to be clarified is what this might mean.

2 Thus, paradoxically, one way the moral reaction can express itself is in the misleading attempt to assimilate moral and empirical judgements: just as it is either raining or not raining, so too, one is tempted to claim, murder is either right or wrong. However, while this statement conceals the difference between moral and empirical judgements, it cannot eliminate them. Thus the latter dichotomy itself already embodies the ethical reaction, for it presupposes acceptance of the terms 'right' and 'wrong' and thereby surreptitiously excludes the position of the non-ethical individual who claims that, while some favour murder, others don't, and that that is all there is to it.

3 Similarly, if someone has a moral scruple which I cannot understand (or which I reject), I may refuse to take it seriously as a moral conviction and instead treat it as an unfortunate hang-up.

4 The central question is not whether doing the act gives you pleasure, but whether your decision to act is based on a consideration of the nature of the act in question or on your personal feelings about the case in hand. Thus if one believes that one ought to do a certain act, one is committed to doing it independently of whether doing it will be a pleasure or a pain.

5 This underlines the futility of trying to justify ethical imperatives by showing them to be in the individual's interest. It would, of course, be possible to seek to prove that committing particular types of act (e.g. murder or theft) was rarely in the individual's interest. This type of argument, however, would have a different sort of interest, and its basis would be empirical. Consequently, there would be no guarantee what conclusions it might yield: perhaps investigation would show that crime pays in the United States but not in West Germany, or that acting dishonestly is profitable for some individuals but not for others.

6 The fact that many would unhesitatingly reject the happiness of the pig in favour of the unhappiness of Socrates is thus another indication of the prevalence and importance of the reaction we are discussing. Furthermore, the concern for the spiritual aspects of human existence, which underlies such a rejection, illustrates the kind of consideration here at issue.

7 Again, it must be emphasized that taking an ethical position does not necessarily express a Puritanical rejection of pleasure as evil. Pleasure is not necessarily to be avoided: rather from the ethical perspective the question of whether the action will bring the agent pleasure is simply treated as irrelevant.

8 Here the point is not that universality constitutes the difference between moral judgements and preferences, but rather that it provides an illustration of what that difference is.

9 It should be noted, however, that the offering of a wider account is not a prerequisite for one's moral judgement making sense. Thus I may hold that I ought to do a certain act (i.e. attribute to it this type of significance) and yet (for the time being, as it were) be unable to offer a further account which would link this conviction into a more

general conception of why there are certain things which one ought to do.

10 Furthermore, Smart's comments betray a failure to understand the reaction he dismisses. Thus he presents it as a strange intellectual confusion, something which doesn't bear reflecting upon; this, however, is hardly a convincing portrayal of the role the concept of guilt can (and does) play within human life.

11 Here one might also mention notions such as 'higher' interests or 'true' happiness, for when used in ethics the notions of interest and happiness are given a new sense. Thus in these cases too it might be claimed that their use in ethics is nonsensical, for acting in one's higher interests may be precisely against one's interests in a non-moral sense, while it might be claimed that true happiness lies in sacrificing one's happiness!

12 Wittgenstein discusses these and related issues at various points in much of the later writings – in particular, in *RPP1*, *RPP2*, and *LW*.

13 Although this may seem to contradict Wittgenstein's private-language argument, in fact it follows from it; for the directly expressive nature of language becomes particularly important when one recognizes that it is a confusion to treat the individual's expression of his experience as descriptions of internal events – reports, as it were, on a private world.

14 Wittgenstein makes a similar point about religious similes: he notes that such similes 'move on the edge of an abyss' (*CV*: 29), for one may easily be tempted to extend them in incoherent or perverse ways. For example, one might append to Bunyan's *Pilgrim's Progress* the statement 'and these traps, quicksands, wrong turnings, were planned by the Lord of the Road and the monsters, thieves and robbers were created by him'. Here the sense of Bunyan's simile has been completely distorted, for this continuation expresses an outlook far-removed from that embodied in Bunyan's tale.

15 The reference to uniqueness here should not be misunderstood. The key point is that the appropriateness of the picture (whether it expresses his moral outlook) is manifested in whether or not the individual in question accepts it. If the individual is equally happy talking about a moral law and about a moral order, then his acceptance of both forms of words shows that he makes no distinction between them. In rejecting all conceptions other than these two, the individual shows that these two notions (for him essentially the same) exclusively ('uniquely') express his moral outlook.

16 A good example here is Williams's vigorous but ill-considered attack on Kantian ethics in the final chapter of his book *Ethics and the Limits of Philosophy*, London: Fontana/Collins (1985).

17 One might object that one *can* claim both that a judgement is correct and that one was caused to hold it. The sense in which this is true, however, leaves the force of the dichotomy intact, for the fundamental point is that if the judgement is to have content the reference to causation is irrelevant. Furthermore, someone who claims that *all* his

judgements are caused cuts the ground from under his own feet, for, while one may claim to have been caused to hold a certain belief and then, as it were, rationally identify oneself with this belief by *judging* it to be correct, the rational content of this latter claim is itself undermined if one then claims that the basis for one's judging it to be correct was also causal rather than reflection on the judgement's content.

18 If one holds to an account in terms of preferences, the statement is simply a disguised statement of preference; while, if one maintains the causal account, the statement loses all rational significance, for one is committed to claiming that only the contingent interplay of causal factors made the individual advance this claim rather than its opposite.

19 In some respects, the possibility of causal explanation has the same sort of consequences as the possibility of having oneself psychoanalysed. In the latter case, unsuspected and potentially reprehensible aspects of one's action may be revealed to one and in this sense 'the knowledge acquired sets us [new] ethical problems; but contributes nothing to their solution' (*CV*: 34). To give one example, the recognition that we may unwittingly be acting towards a certain individual in a consistently hostile way might be seen as creating a new moral responsibility, viz. a moral obligation towards maximal self-consciousness in a situation where the concept of self-consciousness has been altered such that the notion of complete self-awareness no longer has a clear sense. Hence, if one adopted this moral position, a new area of vigilance would open up, for one would be faced with the necessity of taking responsibility for actions which would previously have been seen as unintentional and therefore non-culpable.

20 The justifications offered for retributive principles fill out the picture of why the individual is committed to these principles and so define the particular conception of retribution being advanced. While they show precisely what moral position is being advanced, their logical status is the same as that of the original principles they elucidate; in both cases the logical possibility of rejection cannot be eliminated.

21 Mackie's essay does of course reflect certain cultural trends within our society, for the ethical reaction we have described seems to be at least partly out of keeping with the spirit of the times; from this perspective, that retribution comes to seem paradoxical is itself a sign of declining support and sympathy for retributive principles. The culmination of this development would be the simultaneous disappearance of Mackie's paradox and of the principles themselves.

22 The empirical and moral issues are in fact logically distinct. Even if the retributive reaction were shown to be evolutionarily superior, this would not establish that the reaction was simply a conditioned response, for one might accept the former claim and yet hold that it was of no relevance to ethics. More generally, whatever results empirical research may yield, we would still be faced with the need to

make an ethical decision on the question of whether someone ought to be punished simply in virtue of having done wrong.

23 Blackburn also claims that an explanation of ethics is necessary in order to determine the appropriate scope of ethical claims. This demand clearly reflects the desire for an independent means by which to resolve moral disagreement; as we saw in ch. 4, however, this demand is incoherent. It also illustrates the implicitly substantive role explanation is called upon to play, for here the idea is that it should be able to adjudicate between conflicting conceptions of morality.

24 Of course, if we believe that it is wrong to kick dogs then we will presumably approve of others who hold the same view. This, however, is at best an implication of our judgement not that judgement's content.

25 In fact, Blackburn seems to wish to abandon the very notion of a reason. Thus he prefers to talk of inputs which yield outputs. This disguises the clash between his causal account and the rationality embodied in the notion of making a judgement; it does not, however, eliminate it.

26 Not surprisingly, Blackburn, like Mackie, presents a somewhat strange picture of our existing moral practices. As one might expect, he holds that 'the purpose of moralizing . . . must at least partly be social' (Blackburn 1981: 180). He then develops this idea by claiming that we avoid inconsistent moral views because the teaching of 'fickle' (randomizing) sensibilities would be difficult, and this is to be avoided because 'it matters to me that others can come to share and endorse my moral outlook'. Not only does this once again treat the content of moral judgements as unimportant (here simply a matter of convenience), but it is also a highly implausible explanation of why we hold moral consistency to be so important. One might further note that the 'endorsement' offered me by others would be rather empty, for as good quasi-realists we would all presumably recognize that independently of our dispositions to accept them my moral views were in themselves no better than any others.

7 TRUTH, RELATIVISM, AND OBJECTIVITY

1 The same point can be made in terms of reasons. Thus we have reasons for acting (an ethic) and we show what count for us as reasons by acting according to them (by acting according to the ethic). Between the various possible reasons for action, however, there is no independent means of adjudication; whatever new considerations may be advanced they can only constitute reasons for actions of the same logical status as those already put forward.

2 The idea that our decision may correspond to 'how things are' is a confusion. To note this point, however, is not to rule out any particular moral view, but only to exclude a confused and incoherent interpretation of such views. The sense in which moral views might claim to be 'objective' will be explored below. Here what is ruled out

is not a false or incorrect claim, but one that literally makes no sense.

3 One might reply that the same point holds with respect to claiming that an empirical judgement is true. Saying this, however, conceals the differences between empirical and moral judgements, but does not eliminate them. To claim that an empirical judgement is true is to claim that it states what is in fact the case; whereas to claim that a moral judgement is true is to claim that one should indeed act as it implies.

4 The same is true of Wittgenstein's comments on religion. In denying that religious statements are straightforwardly true or false, Wittgenstein is not claiming that all that is at issue in religion is the question of which concepts are the most fruitful to live by; rather, he is stressing the fact that the language-game played with religious judgements is fundamentally different from that played with empirical judgements. For example, religion does not simply claim that a certain Being exists, but rather that there is a Being towards whom *by definition* one ought to act in such-and-such a way. Correspondingly, the evidence which leads one towards such a belief is not of the same kind as that underlying empirical beliefs. The nature of this difference is further underlined by the fact that *not* believing in the existence of God is treated as morally wrong, whereas 'normally if [one does] not believe in the existence of something no one would think that there was anything wrong in this' (*LA*: 59).

5 See ch. 8 for a discussion of this point with respect to the concepts involved in our notion of agency.

6 To ask successively of, say, colour judgements, mathematical propositions, and ethical statements whether each is objective would be highly misleading; for, since each type of statement has a distinct grammar, the question would have a different sense in each case. Thus, even if one concluded in a particular case that a distinction between objective and subjective was appropriate or useful, it would be crucial from the very start to specify what in that particular context this distinction meant.

7 To put it another way, if the claim that ethics is objective is assigned no sense, the claim that ethics is subjective also loses its substantive content, for then the claim rules nothing out but simply underlines the nature of the topic in question.

8 Of course, the question 'Is it the case that murder is wrong or does it only seem to be the case?' could be taken as an eccentric way of asking whether murder is wrong; in that case, however, the reference to its being the case or not being the case drops out of consideration.

9 With reference to Callicles, it is interesting to note a deep-seated ambiguity in his argument; for he seems to want to argue both that justice (and morality) is a sham *and* that the existing morality is unjust and immoral. In the latter strand of his argument, Callicles is concerned to argue that it is just for the better man to have more then the worse, hence he would seem to be concerned not with rejecting ethics, but with advancing a new kind of ethic. Thus at times

Callicles seems to be rejecting the validity of all moral claims, and at others only to be rejecting the validity of those particular moral claims advanced by Socrates. (It might also be argued that there is a similar ambiguity in Nietzsche; for it is sometimes unclear whether he is attacking ethics as such or simply one kind of ethics).

10 Here, however, it must be admitted that the realist can all too easily become embroiled in the confusions of his antagonist. Two examples should illustrate the point. Thus the debate over the validity of moral judgements can come to focus on the question of whether or not values are in the world, and the realist will, of course, defend his particular substantive position by claiming that they are. However, since the notion of values being in the world makes no sense, to deny this claim and to advance it are both equally senseless. Similarly, it may be argued that since moral judgements do not state what is the case, they must necessarily simply reflect human dispositions. Again, to defend his substantive rejection of this conclusion, the realist may be tempted to claim that moral judgements *do* state what is the case. Rather than doing this, however, a more appropriate response on the realist's part would be to point out that the argument is fallacious, for the grammatical point that moral judgements are not true does not rule out the claim that in making them we do more than merely manifest particular contingent dispositions. Here it is also worth noting the underlying confusion in each of these arguments, for in each case there is an illegitimate attempt to use a grammatical point to establish a substantive claim. This, in fact, is what leads the realist astray, for wishing to reject the substantive claim, he incoherently attempts to reject grammar; perversely, this then seems to justify the realist's antagonist, for at this stage his claims really do become incoherent!

11 Albert Camus would seem to have held a view of this sort: See *L'Homme révolté* Paris: Gallimard (1951). In *The Sovereignty of Good* Iris Murdoch too expresses a moral outlook which stresses that value is not subjective and yet simultaneously treats the notion of the world's having a meaning as an illusion.

12 As we saw in Chapter 5, the notion of values being in the world makes no sense and it is therefore equally incoherent (and misleading) to claim either that values are in the world or that they are not. What gets expressed here is a substantive disagreement, but we must look elsewhere if we are to clarify its substance.

13 This denial has a dual importance: first, it underlies Mackie's claim that certain moral views are just wrong; and second, it expresses Mackie's conviction that the only way of understanding the objectivist's claim is to treat it as the claim that values are in the world. These two points hang together and both will be questioned below.

14 Mackie's account is complicated by the fact that he oscillates uncertainly between an account of this kind and one focused on the question of what dispositions we should wish society's members to

have. Later in this chapter we shall consider both aspects of his account in turn.

15 Thus it is wrong to treat moral judgements as *merely* supported by intuition, for what other kind of support could claims as to how we should act have? Here the reference to intuition presents in an obscure (and negative) fashion a grammatical point about the nature of moral judgements. Since the claim that people ought to act in one way rather than another can have no other kind of support, the word 'merely' invokes a comparison where this comparison has no proper object.

16 This remark gives a foretaste of the problems Mackie's account faces when taken seriously; for if one accepts this point, it is hard to see what meaning is left to the claim that such-and-such ought to be done because it is the just thing to do.

17 This is not to rule out the moral argument that if you wish others to tell the truth, justice requires that you too do so. This argument is based on an appeal to justice; such an appeal, however, is not accessible to Mackie, for it embodies precisely the type of claim he believes to be incoherent.

18 The idea here is a familiar one, for the scheme might be said to be quasi-voluntary in the sense that acceptance of current practices of praise and blame would be taken as tacit consent to the *status quo*.

19 For this reason, Mackie seems to agree with Hobbes that the agreement must be policed, either literally or via social mechanisms of praise and blame.

20 Here one might argue that a moral dimension can re-enter Mackie's account via the fact that we are disposed to desire a just society, etc. What needs to be carefully investigated, however, is the meaning of the claim that we are disposed to desire a *just* society. Here the word 'just' either simply refers to a particular organization of society which we happen to prefer or it involves the claim that one particular way of organizing society is correct. In the first case, no distinctively moral concepts will have been introduced. In the second case, however, the account in terms of dispositions will have been transcended; for the claim that a particular way of organizing society is just involves the rejection of the claim that all that is at issue is our dispositions, and instead claims that the real (and only relevant) question is 'How would it be right to organize society?'. Thus to take this line is to abandon Mackie's approach and return to the traditional conceptions he rejects.

21 At this stage, Mackie's claim that morality is something we choose starts to seem rather empty, for on this approach what gets justified is society causing its members to be disposed in certain ways.

22 Mackie does claim that it is in the individual's interests to be virtuously disposed; and he argues, for example, that a courageous disposition is an asset to its owner. Whether this latter point is actually true is debatable (it might be best to be about average or only slightly courageous); in any event, however, the argument is

only really plausible with respect to courage. To argue that a disposition towards justice is best in prudential terms would be highly implausible. (Furthermore, one might argue that if one is just on prudential grounds, then one is not really *just* at all).

23 For example, he writes 'the demands that I thus make on others are not unfair if there are other transactions in which I am content that others should treat me as a means . . .' (Mackie 1977: 156). Here the reference to unfairness involves standards which do seem to be independent of the individual and hence, strictly speaking, should have no place in Mackie's argument.

24 For the moralist, such a development would not simply be a socio-cultural phenomenon with a causal explanation, but progress towards a general acceptance of the correct moral views.

25 To put it another way, if it is an inference from 'experience', experience here includes everything on the basis of which it would be possible to form a view.

26 Williams objects particularly strongly to the claim that there is no escape from moral obligation and that the moral law applies unconditionally to all individuals even if they reject it. He treats these claims as conceptually confused; in fact, however, they are simply distorted representations of the claim that in particular situations there is one and only one thing that the individual ought to do and that this is so regardless of what the individual's attitude to this may be.

27 The claim that the individual could have acted otherwise is central to our notions of praise and blame; Williams, however, treats it as a fiction, for he denies that there are 'external reasons' for action. Thus he claims that in order to be able to say that someone has a reason to do something, one must be able to show that the reason speaks to a motivation the individual already has. For criticism of this claim see ch. 8.

28 Here there is a temptation to revert to the conception of ethics earlier rejected, for if one asks 'How *ought* people to be disposed?' then one is once again claiming that there are independent standards in terms of which such judgements can be made. If one wishes to avoid claims of this sort (as Williams does), then the question 'How would it be best for people to be disposed?' can only mean 'What way do I want people to be disposed?' or 'What way am I disposed to claim that people ought to be disposed?'

29 When Williams discusses relativism he does indeed note that rival societies will be involved in a *clash* of moral claims, but he explains this by claiming that part of what makes a response an ethical response is its deeply internalized nature. Having noted this point, however, on Williams's approach, the only relevant fact about alternative ethical systems is whether they are an option for us; for if we could arrange our society in the specified way then a decision is called for, otherwise the rival moral claims are of no interest.

30 Or might have been. As a matter of fact, Williams holds that it is

probably not the case. Since there is in fact little hope that a sufficiently determinate moral outlook could be determined in this way, Williams is left with the problem that there are various possible ethics and on his account no way of choosing between them. Here it does seem that moral choice is reduced to the arbitrary or the capricious.

31 It is interesting to compare Blackburn's presentation of a moral problem and Wittgenstein's, for the terms involved contrast markedly. Thus, while Wittgenstein talks of right and wrong and what the individual ought to do, Blackburn largely eschews a moral vocabulary and instead talks of desires and potentially overpowering feelings.

8 REASONS AND THE WILL

1 As Wittgenstein notes, what underlies this fantastical picture is a simple truism, viz. that 'one can say, "I will, but my body does not obey me" – but not: "my will does not obey me" ' (*PI*: para. 618).

2 The emptiness of this explanation is further underlined when one notes, as Wittgenstein does in *Zettel*, that rest may be as voluntary as motion, ceasing to act as voluntary as acting (*Z*: para. 597).

3 In fact, strictly speaking, it is not an assumption at all, for an assumption occurs within a language-game and involves assuming something that one might call into question or later prove. However, the idea that the actions of ourselves and others are voluntary does not play this role in the language-game, and is in many ways more akin to the type of propositions Wittgenstein discusses in *On Certainty*.

4 To make the explanation real, motivational states would have to be identifiable independently of how the individual later acts. Furthermore, one would need a theory of how particular motivational states were produced and how they changed in response to stimuli, etc. Such a theory would treat human action in a new way, and, although success in creating such a theory might conceivably convince us to alter our relation to ourselves and each other, it would make no sense to claim that either approach was 'objectively correct'.

5 Here Wittgenstein makes the surprising claim that here 'an argument is all right if it convinces you.' This draws attention to the fact that in this context argument does not consist in proving something to be the case or in offering evidence that a particular statement is true; rather, it consists in putting forward considerations which are intended to convince someone of the correctness of a certain approach but which of their nature may always be rejected. For a further exploration of this point, and of the nature of moral argument in general, see the Conclusion.

6 There is, however, a further aspect to this question, for as Wittgenstein notes at the end of his lecture, the ability to predict human action would bring with it a radical change in our relation to ourselves and to others. It would be like playing roulette when always

knowing what number would come up – one might continue playing roulette, but the game could hardly be said to be the same. One might also note just how important the notion of unpredictability is to us, for the unpredictable fine shades of human behaviour are central to our response to it as human. How we would act in a world where these fine shares were replaced by less individualized and more predictable behaviour is hard to say; whether, for example, we could take up the same relation to a person in distress if his future actions stood before us like an open book is a moot point.

7 The extent of this change can hardly be exaggerated and might be underlined by noting that even the most scientifically minded philosopher is hardly likely to want to claim that his relation to other people is essentially the same as his relation to machines except that it is more complicated. Furthermore, one might be sceptical as to whether it would be humanly possible to treat human action consistently and exclusively in causal terms. Indeed, anyone who tried to do so might well be treated as suffering from a strange form of mental disorder.

CONCLUSION

1 The same point applies to the claim that one sort of society (or way of organizing society) is more just, or simply better than another; what distinguishes all such claims from non-moral judgements is the claim that one possibility is *inherently* to be preferred rather than simply that possibility which the individual who advocates it happens to prefer.

2 A moral judgement embodies the claim to a certain type of significance, a significance which is more fully spelt out by outlining the particular way of acting and understanding the world within which that judgement has its role. However, as we noted in ch. 6, that an individual should actually be able to supplement moral judgement with an account of this kind is not itself necessary even if the full significance of that judgement would only be fully spelt out by such an account. Similarly, an individual may claim that there is a morally relevant difference between two cases but reject the attempt to capture this difference in words. This may seem to leave undue scope for the individual to mask purely personal preferences by vague reference to ineffable moral principles. However, in these cases just as much as elsewhere, whether (and to what extent) we decide to respect an individual's professed moral principles is itself a substantive decision.

APPENDIX: ETHICS AND SOCIETY

1 Baker and Hacker (1985).

2 Here it is worth noting that the notion that intelligibility has limits may itself be misleading, for it suggests that there are certain claims we might make were it not for the unfortunate fact that they lay

beyond the pale of intelligibility. The point, however, is that unintelligible claims are not claims at all: intelligibility does not exclude a host of mysterious unutterable possibilities – what it excludes are not possibilities at all but nonsense.

3 To the objection that individuals cannot invent moral concepts, one could simply reply that they do. Thus when Proudhon proclaimed that property was theft he was engaged in advancing a new conception of justice. To note that this conception was related to those that preceded it is not to undermine the claim that the conception was new; for any moral concept will of course be related to others in so far as they are all recognizably moral, i.e. play a similar role in our lives and thinking. Furthermore, the possibility of offering an explanation of how this conception arose does not demonstrate that its 'true' origin was society; for whatever conception an individual advanced, it would always be possible to try to place it within some sort of a historical context.

4 This point is illustrated by a predicament faced by Wittgenstein himself. Thus, in a reference to Bach, he concludes the preface to the *Philosophical Remarks* by noting 'I would like to say "This book is written to the glory of God", but nowadays that would be chicanery, that is, it would not be rightly understood. It means the book is written in good will, and insofar as it is not so written, but out of vanity, etc., the author would wish to see it condemned.'

ABBREVIATIONS AND BIBLIOGRAPHY

WORKS BY WITTGENSTEIN

AWL *Wittgenstein's Lectures, Cambridge 1932-5*, ed. A. Ambrose Oxford, 1979: Blackwell.

BB *The Blue and Brown Books*, Oxford, 1958: Blackwell.

BT The 'Big Typescript' (*TS* 213 in the Von Wright catalogue).

CV *Culture and Value*, Oxford, 1980: Blackwell.

LA *Lectures and Conversations on Aesthetics, Psychology and Religious Belief*, Oxford, 1970: Blackwell.

LE 'A Lecture on Ethics', *Philosophical Review* 74 (1965): 3-12.

LLW *Letters from Ludwig Wittgenstein (to Paul Engelmann) with a Memoir*, Oxford, 1967.

LW *Last Writings on the Philosophy of Psychology*, Vol. 1, Oxford, 1982: Blackwell.

M 'Wittgenstein's Lectures in 1930-3', in *Philosophical Papers*, ed. G.E. Moore, London, 1959: Allen & Unwin.

MS *MS 110* in the Von Wright catalogue.

N *Notebooks 1914-16*, Oxford, 1961: Blackwell.

NFW 'Notes on Freedom of the Will', notes taken by Yorick Symthies of an unpublished lecture on free will given by Wittgenstein in Cambridge in 1936.

PI *Philosophical Investigations*, Oxford, 1958: Blackwell.

PR *Philosophical Remarks*, Oxford, 1975: Blackwell.

RFGB 'Remarks on Frazer's Golden Bough', in G. Luckhardt (ed.) *Wittgenstein: Sources and Perspectives*, Ithaca, NY, 1979: Cornell University.

RFM *Remarks on the Foundations of Mathematics* (revised edn.), Oxford, 1970: Blackwell.

RPP1 *Remarks on the Philosophy of Psychology*, Vol. 1, Oxford, 1980: Blackwell.

RPP2 *Remarks on the Philosophy of Psychology*, Vol. 2, Oxford, 1980: Blackwell.

TLP *Tractatus Logico-Philosophicus*, London 1961: Routledge & Kegan Paul.

WWK *Ludwig Wittgenstein und der Wiener Kreis*, Oxford, 1967: Blackwell.

Z *Zettel*, Oxford, 1967: Blackwell.

WORKS BY OTHER AUTHORS

Anscombe, G.E.M. (1957) *Intention*, Oxford: Blackwell.

Baker, G.P. and Hacker, P.M.S. (1980) *Wittgenstein: Meaning and Understanding*, Oxford: Blackwell.

Baker, G.P. and Hacker, P.M.S. (1984) *Scepticism, Rules and Language*, Oxford: Blackwell.

Baker, G.P. and Hacker, P.M.S. (1985) *Wittgenstein: Rules, Grammar and Necessity*, Oxford: Blackwell.

Beardsmore, R.W. (1969) *Moral Reasoning*, London: Routledge & Kegan Paul.

Blackburn, S. (1981) 'Rule-following and Moral Realism', in S.H. Holtzman and C.M. Leich (eds.) *Wittgenstein: To Follow a Rule*, London: Routledge & Kegan Paul.

Blackburn, S. (1985) 'Errors and the Phenomenology of Value', in T. Honderich (ed.) *Morality and Objectivity*, Routledge & Kegan Paul.

Camus, A. (1951) *L'Homme révolté*, Paris: Gallimard.

Cioffi, F. (1981) 'Wittgenstein and the Fire-festivals', in I. Block (ed.) *Perspectives on the Philosophy of Wittgenstein*, Cambridge, Mass.: MIT Press.

Clark, S. (1977) *The Moral Status of Animals*, Oxford: Clarendon Press.

Davidson, D. (1980) 'Actions, Reasons and Causes', in *Essays on Actions and Events*, Oxford: OUP.

Diamond, C. (1982) 'Anything but Argument?', *Philosophical Investigations*, January.

Drury, M.O'C. (1981) 'Some Notes on Conversations with Wittgenstein', in R. Rhees (ed.) *Recollections of Wittgenstein*, Oxford: OUP.

Foot, P. (1978) *Virtues and Vices*, Oxford: Blackwell.

Frazer, J. (1911) *The Golden Bough* (third edn. with preface) London: Macmillan.

Frazer, J. (1922) *The Golden Bough* (new edn.), London: Macmillan.

Frazer, J. (1931) *Garnered Sheaves: Essays, Addresses and Reviews*, London: Macmillan.

Hare, R.M. (1952) *The Language of Morals*, Oxford: OUP.

Hare, R.M. (1963) *Freedom and Reason*, Oxford: OUP.

Hurley, S.L. (1985) 'Objectivity and Disagreement', in T. Honderich (ed.) *Morality and Objectivity*, London: Routledge & Kegan Paul.

Kenny, A. (1984) *The Legacy of Wittgenstein*, Oxford: Blackwell.

Kierkegaard, S. (1941) *Concluding Unscientific Postscript*, Princeton, NJ: Princeton University Press.

MacIntyre, A. (1981) *After Virtue*, London: Duckworth.

Mackie, J.L. (1977) *Ethics*, Harmondsworth: Penguin Books.

Mackie, J.L. (1985) 'Morality and the Retributive Emotions', in *Persons and Values*, ed. Joan Mackie and Penelope Mackie, Oxford: CUP.

Moore, G.E. (1903) *Principia Ethica*, Cambridge: CUP.

Murdoch, I. (1970) *The Sovereignty of Good*, London: Routledge & Kegan Paul.

Nietzsche, F. (1962;) *Philosophy in the Tragic Age of the Greeks*, trans. Marianne Couran, New York: Regnery-Gatesway.

Nisbett, R. and Wilson, T. (1977) 'On Telling more than we can Know: Verbal Reports on Mental Processes', *Psychological Review* 84: 231–59.

Norman, R. (1971) *Reasons for Action*, Oxford: Blackwell.

Parfit, D. (1984) *Reasons and Persons*, Oxford: OUP.

Phillips, D.Z. and Mounce, H.O. (1965) 'On Morality's having a Point', *Philosophy* 40: 308–19.

Plato, *Gorgias*, tr. T. Irwin, Oxford, 1979: OUP.

Rhees, R. (1970) *Discussions of Wittgenstein*, London: Routledge & Kegan Paul.

Rhees, R. (1982) 'Wittgenstein on Language and Ritual', in B. McGuinness (ed.) *Wittgenstein And His Times*, Oxford: Blackwell.

Russell, B. (1918) *Mysticism and Logic*, London: Longmans, Green.

Russell, B. (1926) *Our Knowledge of the External World*, London: Allen & Unwin.

Russell, B. (1959) *My Philosophical Development*, London: Allen & Unwin.

Smart, J.J. and Williams, B. (1973) *Utilitarianism: For and Against*, Cambridge: CUP.

Waismann, F. (1971) *How I See Philosophy*, London: Macmillan.

Warnock, G.J. (1971) *The Object of Morality*, London: Methuen.

Winch, P. (1972) *Ethics and Action*, London: Routledge & Kegan Paul.

Williams, B. (1981) *Moral Luck*, Cambridge: CUP.

Williams, B. (1985a) *Ethics and the Limits of Philosophy*, London: Fontana/Collins.

Williams, B. (1985b) 'Ethics and the Fabric of the World', in T. Honderich (ed.) *Morality and Objectivity*, London: Routledge & Kegan Paul.

Winch, P. (1958) *The Idea of a Social Science*, London: Routledge & Kegan Paul.

Winch, P. (1972) *Ethics and Action*, London: Routledge & Kegan Paul.

von Wright, G.H. (1963) *Varieties of Goodness*, London: Routledge & Kegan Paul.

INDEX